ELEMENTARY PRINCIPLES OF EDUCATION

THE MACMILLAN COMPANY
NEW YORK · BOSTON · CHICAGO · DALLAS
ATLANTA · SAN FRANCISCO

MACMILLAN & CO., Limited
LONDON · BOMBAY · CALCUTTA
MELBOURNE

THE MACMILLAN COMPANY
OF CANADA, Limited
TORONTO

ELEMENTARY PRINCIPLES

OF

EDUCATION

BY

EDWARD L. THORNDIKE

AND

ARTHUR I. GATES

THE MACMILLAN COMPANY

NEW YORK

1929

PREFACE

This volume is intended for use as a textbook in a first course in principles of education. The authors have endeavored, first, to select those general facts and principles which will be of most service to typical elementary and high school teachers. They have tried, secondly, to present these facts and principles in a form intelligible to students who have had few or no other courses in education and little or no professional experience. They have attempted, thirdly, to offer an account based, as far as possible, upon the findings of scientific study.

To satisfy the first two requirements, it was found advisable not to introduce as full discussions of certain philosophic, biological, and sociological speculations as are sometimes found in more advanced books on the subject. It was found advisable also to devote relatively little space to the history of educational theories and practices and to descriptive accounts of the financial, administrative, and legal aspects of the school, its teachers, and pupils. The book is devoted primarily to the purpose of establishing sound principles for guidance of teachers in their most important daily tasks. Its chief topics are, therefore, the major objectives of education, the most insistent needs of education at the present time, the special functions of the school, the characteristics of children from birth to maturity, and the principles which underlie the learning and teaching process and the selection and organization of materials and activities for the school curriculum.

Although the writers have sought to present views which the results of scientific study most fully justify, they have found it impossible, without making the volume too long and difficult, to present much detail concerning scientific methods and results.   The account, although made more simple and straightforward by this policy, may seem dogmatic.   It is expected, however, that the instructor will encourage the students to read additional materials and to take a critical attitude toward the text.   To facilitate outside reading and thinking and class discussion, a list of references and a group of problems and questions are appended to each chapter.

E. L. T.

A. I. G.

CONTENTS

ELEMENTARY PRINCIPLES OF EDUCATION

ELEMENTARY PRINCIPLES OF EDUCATION

CHAPTER I

THE PROVINCE OF EDUCATION

Man, compared to other animals, is the foremost producer of change. His life may be viewed as a continuous and determined effort to change the world in which he lives. He changes the earth's form, whether he merely scrapes out a hole in which to hide or removes mountains to join oceans. He changes its living beings when he destroys flies and breeds cows or when he exterminates weeds and cultivates corn. He changes his fellow men when he teaches or preaches, and he changes himself when he goes to school or joins the church. Whatever he may do, he brings about, directly or indirectly, changes in the world which includes his fellow men and himself.

GENERAL CHARACTERISTICS OF EDUCATION

Education Concerned with Making Changes. — The art and hope of human life is to change the world for the better — to make all things, animals, plants, other men, and oneself, more serviceable for life's ends. Rivers flow without regard to man's intent, but he may change their courses and deepen their channels to make them more serviceable. Insects grow regardless of man's welfare, but

1

he may exterminate the mosquito which infects him with disease and cultivate the bee which provides him with food. Children, too, develop in part by inner impulses apart from man's direction, but man tries to change their original natures into forms which better serve some human needs. Each man singly tries, by promoting certain changes and resisting others, to make the world of things and men better for himself; a group of men living together, so far as they possess wisdom, try to make things and men better for the group as a whole.

Education an Art and a Science. — All of the sciences, arts, and industries are concerned, directly or indirectly, with the production of changes in the world. Science is concerned with the accumulation of knowledge which may enable men to understand and thereby to control changes that are deemed desirable. Arts and industries are concerned with putting the desired changes into effect. Education, which includes both a science and an art, is likewise concerned with understanding, controlling, and effecting changes which promote the general welfare.

Classification of Arts and Sciences. — Sciences, arts, and industries are usually classified and defined on the basis of the objects which they seek to understand or in which they seek to effect changes. Thus astronomy is a science concerned with the nature and changes of the heavenly bodies; meteorology, with atmospheric conditions surrounding the earth; geology, with the earth's crust; biology, with the plants and animals on the earth; physiology, psychology, sociology, and others, with changes in animals, especially human beings. Education, as a science, is closely allied with the latter group. It is primarily concerned with the nature of changes in human beings. It is not, however, identical with other sciences which study human beings nor is it confined entirely to the study of mankind.

Relation of Education to Other Arts and Sciences.— Human beings possess many aspects worthy of study, and the changes going on in men are of many sorts. Thus a man is a mass of matter subject to the laws of gravitation, electrical conduction, and the like, so that some of the changes in him are for physics to study ; he is also a concretion of elements of nitrogen, oxygen, hydrogen, carbon, and the like, so that some of the changes in him are for chemistry to study ; other changes in men belong under anatomy ; still others under physiology. While each of these sciences deals primarily with one aspect of man, each also overlaps and borrows from the others. Education is interested primarily in the general interrelation of man and his environment, in all the changes which make possible a better adjustment of human nature to its surroundings. While education is thus interested primarily in man's instincts and native impulses, his capacity to learn, his intellect, skill, and character, it borrows heavily from all other sciences dealing with the nature of man and is also intimately concerned with the sciences, arts, and industries which deal with other things and events in the world.

Education as Adjustment to the Environment. — It is often said that a man's life consists in continual efforts to adjust himself to his environment. Education is often said to be concerned with the process of an individual's adjustment to his surroundings. According to this definition, education would be limited to the study of the human individual who is to conform himself to fit external conditions as well as he may. Such a definition would be correct as far as it goes, but it would be incomplete and misleading. It is true that education involves efforts to change human nature in such a way as to bring man into more harmonious relations with his surroundings. He *must* learn to live under conditions that exist. But this is only part of the truth. Education is not merely the process of changing human nature to fit into an unchangeable world ; it is quite as fully concerned with changing the world to harmonize with human nature. Man is most conspicuously the animal that refuses to be dominated by the environment. The human will rebels against mere passive adjustment to a stable world. If we look about us, it may appear that more of life is spent in changing the world than is expended in changing human nature. And, as we said in the opening paragraphs, man is not busied with changing the world for the world's sake, but to improve his own condition in it. He is interested and active not only in changing his nature to fit his surroundings, but also in modifying the environment to suit his nature.

Education Concerned Both with Changing Human Nature and Changing the World. — There are, then, three ways in which man may improve his intercourse with or adjustment to his environment. He may change himself, or the external world, or both. The task of the science of education is to discover which of these changes should be made and how to make them. The art of education is the technique of bringing about the changes in human nature when they are found to be desirable. Other arts and industries, such as painting, agriculture, engineering, transportation, are concerned with changing the environment when this is found to be preferable. Education is concerned with any change which influences the interaction of a man and his world. It is concerned with every question of choice between changing nature and changing the environment. If the fruits are poisonous, shall we teach the children to avoid them, or shall we destroy the plants? If the children are by nature disposed to theft, shall we change the world and its institutions or teach the child to adjust himself differently to the world as it is? Sometimes we elect to change the environment, sometimes to change human nature, sometimes each in some degree. In any case, the problem should be considered by the science of education.

The Educationist Must Know the World as Well as Human Nature. — To solve such problems, what facts must education take into account? First of all, education must know human nature as it is and the limits within which it may be changed. It would be unwise to simplify all commercial and industrial operations to the point where they required no reading of directions and no skill beyond a simple twist of one hand, and equally foolish to have all tasks so complicated as to require knowledge of calculus, or the skill of a juggler, which few could acquire. Secondly, education must take into account the external world — its industries, institutions, nations, customs, resources — as it is and the limits within which it can and may be changed. It would be as unwise to neglect education concerning infectious diseases, if many of these are unlikely to be completely abolished in a generation, as to instruct children in methods of defending themselves against packs of wolves that no longer invade their world. The fact that education is charged with taking into account both the individual and his world as it is and as it may be is responsible for the extreme difficulty and complexity — yet, at the same time, the attractiveness — of the science.

Education Requires Broadest Information. — Education, then, is concerned with far more than mere methods of teaching reading, writing, and arithmetic. It is concerned with the interaction of human individuals and their entire world. Education must survey and understand the world as it is — its physical features, its climate, its useful and dangerous products, its peoples, its governments, its institutions, its customs, its moral codes — since it is charged with assisting people to adjust themselves to the world as it is now. Education should be concerned with proposed changes in any phase of the world, as well as in human beings themselves, since it should be able to offer valid opinions concerning the possibility and advisability of changing human nature to conform to new conditions. Education must be alert to all changes in the world, however caused, whether deliberately with or without its approval, or by war, calamity, invention, or what not, since it is charged with assisting people to adjust themselves properly to new conditions. No science requires a broader range of information ; no science is in a position to contribute more to human welfare than education.

Distinction between Education as Art and as Science. — Education, as a science, is concerned with the discovery of the most satisfactory adjustments of an individual to the people, things, and conditions in the world. As an art, education is concerned with bringing about those changes in human nature, as distinguished from changes in the outside world, which result in the desired adjustment. Even as an art, education is concerned with far more than teaching school subjects. It is concerned with producing changes in human knowledge, skills, feelings, emotions, morals, in habits of every type. But before elaborating this fact, let us inquire why the art of education is needed.

THE NEED OF EDUCATION

Education as an art, as a technique of changing human conduct, is needed for three reasons. It is needed, first, because the human being is born and grows up with an inherited, or unlearned, equipment that provides an incomplete and unsatisfactory ability to adjust to *any* — even the simplest — environment. It is needed, secondly, because natural, unguided learning (as distinguished from education by means of guidance) is slow, wasteful, and often misleading. It is needed, thirdly, because the modern world is so exceedingly complex and changeable that rapid learning is required as long as man takes an actively serviceable part in it.

The Limitations of Original Nature. — Each new generation is born with the germs of a native equipment of intellect, skills, and interests which differ but slightly from that possessed by mankind before the dawn of recorded history. Of the products of a lifetime of learning, the masses of information, the multitude of habits, skills, attitudes, convictions, and ideals possessed by parents, nothing is transmitted to the offspring. They enter the world with the same meager equipment as infants born a thousand years ago.

Need of Utilizing the Gifts of Civilization. — If all human beings save newborn infants vanished to another planet, and if by a miracle the babies were kept alive for a score of years, preserving whatever knowledge and skill came from natural inner growth, and lacking only the influence of the educational activities of other men, they would, at the age of twenty-one, resemble a horde of animals. They would get a precarious living from fruits, berries, and small animals, would easily become victims of malaria, yellow fever, smallpox, and plague, and would know little more of language, mechanical arts, or provision for the future than the monkeys. They would be distinguishable from other mammalian species chiefly by a much greater variety of bodily movements, especially of the hands, mouth parts, and face, a much quicker rate of learning, and a very much keener satisfaction in mental life for its own sake. But even under the simple conditions of a primitive environment, the life of the jungle, the learning of a lifetime would be limited largely to the simplest type of food getting and protective skills with scarcely any real understanding of themselves or the natural world in which they lived.

If these infants grew up in a deserted modern city, they would advance little if any further without education. They would be engaged mainly in the search of food, mates, and organic comforts like other animals. They would use the books, tools, engines, and other innumerable products of civilization as toys somewhat more intelligently than would apes, but they would not learn to read the books, to bake bread, repair the tools, or make of engines more than spectacles for amusement, wonder, and fear.

Limitations of Unguided Learning. — Should these infants grow up in a modern community in which men and women went about their business with no attempt to advise, guide, correct, or otherwise educate them, they would learn considerable by means of observation. Their development would consist mainly in learning to do what they could see others do. Much of what they could see others do they would not learn because of inability to understand its significance. Even the simpler activities closely related to primitive wants they would learn uneconomically and often in an inefficient manner by observation alone. At most, they would merely acquire some of the forms of civilized life; they would learn little of its meaning. They would learn to ape us, without learning to live our life. Without some education, the spoken word, the typewriter, the newspaper, the electric light, the medicine bottle would remain mysterious to them all their lives.

The surprise is not that we learn so little and slowly without tuition, but that with it we can learn so much and so rapidly even as infants. Our capacity to learn as adults is largely due to our education as infants. Our development depends more than we realize on acquiring early the most essential tools for learning.

Whatever charms the life of a man left to his own original nature would have, it is certain that no wise man would choose that life for his children. Indeed, the energies of men, as far back as we can trace them, have been spent in preventing that life by education. Even primitive man, in his few-sided existence, recognized the need of educating the young. Because it was so obvious, the value of education was one of the earliest discoveries. So it is not enough to change the face of the world with cities, mines, farms, and factories. Man must be taught to use them. *Advantageous changes in the world's things produce their benefits only when accompanied by changes in the human beings who are to live with them.*

Modern Life Requires Continuous Learning. — As civilization has advanced and as life has become more complex, knowledge more extensive, implements more numerous and complicated, social relations more rich and varied, the need of education has increased rather than decreased. Merely to participate with reasonable fullness in the life of a modern city — and the proportion of urban dwellers is constantly increasing — merely to react with understanding and propriety to the contacts of everyday life requires many skills of body and mind, much information, and millions of modifications of the primitive animals which we are by birth. The need for education, merely to adjust ourselves to conditions to our own satisfaction, does not cease at any time from the cradle to the grave. The motor helplessness of infancy, the emotional unrest of adolescence, the mental and vocational demands of young adulthood, the development of the family and preparations for the future of the adult, the deprivations and weakness of old age require equally new, equally great, and equally difficult adjustments.

Since the traits — the knowledge, skill, habits, attitudes, beliefs, ideals — which we acquire during life are not transmitted to our offspring, who enter the world poorly adjusted even to the simplest environment, education must begin early and be administered effectively to provide a happy adjustment to our complex world as it is. But, as suggested earlier, education is concerned not merely with adjustment to things as they are or even to changes that result [from uncontrollable forces of nature or the momentum of human action already under way, but also with the deliberate production of further changes which may make human life more satisfying and fruitful. In a democracy, where the masses control in a large degree the nature and amount of changes that may be made, wider and fuller education is especially essential.

More and better education is needed to reduce the still appalling sum of error, injustice, misery, and ignorance which blocks progress toward better living.

Education to Promote National Welfare. — Even the most civilized nations have not yet learned to settle international disputes by a court of expert judges, or to prevent national violence and lawbreaking by an international police. Theft, arson, and murder are still honored, provided they be done wholesale by a nation. And the wise opinion is that the only sure preventive of war is to educate men to think of it as a futile crime.

Even the most civilized nations also commit, year after year, the blunder of not letting men work who wish to work and are able to work to the advantage of the common good. A president of this country is reported to have said, when asked what should be done for the million unemployed, " God knows." But man must learn. Until man knows how to arrange national affairs so that no willing, capable worker shall be miserable in enforced idleness, education is incomplete.

Education to Promote Personal Happiness. — In even the most civilized nations the majority of men are not rational even about their own welfare. They do not value absolute goods, taking satisfaction in proportion to the beauty, property, leisure, friends, and the like which are theirs. On the contrary, many of their satisfactions and discomforts are caused by purely relative conditions — being better looking than Jones, not owning so large a house as Smith's, having to work more than other men. It is pitifully true that many a man would object to being twice as well off as he now is, if the conditions were attached that everyone else should be ten times as well off. There is perhaps no greater barrier to human happiness than this irrational bookkeeping of welfare in terms of relative status alone. For it, too, better education is the preventive and cure.

Education to Advance the Control of Nature. — Education, too, is the necessary basis of all the arts and industries whereby man changes his outside conditions for the better. To so change them he must in each generation change himself. He must acquire the knowledge and skill, or the crops will not grow, the bacilli which cause disease will not be killed, the houses will not be built, the poems, paintings, and operas will not be composed, humane national laws and institutions will not be established, and international exploratory, commercial, and scientific enterprises will not be pursued.

Means of Making Education Better

Man improves education as he improves any other human activity — by open-minded thought about it, by learning the results of existing forms of it, by experimenting with other forms, and by clearing up and making reasonable our notions of what changes we should make in human beings and of how we should make them. Such impartial scientific study of man's efforts to change himself for the better has been receiving more and more attention within the last twenty years. In the case of school education, for instance, the actual changes wrought in boys and girls by this or that form of education are being measured, old and new methods are being tested by experiment in the same spirit of zeal and care for the truth that animates the man of science, and the educational customs which have been accepted unthinkingly by "use and wont" are being required to justify themselves to reason.

Such scientific study faces five problems or groups of problems, namely, those of:

1. The Aims of Education. What changes should be made in human beings by schools and other educating forces?

2. The Material or Subjects of Education. What is the original nature of the human beings whom we have to change? What are the principles or laws of human nature and behavior that we need to know in order to change men for the better?

3. The Means and Agents of Education. What forces are at our command in the task of producing and preventing changes in human beings?

4. The Methods of Education. How should these means and agents be brought to bear upon the subjects of education so as best to realize its aims?

5. The Results of Education. What have been the actual effects of different methods, means, and agents acting upon different kinds of human beings?

QUESTIONS AND EXERCISES

1. Is the engineer, the farmer, or the woodsman concerned with making changes in the world? How do the functions of these workers differ from those of the educator?

2. Give some illustrations of the statement that the educationist should be concerned with changes wrought in the world by the architect, the engineer, or the doctor.

3. What is the distinction suggested by the two terms *educator* and *educationist?* Think of the educator in connection with the functions of the doctor, the engineer, the farmer, etc., and the educationist in connection with the functions of the biologist, physicist, chemist, botanist, etc.

4. What is the distinction between an art and a science, in general? In education? Criticize or defend the use of the term *educator* as implying one who practices the art of educating and *educationist* as one who pursues study of the science of education.

5. Why should a teacher know as much as possible about the science of education? Why should the teacher know as much as possible about the contemporary world at large?

6. Summarize the main reasons for the need of education at the present time. Which of these needs are likely to become greater in the future? Which are likely to become less pronounced?

7. Who requires the greater amount of education, the children of savages living on a South Sea island or the children of parents living in New York City? Explain.

8. Among the children in New York City, which probably *needs* the greater amount of education, the very dull child or the extremely bright? Explain.

9. Which will probably repay society at large most fully, the extensive education of the dull or of the bright children?

10. As the term *education* is used in this chapter, does it imply that a child left to play by himself in the back yard is being educated? What is the dictionary definition of the word *educate?* Is it possible to learn at all without being educated? Is this substantially the meaning implied in this chapter?

REFERENCES

The following books contain discussions of the topics of this chapter and of most of the chapters which follow. Appended to each later chapter will be given other references which treat in greater detail the topics of that chapter. A larger number of questions and exercises and an extensive bibliography will be found in O. M. Clem's *Work Book Syllabus in Principles of Education*. Warwick and York.

BAGLEY, W. C., *The Educative Process*. Macmillan.

BAGLEY, W. C., and KEITH, J. A. H., *An Introduction to Teaching*. Macmillan.

BOBBITT, F., *The Curriculum*. Houghton Mifflin.

BODE, B. H., *Fundamentals of Education*. Macmillan.

BODE, B. H., *Modern Educational Theories*. Macmillan.

COURSAULT, J. H., *Principles of Education*. Silver, Burdett.

CUBBERLEY, E. P., *An Introduction to the Study of Education*. Houghton Mifflin.

DEWEY, J., *Democracy and Education*. Macmillan.

DEWEY, J., *Human Nature and Conduct*. Henry Holt.

DEWEY, J., *School and Society*. University of Chicago Press.

FRASIER, G. W., and ARMENTROUT, W. D., *An Introduction to Education*. Scott, Foresman.

GRIZZELL, E. D., *Education: Principles and Practices*. Macmillan.

HENDERSON, E. N., *A Textbook in the Principles of Education*. Macmillan.

HORNE, H. H., *Philosophy of Education*. Macmillan.

HOWERTH, I. W., *The Theory of Education*. Century.

KANDEL, I. L., *Twenty-five Years of American Education*. Macmillan.

KILPATRICK, W. H., *Education for a Changing Civilization*. Macmillan.

KILPATRICK, W. H., *Foundations of Method*. Macmillan.

KILPATRICK, W. H., *Source Book in the Philosophy of Education*. Macmillan.

MONROE, P., *Brief Course in the History of Education*. Macmillan.

MOORE, E. C., *What Is Education?* Ginn.

NUNN, T. P., *Education: Its Data and First Principles*. Arnold (London).

RUEDIGER, W. C., *Principles of Education*. Houghton Mifflin.

SPENCER, H., *Education*. Burt.

TROW, W. C., *Scientific Method in Education*. Houghton Mifflin.

CHAPTER II

THE ULTIMATE AIMS OF EDUCATION

AIMS OF EDUCATION IN TERMS OF HUMAN WANTS

Need of Definite Formulation of Aims. — In the preceding chapter it was said that the effect of education is to produce changes in human nature and in other things in the world. It was said furthermore that by educating himself and others, man aims to produce those changes which result in improving his condition, in achieving a better relation between himself and the rest of the world, in increasing his welfare, or in making his life better and richer. Such statements obviously leave the purpose of education rather vague. The acute reader will at once inquire : " What do you mean by an improved condition, a better relation, an increase in welfare, or a richer life? " " On what basis are we to decide what is a bad, indifferent, or good condition of life? " These are very pertinent questions, which have long engaged the attention of thoughtful men. They are pertinent because every person interested or active in education should have some idea of its aims or objectives. Statements of these aims or objectives should express the ultimate purposes of education in such a way that they may be used as definite, intelligible principles of guidance by those who seek to educate effectively. They should be so stated as to be helpful in deciding on particular steps in education such as the desirability of teaching this fact, establishing that habit, encouraging the other skill, inculcating another ideal.

15

What Determines Values. — Education seeks to secure for men things that are good instead of bad, conditions that satisfy instead of annoy, activities that are right and beneficial instead of wrong and harmful. Things are not good or bad in and of themselves; a man's acts are neither right nor wrong apart from their effects; no condition is either satisfying or annoying in isolation. Things, conditions, and acts can be classified as good or bad, beneficial or harmful, satisfying or annoying, or as otherwise possessing value and significance only when viewed from some point of view. In the last analysis, decisions as to the value and significance of things with which education is concerned are based on desires, wants, cravings, or urges. To justify and explain this statement, we must take a short excursion into the field of psychology, the science which undertakes to explain human conduct as it is.

The Rôle of Human Wants. — According to modern psychology, all human activity is initiated and sustained by some urge, craving, desire, or want. The young infant is largely immobile until it experiences the craving for food, or the urge of thirst, or the desire for physical activity, or some other want. It then becomes active and the activity continues until the infant's craving is satisfied, until it secures what it wants, unless the desire subsides or is overcome by some other urge such as the craving to rest from the effects of its own exertions. Unless the infant wants something, there is no occasion for striving. When it is actively seeking to satisfy one urge, such as hunger, the object of that urge, food, is supremely important, valuable, good, whereas other things such as noises, movements, toys are at the time relatively unimportant and undesired. To the infant, then, things take on value and importance as they serve to satisfy some childish want.

What is true of infancy is fundamentally true of all ages. Human cravings, in the last analysis, initiate and sustain action. Without them, " the human organism would become inert like a wonderful clockwork whose springs had been removed or an engine whose fires had been drawn." Wants, furthermore, are the final determinants of good and bad, useful and useless, right and wrong, beautiful and ugly. Things have value and importance only as they serve to satisfy the urges which lie back of somebody's strivings; they are called useless, bad, wrong, and the like only as they fail to contribute to, or positively thwart, some conscious being's efforts to satisfy his cravings.

A thing or event or act or condition is not then, in the last analysis, desirable because it is valuable. It is valuable because it is desirable — because it satisfies a want or craving or impulse of some man or other conscious being. Suppose, for instance, that all creatures had been, and now and in the future were to be, blind. The most beautiful painting would be no better than the ugliest; for it could make no difference to anybody. Suppose that all beings, past, present, and future, existed equally well and equally happily without, as with, food — that no one wanted food or drink. Temperance would be no longer a virtue, and gluttony no longer a sin. They would simply be accidental qualities like the color of one's eyes. For the temperate man would satisfy no want of his own or anyone else's, nor would the glutton's acts imply deprivation for anybody else. Value or worth or goodness means power to satisfy wants. One thing or condition or act is more valuable or more worthy or better than another because it satisfies wants more fully, or satisfies more wants, or causes less deprivation of wants.

Aim of Education Stated in Terms of Human Wants. — Life is activity initiated and sustained to satisfy wants.

Since this is the case, we may say provisionally that the ultimate aim of education for man [1] is to secure the fullest satisfaction of human wants. Observe that this statement contains the word *fullest;* this implication of this word we should emphasize and explain.

Conflict among Wants of Different Individuals. — Every infant, child, or adult has many wants. Some of these cravings, like that for foods of certain tastes or for a certain amount of unhampered physical action, are native or inherited, born in the very structure of the organism. Others, like the desire for smoking, are acquired. Among both native and acquired wants of persons of all ages are some which, when satisfied in the most convenient manner by one person, tend to deprive another person of the means of satisfying one or more of his wants. If, to satisfy my hunger, I should eat all the berries in the patch, someone else may have to go hungry. If, to satisfy my urge to excel, I should follow fraudulent practices in athletics, business, or love, some more deserving person may be deprived of a satisfaction rightfully earned. If, to appease his craving for domination and power, a man should take advantage of his superiority in wealth to underpay and torment his employees, their wants will be less fully satisfied. Thus, in many cases, if one person secures the *fullest* satisfaction of his individual wants, others will be less able to satisfy their cravings.

Conflict among Wants of Different Groups. — The situation is much the same when we replace the individual by the family, the local community, the members of a religious or political or social or occupational group, or even the nation or a league of nations. If one group, to satisfy its cravings for hoarding and domination, monopo-

---

[1] We shall not attempt to decide what the aim of education should be for the entire universe of conscious beings; or how far man should perhaps sacrifice his wants to those of the universe as a whole.

lizes all of a certain class of goods, such as coal, it may not only reduce the fullness with which the wants of other groups are satisfied but, in the end, it may also cause a diminution in its own satisfaction since the other group may retaliate by monopolizing some other material and the productivity of both may be thereby reduced. If the members of one nation, to enjoy the feeling of superiority, indulge in unreasonable emotional patriotism, the result is likely to be misunderstanding, distrust, rivalry in unessentials, even war, which may reduce the ability of both groups to satisfy the needs of their members. In short, by attempting solely to fulfill the needs of a particular individual, family, community, nation, or even a league of nations, we shall not achieve the fullest satisfaction of the wants of individuals on the whole. On the contrary, by attempting to satisfy the wants of all human beings, the desires of each of us will be most fully satisfied.

Education Seeks to Promote the Satisfying of the Wants of Humanity as a Whole. — Education, then, aims at satisfying the wants of all people in order to give each person the fullest realization of his own desires. A fundamental principle of education, then, is that the best in life is not to be achieved by strivings for the individual aggrandizement of a person, race, nation, or any other group, but, on the contrary, by striving for the advancement of mankind as a whole.

The aim of education is international or universal in scope not for sentimental but for practical reasons; for only by considering the wants of everyone can we satisfy our own desires most fully. If we accept this aim, it will help us to appraise all types of conditions and acts that we may encounter and to evaluate changes in the physical world and in man himself which education may produce.

The chief aim of education, then, is to realize the fullest satisfaction of human wants. To this end external things and conditions and human nature must both be changed. In the last analysis, changes in human nature, to be effective, must include changes in human wants, since satisfaction and activity alike spring from cravings. In general, education aims to diminish or abolish those cravings which are futile or antagonistic to the satisfaction of other wants and to cultivate those wants which do not reduce or which actually increase the satisfaction of others.

Now that a brief statement of the ultimate aims of education has been given it may be clarified and appraised more fully by considering it in comparison with other objectives of education that have received attention. Happiness, preparation for life, growth, reorganization of experience, perfection of oneself, and culture are various terms employed to indicate other objectives of education.

Happiness as an Aim of Education

It is sometimes stated that the ultimate aim of education is to increase human happiness. If this statement takes such a form as " the greatest happiness for the most people," it is substantially equivalent to our statement of the aim of education in terms of satisfying human wants. When we inquire what occasions human happiness, we shall find that it depends upon human wants. Activity which satisfies no need, striving which results in failure or the frustration of wants will not yield the fullest happiness and often will, on the contrary, lead to unhappiness. Happiness results from the full activity of fulfilling human wants. Since the process of satisfying human wants seems to be fundamental to happiness, it is better to define the aim of education in terms of wants.

EDUCATION AS PREPARATION FOR LIFE

To state that education should always attempt to give children happiness by the most immediate and direct means would be as unwise as to say that by satisfying any individual want the welfare of society would be fostered. Many instances of immediate happiness may reduce or deny later satisfaction ; many causes of individual happiness are very dangerous to the welfare of others. Happiness for the individual and society as a whole in the long run is often best attained by denying a person some tempting opportunity of the moment. Among children, who less skillfully conceal their joys and sorrows, inconsistencies between individual immediate happiness and happiness in general for the individual and the group are often apparent. Not all happy experiences are constructively educative and not all educative activities result in immediate happiness. Overimpressed with these obvious facts, some stern souls have declared it ignoble and misleading to define the aim of education as a process of increasing happiness. Education, they claim, is the serious business of preparing children for life. Attempts to make the school add to the store of children's happiness especially are decried as unsafe, " soft pedagogy," trifling with the serious work of education.

Dewey, our leading American in the philosophy of education, has brilliantly and steadfastly opposed this false doctrine. Education, he maintains, is not preparation for life, it *is* life. It is not merely a business of getting ready to live happily and fruitfully, it is the process of living happily and fruitfully at each moment from birth to death. This view is not based on a sentimental attitude toward children but on the hard-headed realization that it represents the best method of realizing the ultimate aims of all life.

The statement that education is not preparation for later life but living here and now does not mean *mere* living but *happy* living here and now. Happiness, as stated above, results from the full process of successfully striving to fulfill our wants. To live happily, then, means not merely preparing to live later, and not merely living, in any way, now. It means living in such a way as to be striving successfully to fulfill our present wants. What Professor Dewey and other modern philosophers contend, then, apparently, is that at all stages in the process of education we must consider the individual's wants.

We should consider the child's wants not merely to make him happy — although this is desirable — but also to make his development more fruitful. If we disregard his wants, we jeopardize his physical well-being, we reduce his interests and activities, we arouse his resistance to the educative process. If, on the contrary, we relate our educational methods and materials to the wants which he experiences, we shall find the learner more vigorous, active, attentive, interested; his activity will be better motivated and longer sustained. To give due concern to the wants of children, then, is one means of making education more effective and of increasing happiness. Fundamentally the dictum *education should be living, instead of mere preparation for life* is justified by the practical results obtained by educating in conformity with, rather than in opposition to, children's wants.

Although it has the practical defense just mentioned, happiness as a guide in education may be considered from other points of view. Children have as great a claim upon happiness as do the adults which they will in time become. If the direct present happiness of children does not conflict with the ultimate ends of education, it is wholly desirable, and even if it does conflict somewhat, it has a right to be put in the balance against future goods and chosen if it outweighs them. It would be folly to deny children happiness for no purpose.

Happiness is not a fiend to be exorcised. The thwarting of every natural impulse and the deprivation of every cherished joy are not necessary means of grace. In fact, if we free ourselves from our adult tendency to think of what is good for us as adults, and consider how cheaply innocent happiness can be given to the young, and consider also that frequently (not always, of course) the childish likes and dislikes are as good guides to later welfare as our artificial prescriptions are, we shall make happiness at the time by no means a small concern of school education.

The apparent conflict between " happy living here and now " and " preparation for life " as statements of the aim of education, then, in the main, reduces itself to a conflict about the chances of attaining happiness and the relative value of present and deferred satisfaction. The greatest happiness for the most people for the most time is an end to be sought by making children's lives as happy as possible and by not denying their wants unless demonstrable good may come from it. The strongest justification of this view is the fact that happiness usually is a good guide and always a symptom of vigorous and active participation in the educative process.

GROWTH AND REORGANIZATION OF EXPERIENCES

Education aims at change. But to define education as the process of producing change is insufficient since change may take many directions, both desirable and undesirable. It is often said that the aim of education is that growth which is brought about by a continuous reorganization of experience. The difficulty with this statement, of education as growth, is that growth may take many forms and directions — it may be wholesome or cancerous. If we express growth and reorganization of experience in terms of our previously stated aim, namely to secure the fullest gratification of wants, we have a helpful concept. Education then becomes the process of so promoting happy living that conditions in the world and our own wants are changed to increase the fullness with which our desires, as a whole, may be satisfied. The direction of growth is now defined; growth comprises changes which lead to the fuller satisfaction of human wants. As the child lives, his experiences should be constantly reorganized and reintegrated so that his wants become increasingly those which, by promoting the welfare of others, rebound to satisfy his own desires. He must grow, too, in power to fulfill his constantly improving wants. Both wants and means of satisfying them, then, are modifiable and changes in the direction of increasing their fullness constitutes growth. Such growth is the aim of education.

PERFECTIONISM

Vague and Inadequate as a Complete Aim. — A generation ago one of the most popular statements of the aim of education was " The Perfection of All One's Powers," or, in Herbert Spencer's words, " Complete Living." These statements always needed qualification. For it is not desirable that life should complete itself by having all possible varieties of envy, jealousy, and cruelty; and it is certain that some features of the life process are more desirable than others. Completeness had to be interpreted as the fulfillment of certain selected features which could work together *harmoniously* — that is, without sacrificing worthy wants. Obviously, no one would advocate perfecting the power to worry or despair. Since certain powers conflict with others, it was necessary to change the phrasing to " harmonious development " or the like.

Specialization Is Necessary. — But even if the misleading character of the term *complete* and the vagueness of *perfection* are corrected by qualifying statements, the doctrine itself — that education's business is to make the best possible specimen of humanity out of each man — is faulty. The aim of life is not to stock the world as a museum with perfected specimens for man or deity to contemplate. It is to make men vital parts of an organized force for the welfare of the group. Powers are not for possession and display, but for use. This requires specialization rather than general perfection. Men have to live together and depend one upon another, not each trying to be the best possible creature in all ways, but each being taught to perform, and take pleasure in, those services in which by excelling he can do the most for the common good. Nor is it desirable, even from the point of view of individuals taken singly, that education should develop equally in every respect. Each individual, by sex, race, hereditary equipment, and the circumstances of time and place in which he is born, is more likely to meet certain situations than others during life, and it is to be competent and happy in those situations that he particularly needs to be trained. It would be wasteful to train a genius and an idiot identically. It would have been stupid to have perfected Pasteur's powers to drive a good bargain, or Darwin's powers as a public speaker, or Aristotle's powers as a gardener. Perfecting the power to shoot with bow and arrow is unimportant in America now for the very reverse of the reason that it was important four hundred years ago.

The doctrine of individual perfection is inadequate because it gives an excuse for the too common tendency of men to educate themselves for competitive display instead of coöperative work, because it opposes the specialization which is necessary for mutual aid, and because it neglects the fact that education beyond certain fundamentals should narrow itself to fit every man for a certain probable course of life, not for all life's possibilities.

Specialization Will Become Increasingly Necessary. — Perfectionism of individuals, one at a time, grows less significant as an aim in proportion as more knowledge is discovered, as the world's work is more divided, and as education is for a wider group. Even to-day such an ideal for the education of the million children attending the public schools of New York City seems a little absurd. Many of them early show special talents to which other powers should be sacrificed for the common good and their personal happiness. Most of them have some weakness which it would be folly to try to remedy. Efficiency in service grows more significant as we see more clearly the world's needs and how to meet them. With every decade it becomes more possible for a special line of action to be chosen beforehand for an individual with a very high probability that, if he prepares himself properly, he will by that career be of greatest value to himself and to the world.

OTHER NARROW AIMS OF EDUCATION

During the long history of discussion of the aims of education, various objectives have been suggested and tested, and usually discarded as too ambiguous or too narrow to serve as the one ultimate aim. Among the objectives suggested have been knowledge, skill, mental power, culture, morality, and character. Without doubt, education does aim to assist the child to acquire character, moral and cultural traits, knowledge, skill, and mental power of some kind and for certain purposes. Merely to say, however, that the aim of education is to develop culture, information, or skill is not useful since such a statement does not suggest what kinds of culture, information, or skill, or what types of character or moral traits are to be sought. To indicate more clearly the significance of these facts, let us consider merely the cases of culture and knowledge, as representative of this list of proposed objectives.

LIMITATIONS OF CULTURE AS A GENERAL AIM

Most educated persons think they know what culture means — and usually think that they have it! But there would be a great variation in such opinions and possessions. To some, culture means a body of knowledge and habits which distinguish its possessor as a member of the leisure class, which ornament his intellect much as tailor-made clothes adorn his body, and which satisfy the craving to display his superiority to others. To others culture means knowledge of *human affairs* as contrasted with science and technology, which are taken to be knowledge of *things*. Thus history, literature, the fine arts, psychology, and government would be regarded as more cultural than physics, chemistry, and geology. To others culture means primarily knowledge and skill in the *fine* arts such as music and painting as contrasted with the *practical* arts such as engineering, nursing, or cooking. According to another idea, culture is a body of knowledge, habits, and interest such as prepares a person to perform, not the special work of any trade or profession, but the general work of citizen, parent, friend, and human being. Culture is thus a name for the broad knowledge useful for being a man or woman in general, as opposed to " technical training " for being a physician, statesman, or carpenter.

The term *culture* is ambiguous. It has too many meanings to serve as a definition of the major aim of education. Culture, as defined by some persons, is an aim of education since the knowledge and skills described are means of increasing the sum of satisfaction of human wants. In so far as culture means the cultivation of impersonal pleasures, or of stainless wants, such as appreciation of beauty in nature and art, interests in human life, a sense of humor, satisfaction in knowledge, which may be satisfied without deprivations to others or, better, with benefits to the welfare of others, it is a worthy aim of education. But in so far as culture becomes synonomous with selfish display, waste, triviality, expense, or uselessness, it runs counter to the ultimate objective of education. To appraise the value of culture, then, we must apply some other criterion such as that embodied in our earlier definition of the aim of education — the increase of satisfaction of the wants of mankind as a whole.

KNOWLEDGE AS AN AIM OF EDUCATION

Knowledge Essential to Education. — There can be no doubt that to increase and diffuse knowledge constitute important aims of education. Although knowledge can be misused, it is in and of itself of utmost value. In the work of making use of the forces and laws of nature to satisfy human wants, knowledge of natural forces and laws is indispensable. In the work of improving our own wants, knowledge of the forces and laws of human nature is essential. If mean men are unwilling and stupid men unable to use knowledge for the best interests of society, the fault is not with knowledge. The cure for folly and ignorance is not less knowledge but more. And for the cure of evil intentions, knowledge is essential.

Examples of Usefulness of Knowledge. — It is only by ignorance or forgetfulness of what man owes to the knowledge thus given to him that anyone can resist a holy enthusiasm in the spread of knowledge. Consider the miseries removed and satisfactions created by the spread of one small fraction of knowledge — preventive medicine — to one small group of men! Cholera, smallpox, and the plague are thereby exterminated. The end of yellow fever, malaria, and tuberculosis in a country becomes simply a matter of dollars and cents. Deaths from wounds, childbirth, and minor surgical operations dwindle to rarities. Consider the fears and suffering that have been undergone on account of purely imaginary gods and evils, whose tyranny over human happiness mere knowledge removes. Ghosts, evil spirits, witches, and demons made the life of many primitive peoples an almost incessant fear, and took tithes in labor and goods that could have added a large increment to human comfort.

Morality Based on Knowledge. — Morality itself, though often contrasted with or set apart from knowledge, is, except for the good will and certain other noble and humane qualities of character and temperament, a creation of knowledge. It is chiefly knowledge that saves the mother of to-day from throwing her baby to an idol, the consumptive from poisoning his neighbors, or the ruler from ruining his country. Most of the greatest disasters have been due more to ignorance than to evil intent.

Thus, it appears that the development of knowledge, while not itself the supreme end of education, is nevertheless a most important means of promoting the aim of education. Knowledge is valuable because it is an essential means of promoting human welfare.

Education Requires Specialization in Pursuit of Knowledge. — While the acquisition of knowledge — any knowledge — is useful it does not follow that it is desirable to teach everybody all available knowledge, even were such an achievement possible. For the teacher, a practical problem becomes: " What knowledge is of most worth for each of my pupils and how is it to be made to function? " As a general guide, we must refer to our most satisfactory general definition of the aim of education — the control of nature to increase the welfare of society at large. In addition to this general point of reference, we must present, in following chapters, as much as possible of the available knowledge which bears upon the selection of materials for particular pupils and the management of children to make the information function most effectively.

A detailed study of skills, habits, ideals, and attitudes, as well as of knowledge, must be made because not all of these can be given to all men, and what is most suitable for a given person at one stage in his development and in one environment and in one stage of civilization is often unsuitable at other ages or in other places and times. Such a study will be undertaken in later chapters.

SUMMARY AND CONCLUSIONS

Before taking up these particular demands upon education at the present time, we may summarize our considerations of the ultimate aim. The ultimate aim of education is to realize a condition in which human wants may be most fully satisfied. Human wants are given this position of supreme importance for the reason that any thing, act, condition, or event in life has importance, value, interest, or significance only as it tends to affect — to satisfy or thwart — man's cravings. Human wants become the central concern of the process of education because they are the primary and essential factors in initiating and sustaining action of all kinds. Thinking, imagination, feeling, acting, forming and breaking habits are subordinate to the dynamic factors — which may be termed wants, urges, cravings, impulses, interests — which generate and maintain them. To change a want is to make the most fundamental of possible changes. Once a want is changed, all sorts of subordinate changes in thought, feeling, and action occur as a result.

A little reflection on the nature of man as he now is and the world as it now exists, led us to the conclusion that to fulfill the aim of education, which is to satisfy human wants as fully as possible, we must change both the nature of the external world and the nature of man himself. To change man vitally we must change his wants. To secure for each person the fullest satisfaction of his wants, we must seek to effect those changes both in man and nature which add to the satisfaction not of any particular person, family, nation, race, or other group, but of humanity in general. Each individual will secure the fullest realization of his wants when they harmonize with and facilitate the fulfillment of the wants of mankind as a whole.

Such is the ultimate aim of education. To realize this objective we must concern ourselves with methods of assisting young people to acquire knowledge, skill, moral ideals and attitudes, culture and mental power of certain kinds and in certain degrees and to secure happiness, to grow, and to perfect themselves in certain ways. Since the changes most desired are those which foster the common good, we must endeavor in the next chapter, and in others, to state more definitely the directions which education — as far as we are able to see — should take at the present time.

QUESTIONS AND EXERCISES

1. What were the main reasons for the view that education should aim primarily to change human *wants* instead of particular acts or ideas?

2. What is the chief criterion by means of which the *value* of human wants is to be judged? What is the justification of this criterion?

3. Enumerate some wants of children that, in the light of the main aim of education, should be strengthened. Should be changed.

4. Why is it that not all of the "natural" wants of children harmonize with the aims of education? Children have certain natural likes and dislikes for foods. Do their tastes provide a perfect guide to the choice of the most wholesome foods? Illustrate. Would they be better off if they had no taste preferences at all?

5. In what respect are the following statements of the aims of education satisfactory and in what respects inadequate?

    a. The aim of education is to increase knowledge and power.

    b. The end of education is to produce a well-balanced and many-sided interest. (Herbart)

    c. The attainment of a sound mind in a sound body is the end of education. (Locke)

    d. The aim of education is to increase social efficiency.

    e. The function of education is to prepare for complete living. (Spencer)

    f. The object of education is preparation for more effective service in church and state. (Luther)

6. Give some concrete cases in which the interests of society would be benefited by educating different people along different lines.

7. Can you recall historical characters who by specializing have been far more useful to humanity than they would have been had they tried to develop all their physical, mental, social, cultural, aesthetic, and other powers equally?

8. Are there some respects in which the education of all persons should be similar? Name and defend them.

9. Why is education likely to be more fruitful when it emphasizes the needs of life here and now than when it emphasizes preparation for the needs of later, or adult, life?

10. Of what practical value is a formulation of the general or ultimate aim of education? Criticize the statement given in the text.

REFERENCES

The books listed for Chapter I treat the topic discussed here.

CHAPTER III

THE MAJOR PRESENT NEEDS OF EDUCATION

The ultimate aim of education is to achieve the fullest satisfaction of the wants of mankind. It now becomes our task to discuss the particular types of culture, information, skill, ideals, and other acquisitions required to realize this aim by people living in the present decade of a highly industrial age, under a democratic government of diversified peoples with strong social and national prejudices and largely in crowded cities with the sources of disease imperfectly under control. Under these present conditions of incomplete control over nature and incomplete mastery of ourselves, we meet several types of notably insistent needs. These needs have been revealed by the results of studies in sociology, medicine, psychology, economics, politics, ethics, and other sciences. To meet these present needs will prove to be the most effective means of achieving the ultimate aims of education.

Classification of Needs. — Merely for convenience of discussion, the main present demands of education may be arranged in two classes of five groups each. The first class deals with the need of proper adjustment to phases of our present-day environment; the second class has to do with several types of equipment needed by every individual. Each of these two classes of needs is divided into five groups of needs, as follows:

33

I. Needed Adjustments to Situations in Modern Life :
   1. Adjustments to the physical world
   2. Adjustments to economic situations
   3. Adjustments to family situations
   4. Adjustments to social situations
   5. Adjustments to civic situations
II. Needed Types of Personal Equipment :
   1. Physical health
   2. Mental health and balance
   3. Recreational resources
   4. Ethical and religious resources
   5. Intellectual resources

ADJUSTMENT TO THE PHYSICAL WORLD

Individual Adjustments. — The last century has witnessed what is commonly termed the great Industrial
Revolution.   One result of an unparalleled number of
inventions has been a radical change in our physical
environment.   The world is now filled with gigantic cities,
enormous buildings and factories, a multiplicity of complex machines, railroads, street cars, automobiles, air-
planes, printing presses, computing machines, steamboats,
sewage, water, and gas systems, electrical appliances of a
thousand types, tunnels, dams, bridges, metals, chemicals,
and thousands of other things unknown in the youth of our
grandfathers.   Never before have our physical surroundings been so complex.   Merely to know the physical world
well enough to get along in it requires a vast amount of
education.   Since parents rarely have the necessary time
or information, the school has been assuming an increasing
portion of the task of introducing children to the ways
and instruments of our complex physical environment.
By means of moving and still pictures, books and
lectures, models and demonstrations, observations and

excursions, teachers must now train their charges to know and to adjust themselves to their material surroundings.

Scientific Principles. — Adequate adjustment to one's physical environment requires more than mere ability to utilize different appliances and objects such as stoves, gas ranges, electric lights, telephones, tools, automobiles, street cars, ferry boats, shops, stores, and the like, and to deal with natural objects and phenomena. It requires a certain degree of knowledge of the principles underlying these objects and mechanisms, that is, some familiarity with many sciences such as geography, meteorology, physics, chemistry, geology, nutrition, medicine, zoölogy, and their practical applications in the case of foods and cookery, transportation, personal and community hygiene, electrical and thermal mechanics, engineering, construction, agriculture, the phonograph, the radio, the airplane, and so on. Many facts from science are useful and many are not difficult to teach. There are valuable facts from the natural and applied sciences which may be taught as early as the first grade. To teach the useful scientific facts, to apply them helpfully to everyday life and to increase the effectiveness of adjustments to the physical world is a task for which special technical knowledge and teaching skill is required and for which the schools must be mainly responsible.

ADJUSTMENTS TO ECONOMIC SITUATIONS

Vocational Education. — The industrial revolution has brought about a diversity of occupations as great as the variety of mechanical products. Our grandparent's task of selecting an occupation by means of which to earn his livelihood was comparatively simple. In many instances he grew into his vocation from his work as a boy. So

numerous are the possible vocations to-day and so specialized the preparation for them that vocational guidance and
in some measure vocational preparation becomes a necessary part of school education.

Practical *versus* Cultural Study. — Due in part to the
fact that, in days gone by, the school was little concerned
with vocational education, leaving it largely to home
training and to apprenticeship in the vocation itself,
" bread-and-butter " studies and practical applications of
knowledge became unfavorably compared to the "liberal"
and "cultural" subjects. This contrast was unfortunate
for both. Culture and refinement thus became identified with futility, with the activities of those persons
who do not share in the world's productive labor. It was
too often assumed that what had practical value could not
also have cultural worth. The fact is that there is no
incompatibility between refinement and productivity,
between cultural and practical value. Not only may the
bread-and-butter studies have rich moral and cultural outcomes, but by making the struggle for a living more fruitful and less intense, exacting and dull, they provide for the
masses not only greater power, but also stronger inclinations to pursue culture and refinement during the working
and the leisure hours. The aim of such practical education is not merely to fit people to get a living, but to fit
them to live. Fitting them to get a living is, however, one
part of fitting them to live. The school is assuming an
increasing measure of this responsibility for the good
reason that it is becoming increasingly superior to other
agencies in discharging the obligation. When education
becomes able to select the work best fitted to each individual as well as to fit the individual to his work, it will not
only increase economic productivity, but also the health,
morality, and culture of society.

The Solution of Economic Problems. — The industrial revolution has brought about conditions which demand more than general knowledge of its material products and fitness for a vocation. It has brought about complex methods of production, distribution, and finance, minute division of labor, trusts and labor unions, extremes of poverty and differential distribution of wealth, conflict of capital and labor, jealousies of " white collar " and manual occupations, and other intricate economic problems which need solution. The startling rapidity with which the industrial and economic world has changed has brought a train of perplexing issues which must eventually be solved by popular voice. Equally fundamental to our future welfare is the solution of problems connected with increasing production, the elimination of waste, unwise consumption, unfair distribution, costly competition, the possibilities of exploitation, and unnecessary depletion of natural resources. Perhaps most important of all is the problem of fitting work to the worker. Up to the present time the worker has been asked to fit himself to the job or leave it, or at most, workers with aptness for a task have been selected and trained. There is considerable doubt whether any men are fitted to certain industrial operations such as those requiring work in great heat, air pressure, or cold or with injurious chemicals or extreme expenditures of energy, etc. Such tasks should, therefore, for the common good, be changed to fit human needs and capacities. All of these and many related problems require study and intelligent action. Since industrial changes are to be made, in a democracy, *by* the people as well as *for* them, comprehensive education of the masses is essential.

Conclusions. — Adequate adjustment to economic needs, then, requires : that each person achieve fitness for that vocation which is the most productive and satisfying means of maintaining economic security for himself and his family; that each person achieve an understanding of the economic and industrial conditions and trends of the time; and that he develop a desire to influence economic life in ways that will increase the common good by improving the types and conditions of labor, augmenting productivity, reducing waste and unwise consumption, distributing wealth fairly, and conserving natural resources for coming generations. These needs require that the school study the vocational interests and capacities of pupils, influence their attitudes toward work and wealth, and study the conditions and trends of the present economic order. The schools are, in fact, making rapid improvements in education along these three lines.

Adjustments to Family Situations

Although the school, the church, industry, the theatre and other institutions have been gradually taking over many of the functions of the family during the last century, the family still is responsible for two of the most important necessities of society at large, the origin of human life itself and the care of infancy. Not only because it is charged with these functions of supreme biological importance, but also because sound family adjustments contribute in many ways to the development and satisfaction of most serviceable human wants, education for the activities of the home assumes great importance. At the present time scarcely any phase of education is more seriously deficient than training for a sound family life.

To promote family life in such a way as to contribute most abundantly to the satisfaction of human wants in general, many facts, habits, and attitudes must be provided. The more important ones may be grouped under the following five heads :

1. The relations of the sexes
2. The biology of inheritance
3. The physical care of the young
4. The education of the young
5. Compatibility of members of a family

Adjustments in Relations of the Sexes. — There are several groups of specialists in mental disorders and maladjustments who maintain that ignorance, misunderstanding, and mismanagement of the sexual impulses are the supreme sources of misery in the world. While this view may be an exaggeration, it is nevertheless based upon a body of facts which reveal striking deficiencies in sex education. The sex impulses are among the strongest of all urges. They ripen in the early teens and are usually not permitted normal expression, in modern society, until from five to fifteen years later. The majority of children attain pubescence with little information and training and often much misconception and many misleading attitudes concerning the period of deprivation which precedes marriage or the period of expression which follows it. The result is too frequently disease of body or mind as the result of indulgence or prostitution, or distortions of character through unnatural practices or unwholesome interests, fancies, mental conflicts, antagonisms, and the like as the result of unfortunate efforts at repression and control of the physical urges. Education is sorely needed both to enable individuals to span the period between pubescence and marriage with untainted body and mind and to fit them for a wholesome sex life after marriage.

Biological Heredity. — A second requirement is education to provide correct knowledge and a constructive attitude toward the facts of biological heredity. The laws of heredity are now well enough known to enable those who understand and follow them to select their mates and manage their marriage relations in such a way as to promote not only the happiness and usefulness of themselves and their fellow men, but also to increase the potentiality of the next generation by improving its stock. No less important than mastering the world which lies about us, no less important than changing the natures of men now in the world, would be the effects of learning to improve, in man's own interest, the native stock of succeeding generations.

Physical Care of Children. — The proper physical care of children during the first few years is of vast importance not only because the mortality from improper care is then exceedingly high, but also because the effects of poor treatment may permanently weaken those who survive. Since many parents do not try to take advantage of medical advice and would be unable to put it into effect adequately if they did, it is not enough that physicians have knowledge of the physical care of infants. Every prospective parent should receive some degree of education in the proper care of the young.

Home Education of Children. — The ignorance of the masses of parents concerning the physical care of infants is exceeded by their ignorance of methods of educating them, of improving their wants and developing desirable habits of intellect, character, and skill. The psychological needs of infants are more seriously neglected and abused than are their physical needs, and the consequences are no less serious. Habits formed in the early impressionable years are hard to break. The school, taking over the child at six or seven, may have as much to undo as to do. This heavy task is made more difficult by conflict between the ideals and methods of the modern school and those of the home. In this conflict the child, the home, and the school all suffer. Education of prospective and actual parents in the methods of education is the only means of improving this deplorable situation.

Family Compatibility. — A happy and useful family life depends upon the compatibility of its members. A wise choice of mates, proper management of sexual life, the birth of sound children reared to health and good habits are the most potent means of fostering compatibility. But in addition, there must be proper division of labor and privileges, communities of interest, mutual respect, and supplementary services. The limitations and responsibilities of marriage represent usually an abrupt change from the most free and irresponsible period of life. Youth but recently relieved of family ties returns to them again in a new rôle. For this rôle they should have adequate education. To be able to play it well, to develop sound family relations, will provide the satisfaction of many of the most wholesome human wants and fulfill many of the most vital needs of mankind as a whole.

Functions of the School. — For all the forms of education here sketched, the school must assume large responsibility. And, no matter how well pupils in the future may be trained for the functions of family life, they should continue as adults to keep pace with new developments. Their education in schools and elsewhere, in other words, should aim not only to give them the facts available at the time but also to cultivate habits of continuing their education for the improvement of the family life of themselves and their children. If other agencies do not provide facilities for education of adults of all ages in the functions of family life, the school should assume this obligation.

Adjustments to Social Situations

Dangers of Too Narrow Social Adjustments. — In the preceding chapters, we stressed the supreme importance of developing good will toward others and habits of striving to promote the welfare of all men. This, indeed, was the ultimate aim of education; an aim defensible on practical grounds as expressing the surest means of administering most fully to the wants of all. To this world consciousness, cultivation of a sound family life may contribute greatly by means of begetting better stock, by developing children of better health and habits, and by promoting mutual helpfulness among members of a family. Should good will and service be confined to the family to further its interest at the expense of other groups, a main purpose of cultivating family life will have been defeated. The fruits of compatibility, mutual regard and helpfulness among members of a family must be appreciated and this knowledge applied to the relations of a larger and larger family; the habits and attitudes which function to increase the effectiveness of family activities must be transferred to other people. To secure this transfer, we must make intelligible and serviceable the elements common to life of the family and to society at large. For this purpose, two things are especially important: (*a*) accurate knowledge about other people and (*b*) suitable contacts with them.

Socialization in the School. — For young children, the school provides opportunity to acquire both knowledge and experience. Progressive schools are placing increasing emphasis on the process of socialization. Children are taught to know and get along with each other, to respect each other's wants and abilities, to assist each other, to coöperate, to follow as well as to lead. Progressive teachers welcome a class of children of varied race and color, size and strength recruited from familes of different social and occupational status, religious and political beliefs, not only as means of giving them the attitudes and habits needed for harmonious living under modern conditions of innumerable and frequent personal contacts, but also as a means of developing a consciousness of the interdependence of all peoples and an appreciation of the value of promoting the interests of the Great Society. For the same reason they favor a large place in the curriculum for the social subjects.

The Social Subjects. — The function of the social studies is, in part, to give true information concerning the fundamentally similar and worthy characteristics of all races, creeds, and nations, to emphasize the value of cooperation and the universal destructiveness of jealousies, selfishness, mistrust, persecution, and war. Similarly the studies should give information which will nullify those popular prejudices which make savages of all Indians, barbarians of all Chinese, rascals of all our country's enemies, past and present, virtues of all our wars and outstanding heroes of warriors, and the general superiority and eternal righteousness of our own race or nation. Correct information, such as that wars are usually stupid and futile, that the English, French, and others are roughly equal to, even if not identical with, us, that negroes if they are less intelligent may be better humored and more generous than we are, should be offered to promote national and racial sympathy and understanding. Instruction of this character should be combined with abundant and varied contacts with all types of people under effective educational guidance. These are samples of effective means of promoting adaptability to the crowded conditions of modern life and of contributing to the larger social consciousness of a universal society.

Adjustments to Civic Situations

Education in America means education in a democracy. It means education in a society which has a variety of political organizations controlled by the people to protect and further its own interests. Our forefathers fought for a democratic form of government because they believed that it provided the best means of advancing the interests of the masses by giving them the balance of power and the best method of advancing the brotherhood of man both by showing the efficacy of putting the wants of a group above the wants of individuals and by providing training in coöperative control. Although democracy in America has fallen far short of realizing the fondest hopes of its founders, its defects may be due in large measure to handicaps which may be removed by education. To this end the means of improving social life and consciousness should contribute. But in addition to social adaptability in the case of all sorts of personal contacts and knowledge of and good will toward people in general, education in the purposes, ideals and means of participating effectively in many phases of civic life is needed. Whether or not we may consider democracy at present a great success, we may safely say that with better preparation of the citizens for participation, it will be more successful than it is. Considering the trial of democracy the most important experiment in the world, many of the ablest theorists in education, notably John Dewey and his followers, place education for civic efficiency as one of the major aims of education in the present day.

Combining Experience and Instruction in Democratic Living in School. — As means of promoting this aim, we are no longer content with teaching merely the abstract principles of a democratic government or the mode of operation of laws, the functions of legislative and judicial offices and the like. Civic efficiency which embraces knowledge, skill, interests, and habits is developed by participation in democratic life to the fullest possible extent. The school therefore must itself provide a real life which, operating on democratic principles, provides a continuous participation from which desirable civic ideals, habits, and knowledge may emerge. History, geography, economics, sociology, political theory and practice, and other content subjects are taught to enrich the civic experiences and to facilitate the development of the social consciousness which are fundamental to the success of democracy.

Correlating Education in the Different Phases of Life. — Thus experiences designed to further adjustment to the family, economic, social, and civic situations of modern life have much in common. The needs of the several fields, the issues which arise and which need solution are closely related. Training for adjustment in these several phases of life should not be sharply separated, but, on the contrary, related and integrated. In addition to providing pupils with information and experience which may foster fairness and good will, the school should provide as far as possible an acquaintance with the important unsolved issues, familiarity with the available facts related to the solution of these problems, and experience, under intelligent guidance, in using such facts in problem solving.

SUMMARY AND CONCLUSIONS

The most insistent demands upon man in our present society are that he learn to achieve some understanding of the present physical world; that he learn to get along safely and efficiently in an artificial, mechanical environment; that he achieve fitness in a vocation well suited to his nature and learn to be as productive as possible; that he acquire interest and ability in promoting a sound family life; that he become so informed and experienced as to be able to participate constructively in life of a wider society and in the solution of the insistent social, economic, and civic issues of his day. As means of contributing to these ends, and as ends in themselves, we must enable each person to achieve such sustaining resources as sound physical health, sound mental health and balance, a suitable philosophy or religion, proper recreational reserves, and an adequate intellectual equipment.

PHYSICAL HEALTH

Value of Health. — Bodily health and vigor are important in education both as means and ends. They are means because happiness and usefulness depend upon a sound body as well as upon a sound mind, desirable wants, and good habits. They are ends since few wants of anyone can be satisfied by illness and pain whereas health and vigor are necessary for efficient production of all desirable changes in man or nature. The general efficiency of the vital organs is a desirable if not the necessary basis of good spirits, good thinking, and good conduct. For the sake of immediate happiness and usefulness, health must be achieved and maintained.

Present Status of Health. — At the present time, the human race is neither free from physical defects, nor immune to many agents of disease; nor has it removed from the world many sources of illness. According to reliable estimates, 75 per cent of our school children possess one or more physical defects. Among the men drafted for the recent World War, men presumably in their most robust years, from 20 to 30, 30 per cent were so seriously impaired physically as to be unfit for service. That the race has not yet evolved to a high stage of resistance to disease was shown by the tremendous mortality during the war time epidemic of influenza. Despite great advances in the control of the disease-causing agents, many scourges, from the common cold to tuberculosis, are still rampant. Some diseases, such as cancer, and organic affections of the heart, blood vessels, and kidneys are actually on the increase. Aside from premature death and serious disability, many diseases, physical defects and various errors in diet, work, play, mental attitudes, and the like, result in vast losses in efficiency due to brief illnesses and chronically lowered vitality. The problem of achieving and maintaining better health is an outstanding task of education.

Function of School in Health Education. — The school must share, with the home and with private and public agencies, the task of maintaining and increasing the natural vigor of children, preventing diseases, and remedying defects. It must assume a very large measure of the task of teaching children — of giving them information and establishing proper attitudes and habits — to preserve their own health and to promote the health of the community at large. Indeed, health education is one of the most important functions of the school not only because of its widespread effects on progress in general, but also because it provides one of the clearest cases, which children can understand, of the tangible returns of good will toward others. The story of communicable disease is a striking and intelligible means of teaching a child that what injures society at large injures him, what protects society protects him.

Health Education as a Means of Social Training. — Indeed, one of the most important phases of health education should be to develop not only information and habits for personal hygiene, but the information and attitudes needed to foster the feeling of responsibility by each individual for the health and vigor of society as a whole. The pupil should have sufficient information and interest to favor and facilitate the best works of physicians, public and private health organizations, and other agencies in promoting the health of society in a large way, as by sanitary engineering, etc., and to contribute directly himself to the welfare of his community by increasing his own vigor, protecting others from his own infection, and by other minor acts which may influence others by either mental or physical contacts. In this important task of quickening the social consciousness, the school will doubtless be called upon to assume the major responsibility and the program of health education will afford an effective means.

MENTAL HEALTH AND BALANCE

That good spirits, fine emotional control, wholesome moods, thoughts, and impulses, and healthy-mindedness in general are promoted by physical well-being is familiar knowledge. Health education, now becoming a widely recognized objective of education and a thoroughly well-established phase of the school curriculum, in the division termed " mental hygiene " touches upon many relations of body and mind and thereby promotes mental health and balance. But quite apart from the influence of the organic processes are many factors which affect mental life and many of these are now seriously neglected.

Desirable and Undesirable " Mental Adjustments." — Each person must make mental as well as physical or physiological adjustments to the world about him and to his own special talents and defects, his own fortunes and misfortunes. These mental adjustments are largely habits which each individual acquires. Under the urge of his dominant wants, a child forms many habits of reacting, mentally, to the things and events in the world. Many of these habits are good, but many, even those acquired by persons in good physical health, are bad.

Illustrations of Unfortunate Mental Habits. — We can, here, merely suggest the nature of these adjustments or habits which constitute a field of study jointly occupied by the sciences of psychology and psychiatry. Among the bad (in the sense of futile or destructive) habits are dispositions to worry or scold, to cherish grudges or jealousies, to give way to futile spells of anger or grief or melancholy, to imagine unreal merits or defects, to imagine unintended implications in the acts or remarks of others, to daydream the realization of desires instead of attempting overtly to secure them, to " sour grape " or minimize the desirability of ends sought but not secured, to " sweet lemon " whatever lot one may have instead of attempting to achieve the really desirable condition; to " rationalize " or defend one's every act, desire, or opinion, however unjust or foolish, in order to secure future indulgence or condone past follies; to evade reality by developing " defense mechanisms " such as partly imaginary phobias, disinclinations, headaches, " sensitive nature," nervousness, or other mental barriers and physical difficulties; to play the " wounded hero " on numerous occasions to secure pity and sympathy and other indulgences that " help neither him that gives nor him that receives " ; to " compensate " for unavoidable calamities or deprivations by resort to despondency, alcohol, drugs, and the like instead of by fresh resolves and renewed activity in constructive lines. These are but a few descriptive terms for mental " ills " that are no less serious and no less frequent than physical ones.

Prevalence of Psychoneuroses. — Dr. Richard Cabot, professor in medicine in Harvard University, declared recently that half of the people who seek medical attention are suffering from no physical illness that medicine or surgery can help, but from psychoneuroses. *Psychoneurosis* is the technical term for many sorts of unhealthy mental habits, " which few doctors have ever been trained to treat." This field of knowledge and service is less advanced than that dealing with physical illness and hygiene. But it is growing, and soon will merit wide consideration as a phase of the education of every child. Its important and educational implications were expressed vividly three decades ago by the great American scientist and philosopher William James. "The hell to be endured hereafter, of which theology tells, is no worse than the hell we make for ourselves in this world by habitually fashioning our characters in the wrong way. The great thing, then, in all education, is to make our nervous systems our ally instead of our enemy. . . . We must make automatic and habitual, as early as possible, as many useful actions as we can, and guard against the growing into ways that are likely to be disadvantageous to us, as we should guard against the plague." [1]

The old adage, " A healthy mind in a healthy body " expresses only part of the truth. Although health in body facilitates health in mind and vice versa, we should give special attention to mental adjustments and habits as well as physical, and for the same reasons. A healthy mind, no less than a vigorous physique, is a worthy end in itself and a potent means of contributing to the fulfillment of other human wants. Healthy-mindedness is essential to productivity and enjoyment in nearly every wholesome enterprise. Its cultivation is largely a matter of education.

[1] *The Principles of Psychology*, Vol. I, p. 127. Quoted by permission of Henry Holt and Company.

RECREATIONAL RESOURCES

Work and Play. — Work and play are often sharply contrasted. The child, we say, needs play as a relief from his school work; the adult must supplement his labor by leisure and recreation. This situation is an admission of the fact that the regular work of school and economic life does not permit full satisfaction of human wants. Children and adults must play in order to round out the expression of their impulses. Yet there are occasional individuals who are so well fitted to their work and their work to them that their regular, daily tasks satisfy their cravings better than any other form of recreation. While it may be vain to hope that work so varied in type and so perfectly adjusted to individual talents as to satisfy completely one's desires can be arranged for everyone, there is reason to believe that much may be done in this direction. Meanwhile, education is necessary to supply recreational resources and a study of recreational needs may contribute to the improvement of work.

Productive and Unproductive Recreation. — No particular kind of activity constitutes play or provides genuine recreation. Any activity is recreational which satisfies wants unfulfilled in one's vocational and other activities. Thus, what is work for one is play for another. The gardener's work is the musician's play; the musician's labor is the gardener's recreation. Few are the activities that are not both work and play. This fact gives us a clue worth following. Recreation need not be wasteful; it may be productive. An error, as unfortunate as it is common, lurks in the belief that activity which results in useful products cannot be play, that recreation must be an end in itself.

Compared to the general outcomes of recreation, results in the way of flowers grown, cabinets made, poems written may seem trivial. Yet recreations which are creative even in these ways, provided they serve all other purposes equally well, are better than those which produce nothing and much better than those which consume goods which others might use productively.

Impersonal Pleasures. — Next in merit to the constructive recreations, other things being equal, are those which, while not adding directly to the world's store of useful goods, are at least not destructive of them. Such recreations as the enjoyment of literature, music, the drama, paintings, and objects and events in nature belong in this category. They may be termed the impersonal pleasures. They are unlike the pleasures of eating, and owning and wearing things, where the pleasure of one person uses up the possible means of satisfying the wants of others. Yet, even in the enjoyment of beauty in the many fields of aesthetic experience, appreciation is usually enriched by active efforts to be productive even if only in an amateurish way. Insight may be deepened, the range and character of appreciation improved, and enjoyment thereby increased by efforts to create aesthetic products.

Recreational Growth. — As a final criterion of the value of recreational activity, it may be said that, other things being equal, that form of enjoyment is superior which provides for the most extensive and varied growth of knowledge, skill, and interests. Thus cabinetmaking would be preferable to chopping wood ; walking to observe nature to playing golf, attending grand opera to attending prize fights, playing the piano to playing solitaire. Indeed the main justification of the fine arts as sources of recreation is not that they are somehow more aristocratic and elegant than others, but merely that for many people they provide almost unlimited opportunities for growth in knowledge,

skill, culture, and appreciations without serious deprivations to anyone.

Individuality in Recreations. — The choice of recreations must be an individual matter for two reasons.
First, since to be a recreation an activity must complete
a gap in life left unfilled by vocational and other work, the
general type of play must differ according to the nature of
the work. A man who is confined all day to a chair in an
office is likely to find spading the garden or playing baseball more recreational than will a man who spends his
day in hard outdoor labor. Secondly, to find an activity
recreational one must have an aptitude for it. Football is
too violent and golf is too exacting for some; bridge is too
simple for some and too intricate for others; many are by
nature incapable of successful execution or deep appreciation of classical music or philosophy. The range of
recreational interests is as wide as the world of activities.
This range of choice makes it possible to satisfy the needs
of every individual.

Conclusions. — The aims of education for recreational
life, namely, to further the satisfaction of human wants
and to improve them, are similar to the aims of education
for vocational life. The means are also similar : to select
the lines most suited to each individual and to assist him
to secure the richest returns from them. The ideal is to
achieve that rare state in which a certain ever-present
aspect of life provides, without cost to others, the experiences which supplement the activities of the work-a-
day life in the most wholesome manner.

PHILOSOPHIC, ETHICAL, AND RELIGIOUS RESOURCES

Philosophy, ethics, and religion are concerned with the
deeper meanings of events in the natural world. They
aim to carry the mind beyond the superficial aspects of

life. They aim to associate the purposes and activities of individuals with the more profound meanings, purposes, and destinies of the universe. A philosophy is a scheme of explanation of life and nature as a whole. Ethics is a guide to conduct based upon a philosophy of life. Religion embraces both a philosophy of life, a set of standards for conduct, and something more, an emotional or spiritual attitude. Experience indicates the value to man as an individual and to mankind at large of coming into contact with, and attempting to appreciate, the broader and deeper issues of life — the ultimate destinies and purposes of the universe in which man and his world are but a trivial part. Familiarity with the larger and more abiding problems of life should increase the breadth of view, foster tolerance, augment ability to distinguish the important from trivial matters, and provide standards and incentives for improving conduct.

It is unnecessary to distinguish sharply between ethics and religion. Ethics has to do with the intellectual analysis of the larger purposes and values and the establishment of moral codes or duties on logical grounds. As commonly understood, and as therefore described in the book of most prevalent opinion, the dictionary, " Morality (the objective of ethics) is the system and practice of duty as required by the moral law, consisting chiefly of outward acts, and thus may be observed without spiritual rectitude of heart. Morality is of necessity included in all true religion which involves both outward act and spiritual service." Ethics means cultivation of the mind and religion embraces both understanding and acceptance by the heart. The value of ethical and religious training both as an end of supreme importance and as a means of promoting all other aims of education has been defended through the ages alike by common men and most gifted prophets.

Considerations of the ultimate meanings and values of the universe, not only by revealing the essential triviality of striving to satisfy one's petty and selfish wants, but also by making clear and inviting the association of man with more powerful forces in fulfilling the destiny of the universe, may strengthen the will to obey the moral codes and increase the satisfaction in living the good life. Add to this intellectual broadening, the acceptance of the central convictions of a true religion with the resulting poise, confidence, faith, and motivation, the good life becomes even more desired and possible. As William James remarks: " Religion thus makes easy and felicitous what in any case is necessary; and if it be the only agency that can accomplish this result, its vital importance as a human faculty stands vindicated beyond dispute." [1]

An intelligent training in philosophy and ethics as a means of enabling one to grasp and to observe the moral principles which have withstood the test of time and logic, and in religion, which as Fosdick remarks, " is a wellspring of character inspired by the assurance that something in the universe abides forever, grows and bears fruit at last," constitutes one of the means of giving each person a type of equipment needed to balance and integrate his conflicting tendencies.

The Rôles of Home, Church, and School. — How to foster religious and related ethical training is one of the most puzzling of present educational problems. Due to denominalization and jealousies of churches, to confusion of religion with form and ritual, and to the conflicts of church and state, religious education has been largely removed from the school and left in charge of the family and church. Both were pitifully unprepared to fulfill the needs. Better religious education is needed to make

[1] William James, *Varieties of Religious Experience*, p. 51.

better religious education possible. Although the church is making some progress in the religious and ethical education of youth, a vast number of children are not effectively touched by its influence. While the school occupies the most strategic position for influencing youthful society, it will probably be unable to exercise its influences until churches succeed in working together in better accord. How the present dilemma will be met cannot now be foreseen. It can only be stated confidently that improvement in religious and ethical training is acutely needed.

INTELLECTUAL RESOURCES

Old Theory of Mental Training. — Less than a century ago, education, so far as the school practiced it, seemed to aim primarily at teaching certain fundamental subjects such as reading, writing, arithmetic, spelling, and grammar, and at developing mental and moral power by means of the discipline of these and certain other linguistic and abstract subjects. Toughened by hard drill, the moral and mental powers presumably needed only a few tools to do the work of the world. The function of the school was to conduct the toughening process and to provide the kit of tools. So completely have the aims and methods of education been changed in recent years that we are inclined to say, at times, that education is no longer attempting either to discipline the mind or to provide what are merely tools. The mind is best trained and the tool subjects most economically acquired, it is said, as by-products or incidents of education for physical and mental health, for recreational and religious resources and for social, civic, and economic betterment.

Present Emphasis on Immediate Values of Educational Tools. — This doctrine is true to a considerable degree. It is true in the sense that educational science does not justify the use of subject matter or content unrelated to needs of children or adults as a means of training the mind. On the contrary, it finds that intellectual resources and abilities are best promoted by materials, information, and skills which function in the pupil's normal life. Consequently, children should be taught to read by reading material related to their needs and interests; they should be taught to do the arithmetical computations which real life will present to them; to spell the words which they need to write and to write with a speed and quality that serves genuine immediate purposes. They are, in sum, taught those things which further the demands of education which we have just described.

Intellectual Resources Important Objectives. — Yet, at the same time, it is not true that education no longer aims specifically to develop intellectual abilities and tools or that intellectual resources are left entirely to develop as an incident to, or as a by-product of, the teaching for other purposes discussed in this chapter. Although the content used in teaching reading and the forms of reading reactions sought should be useful, specific provisions should be made to avoid the acquisition of inappropriate habits and to develop economically the optimum accuracy, fluency and fullness of comprehension. Although we should teach the child to spell only the words he needs to use, we should be interested in giving him the best possible technique of learning to spell other words which he may need later. Although we should not teach useless subjects as a means of developing the pupil's power to learn and to reason, we should make provision in the useful subjects for developing the most fruitful methods of study and the most serviceable skills in reasoning. Although our methods should differ from those of the past, our aim should be concerned no less, but even more, with the development of efficiency in the tool subjects such as oral expression, reading, writing, spelling, arithmetic, drawing, composition, and the like. Although our methods differ they are no less, but more, definite and under control; of no less, but of more, concern to teachers.

Doctrine of Specific Techniques *versus* General Powers. — Although we no longer think of general mental resources as consisting exclusively of improved mental faculties or powers, we prize equally and seek the more actively mental resources in the form of many specific habits, skills, devices, or techniques including especially those which are basal to intellectual interests and appreciations. In the form of fluency and accuracy in many types of reading, skill in analyzing arithmetic problems, ability to manipulate various linguistic and abstract symbols, facility in various methods of study, the technique of sifting data and appraising the results of reasoning in different fields of thought, we should and do seek to give the pupils intellectual tools and resources which will be serviceable in meeting the demands of learning and adjustment encountered in all phases of life in school and out, as well as in providing for a more fruitful satisfaction in intellectual activity for its own sake.

Interests and Values in Intellectual Activity. — Everyone, even the imbecile, enjoys intellectual activity. The widespread enthusiasm for such things as cross-word puzzles reveals both the genuineness of satisfaction in mental activity and the need of education for a richer expression of this interest. Although individuals differ, each should be equipped with the intellectual resources and incentives which will enable him as long as he lives to engage, with enjoyment and profit, in the intellectual pursuits which may assist him to grow in his family, social, civic, economic, recreational, and other experiences.

Concluding Remarks

The main immediate aims of education in our present democratic society are to enable each person to effect the types of adjustment to the physical world, to the economic, family, social, and civic situations and to attain the physical and mental health, the recreational, ethical, religious, and intellectual resources which contribute the most to the welfare of the Great Society. As conditions change, the immediate demands upon education must change. No statement of the immediate purposes of education can be a final one. The statements here given are neither final nor complete. But, with these general objectives in mind, we may be able to select the detailed means more wisely as we achieve further understanding of the materials and methods with which we have to work. To these topics we shall now turn.

Questions and Exercises

1. Do you think people are any happier now than they were five thousand years ago? Any happier than they were a hundred years ago? Explain.

2. In what respects are people now better adjusted to the conditions of life than they were a hundred years ago? In what respects are they less well adjusted?

3. Which of the major needs listed in this chapter are more insistent now than they were a hundred years ago? Which ones will probably call for increasing amounts of education in the future?

4. Arrange the several major needs in order of their importance as you judge them.

5. Which of the needs here listed were most neglected in your own schooling?

6. What needs do you think should be added to the list? Under what categories in the list, if any, might the authors have included the additional needs you have suggested?

7. Suggest a dozen particular adjustments to, and facts about, the physical environment that a child should know by the age of seven years. What health habits and facts, what social habits and attitudes should he have by this time?

8. How can we follow Dewey's doctrine of administering to the immediate needs of a child's life instead of preparing for the demands of

adult life and at the same time give children useful civic habits and ideals long before the age of suffrage or develop useful economic habits and ideals long before they must be self-supporting?

9. For the purpose of achieving the main objectives of education as set forth in this chapter what were the main deficiencies in such subjects as geography, history, civics, physiology, physics, etc., as they were taught to you in school?

10. In what respects, if any, did the extracurricular activities in which you engaged while in school prove to be more useful than the curricular activities in meeting such needs as are listed in this chapter?

11. Is the person who declares that he is happier in his work than in any kind of play to be envied or pitied? Should *every* person develop hobbies? Why? What is the real purpose of a recreation?

12. What are some of the things that tend to disturb mental health and balance in modern society? What are some things that might be done in the elementary school to foster healthy-mindedness?

REFERENCES

CHAPMAN, J. C., and COUNTS, G. S., *Principles of Education.* Houghton Mifflin.

CLOW, F. R., *Principles of Sociology with Educational Applications.* Macmillan.

DAVIDSON, T., *Education as World Building.* Harvard University Press.

DEWEY, J., *Democracy and Education.* Macmillan.

ELLWOOD, C. A., *Sociology and Modern Social Problems.* American Book Company.

HARAP, H., *Economic Life and the Curriculum.* Macmillan.

JUDD, C. H., *The Psychology of Social Institutions.* Macmillan.

KING, I., *Education for Social Efficiency.* Appleton.

PETERS, C. C., *Foundations of Educational Sociology.* Macmillan.

REISNER, E. H., *Historical Foundations of Modern Education.* Macmillan.

RUGG, H. O., and SHUMAKER, A., *The Child Centered School.* World Book Company.

SMITH, W. R., *Introduction to Educational Sociology.* Houghton Mifflin.

SNEDDEN, D., *Educational Sociology for Beginners.* Macmillan.
See also the references listed in Chapter I.

Chapter IV

THE ORIGINAL NATURE OF MAN

The aim of education, as we have seen, is to change human beings for the better, so that they will have more humane and useful wants and greater ability to satisfy them. Human individuals, especially the young, are the material for education; and knowledge of human nature is necessary if educational changes are to be made securely and economically, and without secondary ill effects.

Man as a Species

The different original natures of human beings represent variations around one central tendency or " type " — the ordinary or average original nature of man as a species. Thus, though men vary notably in inborn ability to reason, their variations are around a central tendency, the average capacity of mankind to reason, which is clearly distinct from the average capacity of earthworms or elephants. Though, to the situation " being alone in the dark," different responses would be made by different infants, even though all had been treated alike, yet their responses would center about an average distressed behavior, whereas deep-sea fish would respond to being alone in the dark with stolid equanimity. The original equipment of the central or average or typical human being consists, over and above his strictly physical, chemical, and physiological nature, in tendencies to respond to certain situations by certain sensations, feelings, and acts. By studying the reactions of different individuals at different ages it is possible to determine roughly what tendencies are universal among, and characteristic of, human beings, and by making allowances for the effects of training it is possible to estimate roughly which tendencies are the results of native endowment and which are largely due to education, training, and experience. We must begin, however, by indicating the factors involved in all human reactions.

Situation and Response. — Man is born into the world with a tremendously complex equipment of physical or physiological mechanisms which are so organized that various reactions may be made to influences arising within or outside of the organism. All human activity is *reactivity*. For every action there is a definite incentive or cause. Activity is not the result of a sort of spontaneous combustion; it is the response to stimulation. The total state of affairs by which a man is at any time influenced is called the *stimulus* or the *situation* and whatever action results — attention, perception, thought, feeling, emotion, glandular secretion, or muscular movement — is called the *reaction* or the *response*.

Typically both situation and response are complex. Thus if a person walks into a room his response will embrace attention to and perception of certain things, the arousal of memories or ideals, various feelings, changes in the inner organs, and a variety of movements. What he does depends upon the total situation at the moment and this situation embraces not only the objects and events in the room, but the conditions and activities in his own organism. If he is subject to the stimulating effects of a complex physiological condition which we call hunger, his reactions take one form; if he is not hungry, but fatigued, they take another direction; if he is neither hungry nor fatigued, but interested in finding the date, they take another form. Common experience agrees that a man's reactions are determined jointly by his own inner conditions and the external situation.

Among the inner conditions in the case of an adult we should include not only physiological processes such as those underlying fatigue, hunger, bodily well-being, etc., but conditions in the central nervous system which under-lie knowledge, ideals, innumerable skills and dispositions to act, likes and dislikes, and cravings of various sorts. Let us consider first which of these factors are native, inborn, or inherited, and which are acquired through experience.

Conditions Which Satisfy and Annoy

Satisfiers and Annoyers. — Without experience, a child or adult reacts to an object or event in a complex way determined by the total situation which comprises his inner condition as well as the external object or event. He reacts by movement, inner physiological changes of some sort, and by an effort to comprehend the situation. More than these, the response involves being satisfied or annoyed or indifferently affected. Dangle a bright object before a child and he may grasp it. If it burns or stings, the child is annoyed and drops it. If it is not annoying, the child may carry it to his mouth. If it tastes bitter or strong or possesses a noxious odor, it arouses annoyance and is spit out. If it tastes moderately sweet, it is satisfying and the child continues to taste it. Every reaction may involve satisfaction or annoyance. Whether an act produces satis-faction or annoyance is of profound importance because the subsequent history of an act depends upon its *effect*. Those reactions which bring about a satisfying effect are likely to be repeated and strengthened, whereas those

which produce annoying effects are likely not to be
repeated, but permitted to die from disuse. In this way
— as we shall explain in detail in the next chapter —
native likes and dislikes are of fundamental potency in
habit formation. It is therefore important in education to
know the sources and types of human likes and dislikes.

The causes of satisfaction and annoyance may be classified in three groups : first, the results of sensory experiences; second, the results of efforts to satisfy certain
organic wants; and third, the results of efforts to carry out
certain activities.

Effects of Sensory Qualities. — The sensory experiences,
classified in textbooks of psychology, fall into two types,
those which satisfy and those which annoy. Thus sweet,
mildly sour or salty tastes; fragrant, spicy, fruity, and
other odors; moderate warmth or coolness, and the like
are satisfying.   Strongly bitter, salty, or sour tastes;
putrid and violent odors; extremes of cold or heat, and
sensory pains, severe pressures, itch, and the like are
annoying. In a rough and general way, the sensory
qualities which satisfy are signs of biologically serviceable
things and conditions, whereas those which annoy are
indicative of harmful conditions. The sensory effects
thus provide a rough means of classifying objects into
useful and harmful. Rapidly the child learns by these
means to cherish some things and avoid others. Native
sensory likes and dislikes thus serve as important guides in
learning.

Effects of Organic Wants. — Satisfaction and annoyance spring also from a variety of organic wants or cravings, such as to secure food or drink when hungry or
thirsty, to obtain rest when fatigued and sleep when
drowsy, to find warmth when cold, to secure coolness when
hot, to obtain sexual gratification when aroused. The con-

dition of craving food or of being subject to any organic need is itself annoying and the result is active effort to secure relief. The want for food is thus a potent source of activity. When one is subject to any such organic want, he is satisfied by any act or condition which relieves it and annoyed by any act or condition which interferes with the fulfillment of the urge. Gradually he learns to take those means which serve to satisfy his hunger and to neglect or avoid those which are futile or which interfere with the relief of the want. In this way habits are built up. They are acquired as means of satisfying human wants.

The Nature of Human Wants

Wants or Cravings as Reactions. — Each want or urge or craving is due to a condition or activity in the organism itself. The want is, in fact, a reaction just as truly as the wink of the eye, or the movement of warding off a missile. Hunger, or the want for food, for example, is a reaction set up by a variety of internal conditions and activities. It is a native response to these conditions, a response which may be intensified by external stimuli such as the sight or smell of food. It embraces certain contractions of the stomach and several forms of internal tensions. These contractions and tensions, themselves reactions, act as stimuli which condition or control further reactions. One reaction thus acts as a stimulus to provoke others. The want, as an internal response, becomes an important part of the total situation which determines the next response. For this reason, wants are often termed determining tendencies, selective agencies, or tendencies to reaction since they tend to determine reactions by selecting or favoring those which lead toward the satisfaction of the want. All wants may be conceived in this way. They find a ready explanation in terms of the Stimulus-Response formula or the Reaction Hypothesis which is basal to most modern psychologies.

Tendencies to Action. — In addition to the organic wants, man inherits a number of other tendencies or predispositions to react which are also the equivalents of cravings or wants. He reacts to objects in ways other than by eating them; he has wants other than hunger which objects may satisfy. He may, at times, secure as much satisfaction in manipulating an apple as in eating it. He may, at times, want human companionship as much as bodily comfort. Important as the organic cravings are in determining the direction of human activities and strivings and in controlling the direction of learning, they do not represent the entire stock of fundamental cravings with which education may work.

Distinguishing Native and Acquired Cravings. — An average adult possesses a large number of wants, more than we can list in this volume. Many of these wants are present at birth or appear later as the result of the inner growth of his organism. The want of food when hungry, of drink when thirsty, of rest when fatigued, of free activity when refreshed, of warmth when cold, and many others are native and not acquired. Many particular wants such as the desire of the infant for his own bottle, spoon, cup, table, crib, jacket, rattle are acquired, as means of satisfying the original wants. As adults we similarly acquire innumerable particular desires and habits as means of appeasing one or more of the native, fundamental cravings. Indeed, it is probable that all habits or particular wants are acquired in the service of original cravings. In actual practice, however, we can determine what are the fundamental native wants only by observing what children do, what things, circumstances, and events they cherish, and what they neglect or avoid.

So rapidly do habits develop and so diverse are the directions which they take that it is very difficult to determine exactly which cravings are native and fundamental, and which are acquired and secondary. It is possible, however, to list some that are very powerful and which seem to dominate behavior and learning as life goes on. Some of these may be here mentioned, leaving to future study the determination of the native and acquired elements of each.

INVENTORY OF THE MAJOR HUMAN WANTS

Attention. — To the situations, colored, glittering, contrasting things (such as black on white, sour after sweet, and the like) moving things, blood, loud sounds, pain, human faces, gestures, sounds and movements, and all the situations to which he has further tendencies to respond (as by running away, pursuit, repulsion, and the like) a child responds by such movements or restraints from movement as let the situation produce a strong effect on his sense-organs. Thus he moves his eyes so that the light rays from the moving thing fall upon the area of clearest vision, or holds his head so that the sound reaches his ear in full force.

Many objects provoke avoidance or escape reactions. To those which produce undesirable sensory effects such as pain, sting, severe pressure, limitations of movement, bad odors, startling lights, terrific or strange sounds, and the like, a child responds by efforts to escape, supplemented by fear or disgust. If escape is not easy, vigorous action of the type of fighting may appear. In these cases one wants to escape, is annoyed by inability to do so, and is satisfied by success in so doing.

Collecting and Hoarding. — Any not too large, too disgusting, or too frightful object arouses the tendency to lay hold of it. If it at first evades seizure, the response of pursuing it is evoked. Any easily portable object that has been observed or captured, arouses the response of seizing and assuming possession. To the untutored child, " assuming possession " may mean merely further manipulation, or carrying away, hiding, or resisting efforts of others to take away the object. The universal tendency of children is to take what they want. They are inclined to assume possession of anything which offers an opportunity to satisfy other wants. They also have a tendency to collect and hoard attractive, even if often trivial, objects and to resent the interference of others with these objects.

Visual Exploration and Manipulation. — To an object that is not being responded to by disgusted avoidance, fear, anger, loving behavior, or other specific acts, the child responds, so far as the object permits him, by moving his eyes so as to look it over, and by moving his arms and hands so as to hold it, turn it, roll it, drop it, pick it up, put it in the mouth, squeeze it, poke it, shove it away, pull it back, and so on through the long list of activities that make up the indefatigable experimentation of infancy.

Manipulation includes the tendencies commonly called, or rather miscalled, constructiveness and destructiveness. Man's original nature is innocent of creating and destroying, of changing an object for or against the welfare of the world. Rolling, turning, throwing down and picking up, putting together and pulling apart, digging holes, tearing books, and building with blocks are all due to the same tendency. No one would think it wise to speak of separate tendencies to construct and to destroy the air in the sense of making, on the one hand, words and, on the other, mere mutterings and cooings. So one word, manipulation, best describes the manual responses out of which constructive and destructive activities both develop.

Curiosity. — What is commonly called curiosity is, like most other human traits, the result of both original tendencies and acquired habits. Its original elements probably are: attention to novel objects and human behavior, visual exploration and cautious approach, reaching, grasping, and the food-testing responses, manipulation, and the enjoyment of sights, sounds, tastes, smells, and other sensory facts for their own sake.

This last element needs comment. Whereas a dog or cat cherishes sights, sounds, and smells mainly for their service in connection with food, safety, and the like, man seems to enjoy the mere flow of mental life itself. Merely to hear, see, and touch is, other things being equal, a source of satisfaction to him. His mind abhors a vacuum. Novel experiences are to him their own sufficient reward.

General Mental Activity. — Not only sensing things, but also appreciating the connections of events, of understanding things, is intrinsically satisfying to human beings. A child likes not only to hear a whistle, but also to know how the whistle works and to find the noise coming whenever he blows it. He likes to see a ball roll across the floor, but even more to have it roll as the observed result of his act of pushing it. As soon as a child gets the ability to have ideas and to make plans, he enjoys getting one idea from another, making a plan and having a result come from it, and countless other cases of thinking something or getting some result from his thinking. When he has acquired powers of intellect or skill he may enjoy their unforced exercise as truly as he enjoys food, sleep, or conquest. Other things being equal, mental activity is satisfying in and of itself.

General Physical Activity. — A similar satisfaction

attends any unforced exercise of the body. The healthy child not only runs, jumps, climbs, pushes, pulls, and the like, but also twists, wriggles, bends, and contorts himself in movements that are devoid of any reference to food-getting, safety, or other direct utilities. He puts his body into action for activity's own sake. But activity is especially satisfying if it affects other things. Thus moving an object, controlling a ball, cutting down a big tree, and the like are potent means of satisfying fundamental human cravings.

Overcoming Resistance and Dominating Things. — In whatever activity a person is engaged, it is characteristic of him to want the activity to go smoothly and successfully. Thus the child likes his blocks to stay put, or to tumble when he pushes them; he likes the whistle to sound when he blows; he likes to secure the things he tries to grasp — and is annoyed if his efforts to control things are thwarted. If resistance is encountered, he is aroused to overcome it. If an object persistently resists the child's efforts to control it, anger and violent attack may be the response. Failure to overcome resistance is most annoying and may show itself in continued anger, or change to grief or despondency. Success in overcoming obstacles is the source of keen satisfaction. Successful domination of things, since it usually involves continued mastery over opposition, is equally satisfying, as in successfully breasting a stout stream, climbing a tree, breaking a horse, or making a steep grade " on high."

Vocalization and Facial Expression. — To the situation, being alive and comfortable, the infant responds by gurgling, cooing, prattling, shouting, and the like, especially if some return sounds are heard. In place of the limited repertoire of cries, growls, and the like which a dog or cat displays, the human animal makes sounds including all those used later in language, and many more.   Meantime, he may smile, frown, grin, and contort his face in a multitude of twists and turns.

Visual exploration, manipulation, vocalization, and facial movements seem at first sight to be useless in comparison with such tendencies as : to reach for, grasp, and put in the mouth ; to run and hide from a large, strange animal ; to throw out the arms when falling, or to cry when left alone in a strange place in the dark.   We call them " play " as if they had not the serious value of the responses directly concerned in getting food or protection. But no reactions have surer utility than the apparently random voice, eye, and finger plays.   For the end of voice play is language ; the ends of eye and finger play are knowledge and skill.   In the long run the apparently random voice play is of far greater service to man than the special calls of hunger, pain, fright, and relief ; and the puttering with eyes and fingers is of greater service than making specially adapted movements in flight, pursuit, attack, capture, and eating.

Summary. — Many objects which do not arouse unpleasant sensory effects or fear, anger or disgust or other specific acts, the child wants to study by applying eye, ear, nose, mouth, hands.   He enjoys merely examining their features.   He wants to manipulate them and is satisfied further by making them do things and by observing what they do.   He wants to control them and is annoyed by failure and satisfied by success in managing them.   Manipulative control and examination frequently involve destruction as well as construction.   It may involve noise, dirt, waste, and other results annoying to the sophisticated adult, but either satisfying or indifferent to the child.   If an object persistently resists the child's efforts to control it, anger and a violent attack upon it may be the response.   The child is aroused to overcome resistance offered by things; he wants, and is satisfied by, domination.   All these tendencies represent human wants of great value as materials for use in education.

THE SOCIAL WANTS AND REACTIONS

The tendencies and wants thus far described have been those out of which education may build its edifice of habits of work and thought with *material objects*.   The tendencies now to be described concern primarily man's responses to situations offered by *the behavior of other men*.

Chief in importance for education among such social wants and actions are gregariousness, resistance to social domination, desire for social mastery or domination, submission, approving and scornful behavior, the desire to excel a rival, parental behavior, and general sympathy.

Gregariousness. — Man responds to the mere presence of human beings, except when vigorously occupied with efforts to satisfy some other want, by a positive satisfaction.   To their absence he responds by discomfort and restlessness.   Although it is difficult to be sure that these tendencies are inborn, the satisfaction produced by the presence of other human beings and the annoyance produced by isolation are powerful motives in life.   They show themselves in all forms of social, religious, political, and other gatherings and societies, in the tendency toward city life, in the preference for factory labor compared to domestic service, in the disposition of children to be together in school and play and in the gang activities of youth.   They provide one condition essential for developing desirable social habits.   The fact that people want to be together facilitates the process of teaching them how to act together and toward each other.

Resistance to Social Domination. — When human beings come together, a complex interplay of tendencies is at once manifest. Perhaps most noticeable of all is the tendency to resist domination. Human nature resents interference with its own activities and wants with especial vigor when the interfering object is another person. Try to hold the limbs or head of a very young infant, halt and interfere with the locomotion or other activity of a kindergarten child, an ordinary adult, or a kindly old gentleman and you will see an essentially similar result — immediate efforts to avoid or overcome the obstruction, increasing, if need be, to more active measures, which rarely stop short of violent anger and fighting. By other interferences and means of domination, such as commands or threats, the same disposition to resist is aroused. The fact that the child is fundamentally resistant to being dominated by others provides the need for the most subtle type of human engineering.

Desire for Social Mastery or Domination. — Although by nature man resents being dominated by others he is so organized natively that he actively seeks, himself, to dominate others. He wants to manage other human beings even more than his implements and his dog. To secure the submission of others, to make them obey commands, to dominate them in general is to attain one of the keenest satisfactions, for which men will utilize all the powers and skills at their command. Often the impulse to dominate and control others takes the form of teasing and bullying, which is perhaps the most detestable feature of boyhood. It is found, in innumerable forms, in adulthood, too. It is a bitter fact that apparently few men can be given unlimited powers as rulers, generals, bosses, or schoolmasters without abusing them in the interest of self-assertion.

The Tendency to Submission. — Forced submission under most circumstances is annoying. Man usually does not want to submit. Submission is often merely a means of making the best of a bad situation, a device for eliciting kindly treatment instead of harsh domination from a superior. It may harbor humiliation, jealousy, fear, or resentment. To a person or group of persons of such obvious superiority that submission is inevitable, submission may be tolerable and even agreeable provided the dominant persons are kindly and respectful. To make obedience and submission a positive satisfier and productive attitude instead of a repressed and resentful state of waiting for deliverance is one of the fine arts which every teacher must acquire if she is to be effective.

Approving and Scornful Behavior. — Smiles, admiring glances, and shouts were probably original responses to relief from hunger or the abatement of fear, to victory, gorgeous display, female attractiveness, acts of strength or daring, and other impressive behavior from which the onlooker did not suffer. Frowns, sounds expressive of disgust, sneers and hooting were probably originally among the punishments of him who is empty-handed, deformed, craven, or pusillanimous in his behavior, and of her who has no charm. Thus every child and man tends to weigh the merits of the natures and acts of those about him and in such crude appreciations our judgments of human worth have their source.

To the situation, intimate approval, as by smiles, pats, admission to companionship, and the like, from one to whom he has the inner response of submissiveness, and to the situation, humble approval, as by admiring glances, from all others, man responds by great satisfaction. The withdrawal of approving intercourse by masters, and looks of scorn and derision from anybody provoke a discomfort that may strengthen to utter wretchedness.

The reader will understand that the approval and disapproval which are thus universally satisfying and annoying are far from identical with all forms of behavior which proceed from cultivated moral approbation and condemnation. The sickly frown of a Sunday-school teacher at her scholar's mischief may be prepotently an attention to him rather than to others, may contain a semi-envious recognition of him as a force to be reckoned with, and may even reveal a lurking admiration of his deviltry. It then may be accepted as approval.

As a species, man's desire to secure approval and to avoid disapproval is extremely strong. Proper management of social approval and disapproval may consequently become one of the most useful means which education may utilize of directing action into the desired channels.

The Desire to Excel a Rival. — Closely related to the desire to secure social approval and to avoid scorn and to fulfill the craving for mastery or domination are two other tendencies : first, the tendency to increase the effort put into certain activities, especially such activities as scrambling for or pursuing desirable objects, or fleeing from a fearful object, when other persons are similarly engaged ; and second, the tendency to feel more annoyed at failure and more satisfied by success in an activity in which there were competitors than in one in which one is engaged alone. This desire to excel a rival makes more exciting and zestful many competitive games in which, as we know, the youthful winner is likely to exult and the loser to show resentment. Although this tendency may be utilized to enliven and increase effort in innumerable activities, it is more difficult to get children to compete in studiousness, helpfulness, or modesty than in chasing a stray cat, in struggling to beat a rival football team, or in other types of physical activity. The effect of rivalry may be increased in any activity, however, by making superiority more clearly manifest.

Parental Behavior. — The most striking instance of a native disposition to increase the welfare of other human beings is the tendency to hold, cuddle, and to enjoy the happiness, and relieve the distress of infants. The urge to care for and to protect valiantly the begotten children is strikingly apparent in many animals as well as in human parents. Mothers, human or animal, seem especially responsive to their children after birth, perhaps as a result of their organic condition. Amidst the series of reactions to human beings previously enumerated — approval and scorn, mastery, submission, rivalry, fear, hate, and resentment — the parental tendencies stand out as the first instinctive basis of the brotherhood of man, wherein the advantage of one is the natural satisfaction of another.

General Sympathy for Others. — A weaker, more diffuse sympathetic disposition toward human beings other than one's own children may exist. The more diffuse kindliness, sympathy, or pity consists, in the first place, of attentiveness to a human being, especially a young or helpless one, manifestly hungry, frightened, or in pain, followed by active measures to relieve him. In the second place there may be a positive satisfaction at, and approval of, happy or contented behavior in other men. Even mean and cruel children may, when not in the hunting or angry attitude, be kindly in this second weaker sense. Superior children show it often. Healthy children are in fact endowed by nature with good will to men, so far as is consistent with the attainment of their own selfish ends; and primitive races of men are usually similarly indulgent. These wants are, however, easily engulfed by opposing tendencies.

ORIGINAL EQUIPMENT OF KNOWLEDGE, IDEALS, AND SKILLS

We have now seen that what satisfies and what annoys a person is determined in large measure by his native organization. He has many wants to satisfy. He wants to secure certain sensory effects and to avoid others. He is natively equipped with certain likes and dislikes. He wants to satisfy a number of organic wants such as hunger and sex. Aside from the muscular reactions which serve to satisfy the organic cravings, man everywhere displays tendencies to react which disclose other wants, such as the desires to manipulate, investigate, possess, manage, and dominate things and to be with rather than apart from, to dominate rather than to be dominated by, to be approved rather than disapproved by other human beings. Man seems capable of making without training many reactions to things and events around him — reactions that are preserved and repeated if they satisfy his wants or eliminated if they fail to satisfy his wants or produce discomfort. Likes and dislikes, a variety of cravings and tendencies to reaction, and a number of motor responses are inherited. What may be said of knowledge, ideals, and skill?

Knowledge and Ideals. — In the ordinary sense of the words, knowledge and ideals are not native, but wholly acquired. By original nature man is not given information or ideals of any sort. He does not know what hunger means, why he should eat, or what foods are good or bad for him; he knows nothing about health, or what injures or improves it; he has no information about any of the things or people or institutions in the world; he is completely ignorant and unconcerned about family, social, civic, industrial, and other affairs; he realizes or cares nothing about right and wrong, justice and injustice, cruelty and mercy. Of all the knowledge and ideals (attitudes based on knowledge) laboriously acquired by his forebears, he inherits nothing. Although he inherits no information or ideals, the human being is gifted by nature with an exceptional equipment for learning. Compared to other animals, he possesses extraordinarily good machinery and an unusual disposition to learn, to acquire information about things and events around him. And learn he does, from the time of birth onward, with such rapidity that it is extremely difficult to follow him. This general capacity for learning is, indeed, the supreme gift of nature for educational use.

Skills and Dispositions to Act. — From the time of birth the child displays a considerable repertoire of inner and outer activities such as we have suggested. Aside from the highly complex activities of breathing, circulation, temperature regulation, digestion, and the like, the child reacts by movements of eye, hand, mouth, and all other organs to situations brought to bear upon him. An object presented to the child may provoke the adjustments of the sense organs and of the organism in general to provide attentive observation, perhaps also reaching, grasping, manipulation, or carrying to the mouth. To some objects the response instead of being manipulation or carrying to the mouth may be various movements of pushing away or retreat coupled with the complex inner changes which constitute the emotion of disgust, fear, or anger. Such emotional responses, which are among the most complex in human behavior, are due to intricate but definite patterns of activities of the inner organs resulting in increased bodily strength and endurance. They are inherited modes of response which serve to increase the energy that may be used to put into effect any motor action. While much of the motor activities involved in chewing, swallowing, reaching, grasping, crying, vocalizing, manipulating, pushing, pulling, balancing, locomotion, fighting things off, and the like are native, the major part of the skills which function in the everyday life of an adult is acquired. The means of feeding oneself, of keeping the body clean and clothed, of handling the thousand and one common objects from a spoon to an automobile, of reacting to people in ordinary social intercourse, of carrying out the duties of family, economic, civic, and recreational life are acquired. Nature gives us but a crude, rough and ready motor and emotional adjustment to things and events of a primitive life. Almost all the adjustments and skills which comprise our behavior in modern society represent chiefly the results of learning.

Nature gives us, then, for education a creature with strong impulses, but no knowledge or ideals, many likes and dislikes but only crude methods of adjustment to the world, many cravings but few skills for satisfying them under present conditions. Nature gives us a creature, however, which is extremely active and apt in learning and which seeks to learn primarily what things will satisfy its wants and how things must be used to this end.

The Use of Original Tendencies in Education

In our survey we have attempted primarily to indicate some of the most fundamental human wants and the most universal means by which they are satisfied. Though the means by which human wants are appeased are rapidly changed by education and training, or even as the results of unguided experience from the time of birth, human nature everywhere shows certain characteristic dispositions which are deeply ingrained in man's native constitution. As the potter must know the nature of his clay, the musician the characteristics of his instrument, or the general the nature of the raw recruits out of whom he hopes to make a disciplined force, so education must reckon with the fundamental tendencies here described. To change a child's wants for the better we must know the nature of his wants and the means which most potently satisfy them. We must be able to distinguish superficial expression from fundamental desire since the latter determines what will satisfy and what will annoy.

The task of education is to make the best use of the fund of tendencies, eradicating its vicious elements, wasting the least possible of value that nature gives, and supplying at the most useful time the additions that are needed to improve and satisfy human wants. Some original and early acquired tendencies should be cherished almost as they are. Some must be reduced as far as possible by withholding the situations that would call them forth so that they weaken from lack of exercise; or by making their exercise result in pain and discomfort; or by substituting desirable habits in place of them. The great majority of original tendencies, however, can neither be preserved in their exact original form, nor be altogether annihilated, but should be so modified and redirected as to further the improvement and satisfaction of men's wants under the conditions of humane and rational living.

Thus the indiscriminate manipulation of objects may be modified into instructive play with sand piles, blocks, or ball; and later into the intelligent use of tools, pencil, pen, typewriter, engine, printing press, and the like. Thus the " satisfyingness " which originally accompanies notice and approval by anybody is redirected to form special attachments to the approval of parents, teachers, one's own higher nature, and heroes, living and dead, who are chosen as ideal judges. Thus the original incitement of " another trying to get the food or victory or admiration which we crave " is replaced gradually by rivalry with others in all work and play, then by rivalry with our own past records or with ideal standards. Thus the interest in collecting and hoarding at random whatever is handy and attractive to the crude interests in color, glitter, and novelty may be enlisted as a motive for habits of intelligent, scientific collecting and arranging and the interest in collecting may be made a stimulus to getting knowledge about the objects collected. Thus the original interests, the tendencies to be satisfied by and annoyed by, to like and dislike, are turned into acquired interests in efficient workmanship, kindly fellowship, the welfare of one's family, friends, community and nation, and finally into the love of truth, justice, and the happiness of mankind as a whole.

To Neglect Them Causes Failure or Waste. — It has been a common error in education to try to make such changes all at once — to demand rationality and morality offhand — to stick ideal considerations and motives into children in a few large doses — to expect them to work, study, be just, and be wise because we tell them to. Nothing but harm comes from expecting such miracles. Little more is gained by telling a man to think, or to be accurate, or to have good taste, or to honor truth and justice than by telling a tree to bear fruit, or a duck to keep out of the water. The eventual nature which is desired for man has to be built up from his original nature.

Since the strengthening, weakening, and redirecting of original tendencies begin soon after birth, a child by the time he enters school is already in many respects a product of our complex environment of clothes, furniture, toys, tools, language, customs, and ideas. School education starts from acquired as well as original tendencies. But the original roots of intellect, character, and behavior are still potent. Education which works with rather than against them — human wants which conserve their energy while modifying them into more desirable forms and changing their direction — will have a tremendous advantage. The most potent means of improving human wants are the human wants themselves. A sound theory of education must be based on this fact.

QUESTIONS AND EXERCISES

1. How would you explain the fact that certain school children when asked what school activities they most enjoyed frequently mentioned distributing pencils, feeding the bird, going on errands, etc.?

2. What are some of the activities which pupils in the high school pursue in out-of-school hours and for which they form groups, societies, etc. during school? Do these activities suggest tendencies which the school might direct to better uses? If so, suggest means.

3. Name several tendencies which result in truancy. Suggest means of utilizing these tendencies more effectively in school.

4. Which of the following statements are true? Which are false? Which are partly true and partly false? Explain your position in each case.

   a. Nothing can be more unwise than to tell a child he *must never* fight.

   b. It behooves us to study nature's plan, and seek rather to aid than to thwart it. For nature must be right; there is no higher criterion.

   c. Children by nature enjoy being submissive to the control of the teacher.

   d. Children in the first grade desire to be physically active not because of their inner nature, but because of lack of proper training in earlier years.

5. Enumerate a number of things and situations in modern life to which children should make adjustments, but to which their native tendencies are likely to be misleading rather than helpful.

6. Are the native tendencies, likes and dislikes of all children of a given age identical?

7. Name some respects in which the tendencies of the human species are more like those of sheep than lions. In what respects are our tendencies more unlike those of either of these animal species?

8. Give certain native tendencies which are most likely to be left unsatisfied in the life of the shepherd; the private in the army; the sailor; the stenographer; the actress; the doctor; the postman; the writer. Suggest recreations that are specially suitable to each of these classes. What other facts should you know before selecting recreations for any individual?

9. Which of these activities is most natural to, or requires the least learning by, a child of six: swimming or climbing; dancing or wrestling; building with blocks or writing with a pencil; learning the names of common objects or learning the parts of speech; playing alone or playing with other children; playing tag or playing marbles; bossing other children or helping them?

10. What are some of the situations in school that tend to˸provoke fighting? Sympathy?

11. Is the tendency to be satisfied by approval and to be annoyed by scorn more pronounced in the elementary grades than in the high school? If so, why? How may these tendencies be most wisely guided and utilized in the school? Give some illustrations of unwise management of them.

12. What are the main tendencies which seek satisfaction in the gang activities of youth? How may the school make better use of these tendencies?

13. What native tendencies, on the whole, are least fully satisfied in the conventional school? Is it wise to continue to disregard them or should they be more actively inhibited or should they be more actively redirected? Suggest means of doing what you think is best.

REFERENCES

CONKLIN, E. G., *Heredity and Environment in the Development of Men.* Princeton University Press.

DEWEY, J., *Human Nature and Conduct.* Henry Holt.

GATES, A. I., *Psychology for Students of Education.* Macmillan. Chapter VI.

JAMES, W., *Psychology: Advanced Course.* Henry Holt. Vol. II.

RAUP, R. B., *Complacency: The Foundation of Human Behavior.* Macmillan.

THORNDIKE, E. L., *The Original Nature of Man.* Vol. I of Educational Psychology. Teachers College Bureau of Publications.

See also references for Chapter I.

Chapter V

THE MAIN CHARACTERISTICS OF LEARNING

In treating the aims of education we described roughly certain characteristics of the human being which, by education, we should try to produce. In discussing original nature, we presented briefly some of the characteristics of the human being as he is, apart from training. To convert the individual as he is by nature into the person that education seeks to produce, we must know not only the nature of our raw material and the finished product but also the methods of effecting the change with certainty and economy and without secondary ill effects. We must, in other words, have a sound theory of educational method. To be sound, our theory of educational method must be based upon the principles of efficient learning and these we shall consider in the present chapter.

Learning as Reacting

The Need of a Motive. — Learning is always an active process. It is never a passive reception — a mere absorption. Before a child or an animal can learn anything it must be aroused to action. Now, an animal or child by nature is active only when some want is unfulfilled. Children are usually active, to be sure, but they are active because they have many wants, some of which are nearly always unsatisfied, and because they have a great deal of energy to use in seeking to appease their cravings. Some animals whose wants are fewer, especially those who have relatively slight cravings for mental and sensory exploration, manipulation, and the like, when placed in comfortable quarters, thoroughly fed and watered, and left undisturbed, relax into a period of inactivity during which they make no progress. To secure learning we must have activity, and to secure activity some want must be alive. The most effective learning occurs when learning is the means of satisfying some want. A primary consideration, then, in all learning and teaching is the provision of a motive; of an energizing want, desire, or interest which will provide vigorous and whole-hearted activity.

Learning as Acquiring Reactions. — Learning is an active process and, as we said in the preceding chapter, activity is always reactivity. An act is a reaction to a complex situation. Learning goes on during a process of reacting and — this is a most important fact — what a person learns *is a reaction*. When we say that a person learns subject matter — names, dates, or other facts — or that he learns a skill, or acquires an ideal or builds up an emotion or attitude, what we really mean is that he *acquires certain reactions to learning-situations* such as a passage of printed words, movable sticks, the actions of other human beings or other things. Let us illustrate.

Acquiring Knowledge. — Have you learned the A.B.C.'s? Well, you can read the A.B.C.'s readily; you have learned to react to the printed forms in several ways. You also learned to react to the voice of the teacher who said the A.B.C.'s in different ways. You can recall these reactions. You can say the A.B.C.'s in the way that you practiced saying them. You can say them forward rapidly since that was a reaction much practiced. Trying to say them backward will occasion considerable difficulty and perhaps require you to take roundabout methods. If you are asked to give immediately the second letter before m, r, t, or j or the third letter following them, you are quite sure to fail on occasions, except as you resort to saying them forward or backward one at a time. The fact is that you do not *know* even the alphabet. You can merely repeat some of the reactions to this letter series that you have previously made frequently. Similarly, you do not *know* the face of your best friend. It is not an entity that you have absorbed into your mind and with which you can do anything. If you recall that face as clearly as you can you will find yourself unable to describe exactly all sorts of facts about it, such as the exact shape of the nose and mouth, the distance between the eyes, the particular contours and colors. All that you can do is to revive some of the reactions, with certain omissions and distortions, which you have previously made to the face. And so in general, one does not absorb, master, or learn any objective thing or fact or subject matter. One learns to make reactions to objects, pictures, printed passages, and so on, reactions which can in some degree be recalled or revived.

Acquiring Other Reactions. — What is true of learning to know is even more obviously true of learning to feel, to experience emotions, or to make muscular acts. As one responds with certain feelings toward a man or by moving the members of the body in a certain way at the approach of a baseball, one practices certain forms of reaction. A reaction once made may — with certain reservations to be mentioned presently — be repeated and, eventually, learned. We learn only through the process of making responses and a reaction is what we learn.

Varied Reactions and Their Effects. — An animal, child, or adult learns by reacting as he can to a thing or situation.

Many different reactions may be made to the same thing or situation because everything has many aspects and because the inner condition of the learner (which, it will be remembered, is always a part of the total situation) changes from moment to moment. Although the learner makes different reactions, he does not learn them all equally well nor each in proportion to the number of times it was made. Out of the many reactions made, some will be selected, repeated, and learned; the others will be rejected, unpracticed, and unlearned. Suppose a hungry cat is placed in a box from which he sees an attractive piece of fish on the outside. The box may be opened by exerting pressure on a latch. The cat reacts in many ways to the features of the box. It bites, pulls, scratches, tugs, pushes, one thing after another. Some reactions it may make many times before it pulls the latch which opens the door. If you continue to repeat the performance when the cat is hungry you will see that eventually, of all the reactions made, some of them a great many times, most are rejected and only those retained and learned which provide release and food.

The Law of Effect

The Law of Effect. — This rather obvious behavior of the cat illustrates the most significant of all the facts of learning which need to be heeded in education. It illustrates the fact that one learns those reactions which produce certain effects, and rejects and fails to learn those reactions which bring other effects. The individual tends to repeat, and learns quickly those reactions which are accompanied or followed by a satisfying effect, and he tends not to repeat and hence not to learn those responses which are accompanied or followed by an annoying state of affairs. This statement constitutes the Law of Effect, the most fundamental principle of learning.

The Relation of Wants to the Law of Effect. — What determines the satisfaction and annoyance? In the case of the cat, the hunger, the want of food, and the impulse to escape from confinement clearly determine the effects of the acts. Those reactions and states of affairs which did not in any measure satisfy the desire to get out at the food, but which meant futile or painful effort were annoying; those which were obviously closely associated with the fulfillment of the wants were satisfying. This illustrates the general fact : those reactions are satisfying and consequently learned which contribute to the fulfillment of some want; those acts are annoying and consequently not learned which do not contribute to, or which interfere with the fulfillment of some want.

Man, natively, never does something for nothing. He acts only to satisfy his wants; he learns only those reactions which contribute to the fulfillment of his urges. Throughout his life, however sophisticated he may become, man's learning is motivated by his urges. Genuine wants must be enlisted to get him to learn at all and they must be used to guide and sustain his learning. The primary law in all human control is to utilize man's wants as a means of getting him to make the desired response and to utilize his wants again to make the response satisfying.

The Law of Readiness

Human wants are not equally acute at all times. Consider hunger. A cat which has had no food for many hours is most active in trying to learn the way out of the box. To succeed in getting out of the box and in securing the food is then highly satisfying. After having feasted on one fish the cat will be somewhat less active in trying to get at the food again and less satisfied by eating. After a third or fourth feeding the activity and satisfaction may be greatly reduced. The cat may reach a stage of satiation finally, wherein it will do nothing to secure food and even resist being fed. Wants vary in intensity from time to time and their effects both as a means of motivating learning and as a means of rewarding or punishing the learning reactions may dwindle and even change. It is apparent, then, that the potency of wants and the main means of controlling the educational process depend upon their intensity or readiness. The facts here indicated may be stated as a general educational law or principle as follows : *When an individual is ready to act in a certain way, for him to act in that way is satisfying and for him not to act is annoying. Conversely, when an individual is not ready to act in a certain way, for him to act in that way is annoying. This statement may be called the Law of Readiness.* Readiness thus refers fundamentally to the degree of craving for a particular activity.

Changes in Wants and Changes in Readiness. — Readiness refers to conditions at a given moment. We have many powerful wants each more acute at some time than at others. Hunger is a futile motive for use in teaching an animal which is satiated with food. The organic cravings are much subject to variation and, in the case of most human beings, are rarely useful educational motives. Some tendencies, such as the desire to overcome a difficulty successfully, to master or dominate, to secure social approval, to excel another person or one's own past record, and the like are nearly always in readiness and are therefore rather reliable means of promoting and guiding learning.

Acquired Desires and Motives. — Although in the final analysis some original craving is basal to all wants, acquired habits, attitudes, information, and skill may be utilized to secure readiness for an activity. If children are regularly given a recess at 10:30 A.M. during which they have learned to play baseball, they come to be, at that hour, highly ready for baseball and unready for other activities such as spelling. While playing baseball is an acquired habit, its zest depends upon the fact that it satisfies many native cravings such as the desires for physical activity, for excelling rivals, overcoming difficulties, securing approval. The activities of baseball are nevertheless habits and to exercise these habits is the immediate craving. All sorts of habits provide readiness in a similar way. It is often truly said that we become slaves to our habits. This statement means that we become accustomed to certain acquired means of satisfying our wants. Conditions of readiness may be in considerable measure prearranged and predicted by having a well-ordered schedule of activities for satisfying one's wants to eat, drink, engage in vigorous physical activity, rest, engage in quieter mental activities and in social intercourse, and so on. The particular requirements of school work may then be fitted into the most relevant states of readiness.

The Rôle of Success and Failure. — In another sense, acquired activities constitute readiness. The acquired school abilities such as reading, writing, arithmetic, and so on, are at no time static performances which merely work mechanically without results. Each is, or should be, a means of accomplishing other things, of satisfying other wants. At the very least, the scholastic abilities should enable the pupil to satisfy his native interest in overcoming successfully other difficulties in the same subject. While no school subject could be justified merely because it enables the child to overcome successfully other difficulties of a similar sort, it is very important that in a subject which is justified on other grounds adequate provision be made to secure this source of readiness for further activity. Readiness for any activity cannot be secured unless the child can successfully function in that activity. A pupil will not long show an interest in an activity which brings only difficulty, failure, subordination to rivals, disapproval, scorn. This fact has two implications.

Aptitude and Readiness. — The first implication is that readiness for an activity can be developed if a pupil has enough aptitude — the motor speed and facility, strength, mental maturity, and the like — to learn to perform successfully. Few educational requirements are more important than the need for a proper adjustment of desirable activities to the developmental and other individual differences of children. These topics are so important that we shall discuss them in special chapters later.

Ability and Readiness. — The second implication is that readiness for an activity often *must* be developed. It is often best secured by developing, first, such abilities as are needed to enable the pupil to function — to taste success and the possibility of further achievement in the activity. It is never safe to say that a child is intrinsically unready to read because he has not tried and shows no inclination to try to read. Readiness cannot be predicted from a child's foresight of his interests. Readiness does not always precede the acquisition of ability; it often follows and depends upon ability. It is really a state of readiness of the abilities acquired. Abilities cannot get into a state of readiness before they exist. Readiness, then, is derived in considerable measure from building up efficient, successfully operating habits.

Rôle of Teacher in Developing Readiness. — The teacher's function consists in doing a number of things which facilitate readiness for a particular activity and of getting rid of conditions which tend to reduce or interfere with readiness. She must control the environment to eliminate distracting noises, things, or activities. She should take into account fatigue, boredom, excitement, discouragement, poor physical tone, and other factors which reduce readiness for any work. She may " talk up " an interest in the work ; she may arouse readiness by her own enthusiasm. She may help the pupils to anticipate happy results of the work although anticipations of *distant* returns are not very potent. She should utilize related acquired habits and information in order to start action or thought on familiar grounds. The pupil should not be discouraged by serious perplexities and difficulties in the beginning. Activity, once under way, should be observed so that annoying errors and failures may be nipped in the bud and learning may be made as rapid and efficient as possible. Errors and difficulties should not be emphasized or criticized except as a means of removing and relieving them. Progress and success should be recognized and rewarded. Provision should be made for individual initiative, variations in method, and applications of results which *lead toward* success and which do not clearly lead astray. These are but a few of the factors in the technique of teaching to be treated in greater detail later, which directly or indirectly influence readiness.

Readiness and Effect. — To achieve a condition of readiness for an educative activity is of importance as a means of securing alert, vigorous, whole-hearted activity, and as a means of increasing the potency of the Law of Effect. The more fully an animal is ready to perform a certain act, the more satisfying are the reactions which facilitate that performance and the more annoying are those which are futile or misleading. Readiness and effect are thus intimately related. The greater the readiness the more potent the operation of effect.

THE INFLUENCE OF PRACTICE

Although readiness and effect are of primary importance in teaching, exercise is also a necessary condition of learning. A reaction needs to be satisfying and ordinarily it needs to be repeated, practiced, exercised, to be permanent. Indeed, an older educational slogan was: "Practice Makes Perfect." This slogan is true in the sense that practice is usually necessary, but false in the implication that practice is alone sufficient. This fact merits illustration.

Limitations of Sheer Exercise. — Suppose that we teach each of four kittens equally well, to come to a certain place as a response to the call "Kitty, Kitty." Then we proceed to exercise this reaction for each cat in turn. When the first kitten arrives, we fondle it and give it milk; the second we merely pet; the third we disregard entirely; and the fourth we douse with water. Now, if exercise alone makes perfect, we should expect that each cat would learn equally to make the reaction of coming to the call more promptly and surely as the result of repeated exercise. But will they? The first cat, which was fed and petted, will respond with increasing promptness and certainty; the second cat, which was merely fondled, will probably continue to come but not as promptly as the first; the third kitten, which was entirely disregarded, may come for a while but less surely and promptly and finally not at all; the fourth cat, which was doused, will fail to respond sooner than the third. Clearly exercise alone does not guarantee the perfection of a reaction. An annoying effect may kill off a response in the very process of practice. Practice which brings satisfaction, which satisfies some real

want, is what makes perfect.   And, in general, the greater
the resulting satisfaction the more productive the exercise.

The Law of Effect is the fundamental law of learning
and teaching.   By it a crab learns to respond to the
situation *two paths* by taking the one choice of which has in
the past brought food.   By it a dog will learn to respond
to the situation *a white box and a black box* by neglecting
the latter if opening it in the past has been promptly
followed by an electric shock.   By it animals are taught
their tricks; by it babies learn to smile at the sight of the
bottle or the kind attendant, and to manipulate spoon and
fork; by it the player at billiards or golf improves his
game; by it the man of science preserves those ideas that
satisfy him by their promise, and discards futile fancies.
It is the great weapon of all who wish — in industry, trade,
government, religion, or education — to change men's
responses, either by reinforcing old and adding new ones,
or by getting rid of those that are undesirable.

The rôle of the Laws of Readiness and Effect, which have
been illustrated in the case of rather simple reactions, is
equally important in the acquisition of complex skills, practice in which may extend over months or years.   The increase of efficiency in any complex activity involves: (1)
the addition of new reactions; (2) the elimination of old
ones that are undesirable; and (3) the simultaneous building up of new and the abandonment of old, which we call
combination or *integration*.   These facts are easily observ-
able in almost any practice experiment.   In typewriting,
the unguided learner may at first use only the forefingers,
but comes to add movements of all the other fingers.
In arithmetic, one gets the new power to think "thirteen"
immediately upon seeing 4, 7, 2 in a column; or even to
think thirty-nine, sixty-seven, ninety-six, one hundred
seventeen, one hundred forty-two, upon seeing 17, 22, 28,

29, 21, 25 in a column. The elimination of harmful or irrelevant reactions is equally important. One learns not to fidget, not to worry about the result, not to listen to noises in the street, in almost any task. In handwriting, improvement with practice consists in part in omitting the tremblings, overpressures, and erratic pushes and pulls. In adding, one ceases to say to oneself, "Three and nine are twelve; twelve and seven are nineteen," and the like; or even to think anything save, "Twelve, nineteen," and so on. The combination or integration of reaction occurs in the process of acquiring any type of ability or skill. It has been demonstrated clearly in reading, typewriting, telegraphy, writing, and other functions which have been carefully studied in the laboratory.

Thus in typewriting, the learner who at first had to make a series of separate reactions, one for each letter, in typing the phrase "Dear Sir," later becomes able to write this phrase as a single unified act. Similarly the person who first found difficulty in steering the automobile, applying pressure to the accelerator, releasing the clutch, and shifting the gears at the same time gradually learns to combine all of these reactions into one complex whole. The integrated reaction, however, is not merely the original reactions welded together. As learning goes on, the components of the responses change. Some of the old components drop out and new reactions are worked into the total. The combination is a whole of changing component reactions. The combinations are different at different stages in the course of learning.

The Conditions of Improvement. — *Mere practice does not make perfect.* The repetition of an activity need not improve it. Indeed, if just the same thing happened each time, the pupil could not improve. Repetition is useful because the pupil *does not exactly repeat* — because a chance is given him to vary what he does, to select for use the variations which improve the ability, and to eliminate those which weaken it. He may, in many instances, seem from the outside to do the same thing; but, if he is to improve, he must not, trial by trial, repeat exactly the same performance.

Improvement Requires Variation. — To improve he must vary. The variations will usually include minute reactions that are both beneficial and detrimental. If the urge to improve is present, the beneficial variants are more likely to be selected and repeated and the others eliminated. A primary requirement for improvement is the readiness or desire to improve. This desire provides the exertion needed to break up the old performance by striving to better it. In this way variations are produced and more actively selected and rejected. Typesetters, telegraph operators, and others who have worked for years on a dead level have been induced, by making *improvement* the means of satisfying some real want such as securing a higher wage or better job, to push beyond their old habits to a new pattern of reactions which is more efficient and quite as easy going once it is achieved. When a person's desire to improve is coupled with certain definite aims or ideas concerning what variations will bring improvement, the variations which do appear have greater effect and are consequently more quickly selected or rejected.

Detecting Desirable and Undesirable Reactions. — One of the difficulties experienced by all learners, no matter how great their desire for progress, is inability to sense or distinguish the minute reactions which are beneficial and detrimental. Many good reactions are hit upon and discarded because their value is not realized; many bad ones are retained because their detrimental effects were unsuspected. Herein lies one of the primary functions of the teacher. She must observe the pupil's work, discover the favorable reactions — indeed, whenever possible indicate their nature beforehand — and assist the pupil to master them. She should also perceive the unfavorable reactions and help the pupil to avoid or remove them. In this way the teacher facilitates the operation of the Law of Effect.

The good variations must be selected for survival by the Law of Effect. Hence the supreme importance of readiness for and interest in the task and in making improvement in it. Interest multiplies the " satisfyingness " of every success and inspires effort to discover and eliminate the causes of every failure. Ten minutes of practice with full zeal, when the worker is keen to do his best and when he is thrilled at every advance in his accomplishment may be worth an hour of work done merely to avoid disfavor or reproach, or idly to pass away the time.

THE COMPLEXITY OF REACTIONS

Learning is reacting; what we learn are reactions. In the careful studies of typing and other functions it is very apparent that the reaction is complex. It is more complex than our accounts, above, indicate. In reacting to any situation, in learning any function, the response may, and usually does, involve all the types of action of which we are capable. To test an ordinary type of learning, try to write with the unpracticed hand, left or right as the case may be. The reaction involves not only actions of the muscles of that hand and arm; it includes adjustments and movements of the head, neck, back — practically the whole body. It embraces various sensations, tensions, strains, pressures, sights. It involves changes in respiration and other less readily observed inner activities. It includes adjustments of the sense organs, especially the eyes, attention, perception, thinking. The learner attends to and observes his movements and written products. He observes facts, recalls ideas, imagines possible new steps or results, thinks of devices which may facilitate learning, plans new procedures, determines to make a particular letter, purposes to improve quickly. All of his mental machinery may be engaged. And this is not all. The learner *feels*. He is satisfied or annoyed by different reactions. He may experience excitement, anger, chagrin, pleasure, hope, exhilaration, mirth, despair, the " blues," disgust, envy, resentment. He may elaborate feelings and fancies such as rationalized resentment against a person who suggested or required such work, or disinclination to pursue such a subject any farther, or to do any more work during the day; or, on the other hand, he may develop renewed interest in studying or in teaching or in living in general. In sum, even in relatively simple tasks of learning, the whole person is engaged. One reacts as a whole to the learning situation. All sorts of motor acts, muscular and internal adjustments, emotional attachments, facts, learning techniques, interests, resolves, purposes, aims, ideals, may be acquired in this one act and setting. To say that a person is merely learning to write is to misinterpret almost entirely the process of education and learning. To say that one's entire person or life is being changed in some degree during this experience is more nearly correct.

PRIMARY AND CONCOMITANT LEARNINGS

To borrow terms aptly used by Kilpatrick, every instance of learning involves " primary " and " concomitant " learnings. In the illustration above, the primary learning is the mastery of the assigned task namely, writing with the unaccustomed hand. Under concomitant learnings would be included all of the other reactions, attitudes toward the task or toward the teacher, the subject, or life in general, habits of judging, thinking, planning, techniques of work, resolutions, self-reliance, pride, humility, habits and ideals of neatness, accuracy, emotional control. And, as Professor Kilpatrick rightly insists, the concomitant learnings are often more important than the primary. In the illustration used above, it may be of little importance how well one learns the primary or assigned task of writing with the unaccustomed hand; but whether the experience increases or decreases insight into the process of teaching or learning, or increases or decreases interest in education, or results in strengthened or weakened resolves to study the science basal to education, or develops attitudes of confidence in one's ability to improve instead of augmenting one's " inferiority complex " may be of profound importance.

Concomitant Learnings Always Present. — Every learning situation, no matter how insignificant or important its primary task may be, is fraught with possibilities for developing both desirable and undesirable information, attitudes, habits, techniques, or appreciations as concomitants. There is no escaping the concomitant reactions. They may be disregarded by a teacher but many, both desirable and undesirable, will occur just the same.

In most instances, the primary learning means improvement in the assigned task — to practice writing, learn to spell ten words, study a chapter in history, draw a picture on the blackboard, act as leader in a game, and so on. Some of the most important forms of learning cannot be so definitely assigned. It is futile to say, for example: " Now children, I want you all to spend 20 minutes improving your ability to reason " — or " to control your temper," or " to acquire appreciation of your fellows," or " to increase your interest in arithmetic," or " to increase your love for beauty." Most of these desirable but subtle reactions must be secured in the midst of activity directed to other ends. Although they are developed simultaneously as concomitants of many assigned tasks, they are nevertheless as fully subject to control in their development as any other educational product. They are difficult to control but they are not uncontrollable. To control them so as to secure the desirable growth is the responsibility of every teacher in every subject. Indeed, a person who is interested and competent only in the management of the assigned lesson and not in the concomitant learnings does not deserve the title of educator. Each learning task or situation is the means of changing in some degree the whole reaction equipment, the whole personality and life of the pupil. There is no escaping this fact; there is no escaping the responsibility of being prepared to control the many-sided reactions to every learning situation.

Laws of Learning Applied to Concomitant Learnings. — The principles of learning and teaching which must be observed in developing concomitant reactions — details of which will be treated in later chapters — are the same as those which underlie the acquisition of the primary or assigned reactions. The assignment or task and its subject matter, tools, and materials are to be considered as situations to which the pupil reacts in a very complex way. Preparations should be made to elicit, identify, and reward every type of desirable response and to discover and eliminate the undesirable. Skill in managing the materials, environment, and the pupil's activities to secure readiness and, whenever possible, to create a definite aim and purpose as a means of eliciting and making obvious the desirable variations; skill in detecting both desirable and undesirable reactions, and skill in rewarding the one and eliminating the other are the basal requirements of method.

THE TRANSFER OF ACQUIRED REACTIONS

The Meaning of Transfer. — We have said that learning consists in reacting muscularly, mentally, emotionally, in fact, in all the types of ways made possible by our organism, to situations which are invariably complex. Progress in learning consists in the selection and organization of those reactions which bring satisfaction and the elimination of those which are annoying. To every learning situation we tend to establish a complex of reactions which involves every phase of our nature. Thus, every lesson or task, every learning situation, provides the means of changing our life and character in some measure. The last problem of this chapter is concerned with the degree or extent of this change. This is essentially the problem of the extent to which a reaction made to one situation will transfer to, and function again in another situation. Will a movement or feeling or attitude of determination or an emotion of resentment or any other reaction made to the situation of practicing with the unaccustomed hand remain forever exclusively bound to that particular situation or will it be a permanent tendency to reaction which may be called out by a few, or many, or all other situations?

The Degree of Transfer. — Although many careful experiments have been performed since 1900 to determine the amount and nature of the transfer of a reaction from one situation to others, it is difficult to state the facts exactly because transfer varies with the method of training, with the intelligence of the subject, and with the nature of the reactions. In general, it may be said that reactions established in one situation will not carry over to *all* other situations, but that they may transfer to other settings which have a great deal in common with the one in which the reaction was built up. Thus, a movement, a method of attack, a feeling of confidence, or a disposition to be neat or accurate developed during writing with an unaccustomed hand may not reappear at all in studying history, buying a picture, practicing on the piano or typewriter because these learning situations have too little in common with writing. But some or all of these reactions may transfer to some extent to drawing novel figures, or learning to write backwards; inasmuch as these tasks have tools, bodily positions, paper, and operations in some measure identical with writing with an unaccustomed hand. Even among similar tasks, the transfer is often less than one would expect.

Samples of Transfer. — Suppose that the reader should now test his speed and accuracy in finding and marking words, on these pages, which contain both *i* and *t*. Suppose that he should then practice finding and marking words containing both *e* and *s* until he has made substantial improvement. On retesting his ability to find the words containing *i* and *t*, he will find that the improvement is only about a third as much as the improvement in ability to mark words containing *e* and *s*. Even so slight a difference in the abilities restricts improvement mainly to the one exercised. Or suppose that a child practices until he achieves marked improvement in reading to note the detailed facts in paragraphs. It will be found that he manifests only about one fifth, or less, improvement in reading to get the main point or in noting the outline of similar passages. While there nearly always is some positive transfer from one situation to others roughly similar, it is usually small and, occasionally, it is negative or detrimental.   Thus training in reading to note misspellings (proof-reading) may have an injurious effect upon reading to get the meaning of paragraphs.

Significance of Facts of Transfer. — Despite the fact that certain reactions — such as to neglect the impulse to idle or heed sensory distractions, to work with a will to succeed, to restrain anger, fear, worry, and overexcitement, to search for outstanding clues for improvement — are useful and possible in any learning situation, they cannot be guaranteed by developing them in occasional situations. A new learning task may offer so many new elements and difficulties that the learner may idle, fumble, become distracted, lose his interest, give way to resentment or excitement, and be unable to perceive the principle in the situation which is identical with that in problems previously solved.   Nevertheless, general ability, character, poise, reasonableness, emotional control, neatness, honesty, efficiency, and insight are secured by exercising them repeatedly in particular settings, and the opposites of these abilities become more and more pronounced aspects of a person's behavior, in general, by permitting them to occur in one situation after another.   The spread of training is genuine even if small in magnitude.   And it must be remembered that undesirable reactions tend to spread just as do the desirable.

The meagerness of the transfer of good reactions emphasizes the importance of the teacher as the instrument of controlling all of the pupils' reactions in all learning situations under her observation.   Good techniques, habits, and attitudes of intellectual, volitional, emotional, temperamental, appreciational, moral reaction must be built up out of the specific adjustments to all types of situations.   They cannot be safely relegated to any one school subject, teacher, or period. They must be the objective of teaching by every teacher in every subject all of the time.

Importance of Individual Differences. — Studies of the transfer of training show also that the native ability of a pupil has a pronounced effect upon the degree of transfer. In most subjects, the brighter pupils, other things being equal, can make wider use of their acquisition than duller pupils. Brightness, indeed, means in a considerable measure sensitivity to the factors or principles which are common to many situations. Not only do the bright pupils isolate the essential elements in a learning situation more quickly, but they also perceive more acutely the same elements in new settings. Transfer of experience therefore occurs more fully among bright than among dull individuals; it is in considerable degree determined by intelligence.

Importance of Method of Teaching. — Studies of the transfer of training also have shown that the methods used in guiding the pupil's learning activities have marked effect upon the degree of transfer. The more clearly the crucial element or fact or principle in a situation is brought to the pupil's attention the more readily the same element or fact or principle may be identified in another situation. Transfer in many cases depends very largely upon becoming sensitive to the essential factors in an experience which were also the crucial factors in preceding experiences. Thus if a child observes, despite many differences in details in a new mechanical puzzle, that the vital principle is the same as in puzzles previously solved, the solution is more likely to be achieved than when the common principle is not identified. By proper selection of experiences and by skillful management of the learning process, the teacher can greatly facilitate the pupil's efforts to identify the essential elements common to different situations, and thereby to increase the transfer of experience from one situation to others. To the methods by which such a result may be achieved, considerable attention will be given in the next two chapters.

QUESTIONS AND EXERCISES

1. If ten children are shown a picture for twenty seconds and then asked to describe what they observed, the accounts will differ considerably and no child is likely to be able to recall correctly and fully all of the items in the picture. What principles of learning does this fact illustrate? In particular, how is it related to the statement that learning is reacting?

2. Explain how it happens that learnings which give a child power to satisfy wants are likely to be more effectively undertaken than those which do not. Does a strong motive provide all the essential elements for effective learning? If so, how do you explain the difficulty of the old gentleman who, despite a strong desire to learn to play golf, made little progress while practicing without keeping his "eye on the ball"?

3. Give some instances of the management of crying, refusing food, throwing things, etc. among infants which illustrate wrong application of the Law of Effect. Suggest more effective management of the child in these cases.

4. Give some recent instances in your own experience or in those of others in which you were not in a state of readiness to learn. What were the reasons for the unreadiness and what were the effects?

5. What inquiries would you think it advisable to make about a healthy boy who had shown no inclination to learn to read in the first grade?

6. In what respects is the statement "we learn by doing," likely to be misleading? Frame a statement which states more fully and accurately the relation of learning and activity.

7. In what respects is the statement "Practice makes perfect" true and in what respects is it untrue?

8. What would be possible differences upon the process of learning between "a strong interest in reading" and "a strong desire to increase the speed of reading"? What defense can you offer for the statement that "few things are ever learned well unless they are made a specific and desired objective of learning"?

9. Enumerate some possible primary and concomitant learnings in each of the following situations: (a) second grade reading lesson; (b) drawing an illustration for a class poster; (c) construction of a box for a plant brought to school by a pupil; (d) test in arithmetic; (e) discussion of what shall be done with a pupil who cheated in a test.

10. If honesty or neatness could be developed equally well in the several high-school activities which came within your experience, from which ones would the transfer to the situations in life in general probably be greatest? Why? In order to secure still greater transfer of honesty or neatness, what changes in your high school work would you recommend?

11. Do you think that certain subjects or activities are intrinsically superior to others for developing certain habits such as persistence, sociability, initiative, originality, trustworthiness, open-mindedness, etc.? Explain.

12. Can you give instances in which the method of teaching was probably more important than the subject matter in developing and transferring desirable habits of behavior?

13. What principles are to be followed if the concomitant learnings are to be fostered more than they now are?

REFERENCES

GATES, A. I., *Psychology for Students of Education*. Macmillan. Chapters X, XI, XV.

KILPATRICK, W. H., *Foundations of Method*. Macmillan.

LARUE, D. W., *The Child's Mind and the Common Branches*. Macmillan.

MEAD, A. R., *Learning and Teaching*. Lippincott.

THORNDIKE, E. L., *The Psychology of Learning*. Teachers College Bureau of Publications.

See also general references for Chapter I.

Chapter VI

THE ACQUISITION OF KNOWLEDGE AND THE ABILITY TO THINK

In the preceding chapter, the main characteristics of the learning process and the chief functions of the teachers in facilitating it were presented. In general terms, the teacher's task consists in securing the optimum readiness, interest or motivation needed to initiate and sustain whole-hearted learning activity, in guiding the learner as far as possible to make the desired reactions and to avoid the erroneous ones, and finally in managing the situation so that the desired reactions are made satisfying and the undesired ones annoying. Although the teacher's work may be classified under these three functions, the number of different things she must do is enormous. In this chapter we shall be concerned primarily with illustration and extension of some of the points made in the preceding chapter in order to bring out more clearly certain facts which underlie both the determination of detailed methods of teaching and the criteria for use in selecting the subjects and activities for the school curriculum.

A Reaction May Be Primary or Concomitant. — In the preceding chapter, emphasis was given to the fact that learning is reacting and that any learning-situation may elicit a wide variety of reactions. Some of these reactions are closely related to the assigned or primary task, while others, the concomitant or incidental reactions which occurred simultaneously, are not exactly part of the assigned task and, often, are not noted by the teacher since her attention is usually mainly on the primary results — on the assigned tasks. Any kind of reaction, from a simple motor act to the most complex mental or moral or emotional adjustment, may be acquired either as primary or concomitant learning. It should be realized, furthermore, that what is primary learning in one case may be incidental in another and vice versa.

Thus when we ask the pupil to study his history, the reactions to certain historical facts are primary and reactions which affect skill in reading, studying, spelling, and thinking are concomitants. If another pupil, asked to practice accurate and rapid reading, selects the same material, the reading reactions are primary whereas the facts of history and other information and skill are incidental. The results in the two cases are unlikely to be identical. The child tends to change most in the direction of the assigned objectives. The assignment of a task or purpose tends to influence greatly the reactions made, selected, and rejected. Since this is the case, we must, in this chapter, outline the different kinds of reactions which are to be acquired, indicate similarities and differences among both the reactions themselves and the means of developing them as primary and as concomitant learnings. In this way we may be able to discover means of improving both our methods of teaching and of selecting subjects and activities for the curriculum.

CLASSIFICATION OF TYPES OF LEARNABLE REACTIONS

The particular reactions which a human being can acquire are innumerable. They may be classified in various ways. Common usage would give us such a statement as this: " One can acquire information, skill, habits, attitudes, feelings, inclinations, prejudices, appreciations, purposes, ideals, etc." These are all common words which refer to various types of groupings of the acquisitions from learning. Some persons would utilize all of these groups and more; some would get along with half of them or less. Some persons have selected one term or another, such as ideals, as the main product for which education should strive. The danger in such usage is that one may come to think of information, ideals, or skills as separate and distinct entities, or products of a different order. The fact is that they are merely very rough classes of reactions which overlap in many ways. This fact we must try to keep in the foreground despite the fact that, merely for convenience in discussion, we shall also adopt an arbitrary scheme of classification of reactions.

For our purpose we may classify the multitude of reactions under the following headings:

1. Reactions of information or knowledge of facts.
2. Intellectual reactions or techniques such as thinking, reasoning, judging.
3. Reactions of skills or motor abilities.
4. Reactions of conduct; moral, volitional, and other behavior.
5. Reactions of feeling and emotions; aesthetic and appreciative experiences.

These we may consider in turn, pointing out similarities, differences, and interrelations.

Acquisition of Reactions of Information or Knowledge of Facts

We have frequently stated that the process of informative learning is a process of reacting. We learn facts by reacting with our intellectual equipment to any sort of thing or event. We learn to know a face by reacting to it. We learn to know new facts about a face by react-ing to it at different times from different points of view, or with different interests in a state of readiness. We learn all facts by reacting either to concrete objects and events or to pictures, words, or other symbols which repre-sent or mean the objects and events in whole or part.

To Know a Fact Is to Be Able to React Correctly to a Situation. — Perhaps this truth will be more convincing if we ask: "What is involved in knowing a fact?" "What does knowledge of a fact imply?" To know a fact means exactly to be able to respond in a certain ap-proved way to one or more particular situations. To illustrate: Two and two equal four. This is a fact that you know. Now, this means that when you are con-fronted with such situations as

$$2 + 2 = \quad , \text{ or } \underset{=}{2}, \text{ or } \Box\Box + \Box\Box = \quad , \text{ or two plus two} = \cdot ,$$

or with any arrangement of two pairs of concrete objects, or thoughts of such situations or objects, you can respond by awareness of the fact *four*. Because you have re-acted to so many different types of two-plus-two situa-tions, you can react correctly now to almost any such situ-ation you may meet. We may say you know this fact very thoroughly. But some facts are not so well known.

Illustrated by Knowledge of Weight. — Consider weight. Ask a child such questions as these. "Does a chair, a dog, a feather have weight?" "Does air have weight?" "Does steam or a toy balloon which rises in the air have weight?" "Does anything which pulls up instead of pushing down the weighing scale have weight?" "Does sunlight have weight?" He will be unable to respond correctly to all such situations. His knowledge, we say, is incomplete and not universally applicable. He can respond by knowing weight in certain situations, but not in others. The fact will not transfer to all situations; it occurs as a correct response to only a few. Information, then, means ability to react in a certain approved way, intellectually, by thinking of some fact, to some situation. It is just as truly a reaction, just as truly subject to limitations of transfer as any other reaction such as skill in handling tools or catching balls or exercising neatness or controlling one's temper.

The Function of the Teacher — Setting Up the Proper Situation. — Efficiency in teaching requires, in addition to arousing the readiness which provides for whole-hearted activity, the arranging of the situation so as to facilitate the right response as far as possible. The first dictum is: *Consider any situation before letting it act on the pupil; see that it tends to evoke the desired response.* The teacher's function, then, is to set up a situation which tends to provoke the desired response.

Illustration of Undesirable Set-Up of Situation in Spelling. — The application of the dictum, "set up the learning situation so that it will tend to evoke the right response," may be shown by illustrations of incorrect and correct arrangements. Consider the plan of asking pupils to correct the spelling errors in a passage like the following, while they read it, as a means of improving ability to spell.

> If hope be a star that would leed us estray,
> And, "deceiveth the heart," as the aged ones preech,
> Yet it was mercy that gave it to break on our way,
> Tho' its halo ilumes where we never may reach.

This situation tends naturally to provoke efforts to understand the thought and not to puzzle over individual words seductively misspelled. The misspellings, furthermore, tend to practice the act of seeing words as they should *not* be observed instead of as they should be. Instead of being assisted to get the right response the pupil is hindered and the concomitant reactions are detrimental to reading habits. Finally, the situation does not provide convenient means by which the pupil can tell whether his spellings are correct or not.

Illustration of Better Set-Up of Situation in Spelling. — To induce the learner to make the correct response, the situation should, first of all, indicate the correct reaction. Thus, the word *astray* should be presented, correctly spelled and the pupil should react to it by *seeing* clearly its visible form and by pronouncing it in order to hear correctly its audible character. The next step would be to react by saying the letters in correct order. But this is not enough. If the pupil merely repeated the letters while *seeing* them, he would be practicing only the reaction of saying (or writing) letters correctly while looking at them; that is, he would be practicing the act of *copying* the letters in a word. The reaction really desired is that of saying, writing, or thinking of the letters when the word is not visible. The learning situation, therefore, requires an additional step. It requires *recall* of the letters while the pupil is not looking at them. Having made this attempt, the pupil should check his recall by repeating it while again looking at the word. If he is incorrect, he should, by observing the word, correct his error and repeat until he can correctly recall the letters. Thereafter, the letters should be repeatedly recalled until the reaction is perfected.

The Situation Should Elicit the Reactions Which Meet Practical Needs. — In this illustration, it may have been noted, several different reactions were possible. The pupil might say the letters aloud, say them subvocally, " see " them in his mind's eye, " hear " them in his mind's ear, trace them in the air with his hand, or write them on paper with a pencil. The dictum was: " Set up the situation so as to exercise the *desired reaction*." How can one tell what the desired reaction is? The reaction desired is that one which meets a practical life need; the one which the world demands. Chiefly the practical need of ability to spell a word is to enable a person to *write* that word. (Spelling words orally is rarely required except in school and but very little in most progressive ones. If a person doesn't know how to spell a word, modern etiquette suggests that he use the dictionary instead of bothering, and sometimes embarrassing, his companions — who are rarely so reliable as the dictionary anyhow!) Hence the reaction to be exercised for permanent retention and use is the *writing* of the word. The total situation, then, requires a correctly printed model, which can be put out of sight at will, pencil and paper, and instructions, which can soon be learned by heart, concerning the procedure. Since a person writes words chiefly in connected discourse, only those words should be taught which are very likely to be used immediately in the writing of letters, and other compositions, which the world will demand. Thus the practice of writing the word correctly while thinking ahead of other words in each sentence will be exercised later in normal activities of writing notes, letters, and other compositions.

Illustration from Learning the Alphabet. — Let us take another illustration to show how even in learning the most elementary facts, such as the A.B.C.'s, the teacher should consider the situation in order to have it result in reactions which will function most usefully in life. As a matter of fact, except when the teacher or a fond parent asks a child to "say the A.B.C.'s," there is little real demand for this stunt even in the lower grades. The child needs to recognize the letter when he sees it in a word, on his hat hook in the room, on lockers in the gymnasium, on the seats in the auditorium, on the doors of rooms, on the street corner posts, and, later, on thumb holes in the dictionary. He needs, moreover, to be able, in a general way, to think where a given letter such as K is in the series and in which direction and about how far off it is from another letter which he has come upon, such as N. To develop ready reactions of these sorts, situations must be devised which provoke and check reactions of thinking of the position of letters in the whole series, or of which way and about how far any letter is from another. Merely to say the A.B.C.'s is a different reaction from these. It would be better to use letter cards, indexes, seating and locker arrangement, hat hooks, the dictionary, and so on as means of practicing these reactions.

Illustration from Arithmetic. — Until recently, it was often assumed that a child should be taught to do problems in division by giving him first the table of divisions, such as the following, to learn :

$2 \div 1 = 2$	$2 \div 2 = 1$	$3 \div 3 = 1$
$3 \div 1 = 3$	$4 \div 2 = 2$	$6 \div 3 = 2$
$4 \div 1 = 4$	$6 \div 2 = 3$	$9 \div 3 = 3$
etc.	etc.	etc.

Even if a child learned these tables by heart, he might have difficulty if he were suddenly asked to respond to " 15 divided by 3 equals what? " Since he had learned the combinations in series, like the A.B.C.'s, he might have to say, " $3 \div 3 = 1, 6 \div 3 = 2$," and so on until he reached 15, just as, in order to tell what letter follows F, he might have to say " abcdef *g*." Therefore, practice on the combinations presented one at a time in miscellaneous order would be essential to insure prompt reactions to such problems. But mere mastery of these tables is not the same as ability to react correctly to such situations as the following, which require division of the same numbers

10 = how many 5's?
12 = how many 2's?

_____

Ten cents contains how many nickels?
Twelve cents buys how many two-cent stamps?

_____

If 5¢ pays one car fare, then 15¢ pays how many car fares?

_____

How many 5¢ balls can you buy with 30 cents?

_____

For 2 cents you can buy one postage stamp.
For 12 cents you can buy —— postage stamps.

Each of these situations sets up the problem in a different way. Some of the latter ones are more like the kinds of situations which a child encounters in life than are some of the former. This being the case, pupils should have abundant practice in meeting just such situations rather than little practice on problems of this type and extensive drill on the artificially arranged tables. If they have reacted frequently, with accuracy, to the lifelike questions, they are more likely to react to them correctly henceforth than if they were merely experts in reciting the tables.

Growth in Understanding and Use of a Fact. — Knowing a fact is not a static thing. The intellectual reaction of knowing a fact goes through a process of growth quite similar to that described in the preceding chapter for the development of ability to typewrite. As new situations are reacted to, and as older ones are responded to in new ways, various changes in the nature of the knowing reaction occur. Little variations appear. Some of them are faulty and misleading — as when a child reacts to one of the preceding problems in division by multiplying the numbers given or when he reacts to his cat's tail as a thing to lift her up by. Such erroneous ways of reacting are likely to be eliminated if a clear-cut indication of their faulty character is given. The teacher should point out the child's error in the first case, and the cat certainly will in the second. Each such elimination of an erroneous intellectual response contributes to the growth and usefulness of the child's idea of division or of cats. Other reactions, such as those made to a new statement of a division situation or to a cat's paws, may be correct and are therefore selected and woven together with others that have to do with division or cats. Thus the knowledge grows, enlarges, becomes increasingly refined, and reaches higher levels quite as hierarchies appeared in the development of ability to typewrite. As the idea of division or of cats becomes integrated on higher and higher levels, it becomes more refined, more detailed, more complex, and inclusive : — it becomes more useful because it can be applied more widely, and because it appears more frequently and surely as a reaction to more numerous and more subtle situations. Thus the child learns correctly to react by division to a very great variety of problems with better understanding of what division is and does and he learns more subtle facts about cats and to recognize cats by merely seeing the cat's paw or footprint or hearing of some of her traits or emotional dispositions.

Facilitating Development of Knowledge. — To facilitate the growth of an idea — that is, of the processes of reacting to a situation by knowing a fact in some degree

— it is necessary to choose situations and experience so as to emphasize the essential elements in the idea or fact and to carry the conception gradually onward to increasing levels of refinement and wider application. This is true of all facts, both simple and complex. The fact of recognizing the word *cat* and of spelling it may be considered a relatively simple type. At the other extreme may be placed knowledge of an abstract character or element, such as sum, difference, average; per cent, interest, profit; length, weight, mass; noun, verb, predicate; soft, big, smooth; triangle, circle, square; why, nevertheless, therefore; government, law, honesty; and so on. Knowledge of these facts permits great growth and extension. Our problem, now, is to discover methods of facilitating the process of learning to know such facts.

Extending Awareness of a Fact by Showing Its Presence in Many Situations. — The first requirement is the one already given: Set up the situation which emphasizes the fact clearly in the form desired for practical purpose. Now, to extend the significance and usefulness of seeing and spelling *cat*, we can go further than merely to see it and spell it as a whole. The word *cat*, to illustrate, contains two elements, the *c* and the *at* which appear in many other words such as *cot, can,* etc. and *rat, hat, bat,* etc. To have a child solve such a problem as: " Which has the longer tail:

> The rat?
> The cat?
> The bat?"

might attract attention to the element *at*. In a similar manner, if we wish to extend and clarify the awareness of *squareness* (which can be taken as representative of learning to know any abstract fact) we should secure a number of different situations which clearly indicate this factor but which differ in other respects. Thus, we can show the child in succession or together a square sheet of paper, a square board, a square drawing on the board, a square card, and so on. We ought, in this case, to show squareness as part of solid as well as flat objects to prevent the child from thinking that only flat objects are square and consequently reacting erroneously to solids. Square boxes, tables, blocks, and the like should therefore be shown. The first principle, then, is to extend knowledge of a fact by presenting many situations which differ from each other in all respects except by containing the element or fact to be emphasized. By repeatedly reacting to the fact in otherwise different settings, the child comes to know the fact better and to recognize it in more situations. Although this is a matter to be discussed more fully later, the child learns more effectively when he is led to take the active attitude of discovery in identifying the essential element himself than when he merely passively observes the element as it is *shown* to him. It is not enough, in other words, merely to present various situations which contain the fact which we desire to teach. It is essential that the pupil react vigorously to the situations presented with his mind set to observe the essential factor.

Extending Awareness of a Fact by Emphasizing It. — While the various situations are being shown for the child to react to, the fact may be emphasized in many ways if necessary. The teacher may pronounce *cat* by saying *ku-at*. She may point to or underline each part while saying it. She may point to the *at* in the series of words on the above exercise. She may say: " Now, many words contain *at;* look at these words carefully, etc." In the case of squareness, she may, by tracing the outline, by verbal description, by calling attention away from the paperness, or other irrelevant elements, center it upon the *squareness*. Since in a later section of this chapter we shall discuss in greater detail the merits of verbal descriptions, actions, construction, models, etc. as means of emphasizing different facts, we shall not pursue the topic further here except to repeat that the process of learning may be facilitated not only by the choice and mechanical arrangement of the situations and by inducing an active, searching attitude on the part of the pupil, but also by emphasizing the essential fact or element.

Extending Awareness of a Fact by Contrasting It with a Different Fact. — Another means of emphasizing a fact is to contrast it with some other fact which is its opposite or very unlike it. This method is most effective when the two facts contrasted are really incompatible or mutually exclusive. Thus in demonstrating and getting the young child to react to *squareness*, situations may be arranged in which this fact is contrasted with *roundness*. Thus the teacher shows a square and a round piece of paper. Now a piece of paper cannot be both round and square at the same time. This can be brought to the child's attention. By placing the emphasis upon square *versus* round, the fact of *paperness* in each situation is less likely to become prominent. Contrasting squareness and roundness tends to emphasize the distinctive character of each.

In the case of spelling, the effective use of this principle can be made in a few cases in which two different spelling procedures, often confused, are mutually exclusive practices, as in the case of the familiar trouble with *ie* and *ei*. The procedure is to show or ask children to spell a number of words such as *receive, believe, deceit, chief, ceiling, grief,* and so on, and then to ask them to observe a series of words spelled with *ie* and another with *ei* and try to discover other differences between the two groups. They may spontaneously note, or be assisted to observe, that in all words containing *ei*, these letters are preceded by *c*. By introducing further words like *neighbor* and *weight*, they may detect a third group in which *ei* is the rule when the digraph takes the sound of $\bar{a}$.[1] Thus by the experience of reacting to many words of each type and of contrasting particular instances of the different types, the general facts which cover the spelling usages may be derived.

The Use of Rules, Definitions, and Other Verbal Formulae. — The last illustration leads us directly to a consideration of the value of rules, definitions, slogans, summaries, and other verbal formulae as means of developing awareness of a complex or subtle fact. These and other verbal devices may be useful in many cases if properly applied. They are often overused and misused. The teacher must distinguish between learning verbal definitions and learning facts. You can teach a child to recite a spelling rule before he has spelled a single word or to say the definition of *mass* before he has any conception of the fact. To do so would not necessarily give the child any knowledge of the fact or assist him in acquiring it. The rule or definition is to be considered as one means of attracting a pupil's attention to the feature of experience being emphasized. It is never a substitute for the experience. Except as it really guides or illuminates experience it is of no value. Its usefulness should be compared with that of pointing, drawing, lengthy discussion, underlining, arranging in groups,

[1] The fact that there are a few "exceptions" to this rule, such as *either, neither, seize, leisure,* makes the practical value of the method relatively small in this particular case as in most other cases of spelling rules.

demonstrating by a model, and other means of emphasizing the aspect of experience that is the object of the teaching.

It should be noted that the facts contained in such a definition as " square means having four equal sides and four right angles " or in such a rule as " I before E, except after C or when sounded like A as in *neighbor* or *weigh* " are themselves highly abstract. To enable a child to understand this spelling rule requires the full process of carefully guided experience and the use of all the devices we have just been considering. The common error in teaching is to forget this fact; to assume that the rule need not be taught with the elaborations of experience which we have described. To be useful the rule must be taught in this way. The spelling rule just given, for example, is of little value unless taught with greatest care and thoroughness and even then proves serviceable to few children lower than the seventh or eighth grade. In some cases, the succinct rule or definition is as hard to teach as, or even harder than, the fact which the rule merely verbalizes. The special values and limitations of verbal methods in general should therefore be considered in some detail in comparison with other means of demonstration and explanation.

Advantages of Expression by Language

The advantages of expression by words and similar symbols are:

1. Their economy of time.
2. Their convenience.
3. Their special fitness to express and arouse general and abstract ideas and judgments and knowledge of relationships.

Economy of Time. — Language is the only means of expression that approaches thought in quickness. There is hardly an object that cannot be named more quickly than it can be drawn; there is hardly an event that cannot be retold again and again in the time it would take to act it out in pantomime.

Convenience. — The development of the random prattling and noise-making of infants into articulate speech expressing nearly the entire realm of human experience, is one of the greatest triumphs of the human species. One is tempted to think that the human species hit upon the best possible means of expression when one considers its extreme convenience.

Oral speech can be carried on regardless of position, regardless of whether one is at the time using arms and legs vigorously; it requires practically no space and no material but air; it expresses thought to hundreds and thousands at once; it produces little fatigue; it needs no very high degree of muscular control; and requires not a great amount of time in acquisition. Written speech adds permanence to the expression and makes hardly greater demands upon space, time, and material. Next to words, drawing is probably the most convenient means of expression, but consider the appliances and technique required for the graphic expression of even a very simple fact. In such expressive work as a good course in manual training offers, the space, apparatus, and technical training demanded become a most important consideration. Verbal expression will always be preëminent in the school as it is in life, because of its tremendous advantage on the side of time, space, material, and technique.

Special Uses. — Verbal expression, including technical symbols, is peculiarly adapted to the expression of relationships and general and abstract ideas. The very unlikeness of the expression to the fact expressed which differentiates language from pictorial art gives language the possibility of expressing likeness, cause, condition, concession, and other nonrepresentative aspects of experience as easily as red, blue, apple, pear; of expressing a reference to 40,000,000, bravery, or square root as easily as to two, the rescue of a drowning sailor or the division of an apple into halves.

Hardly in any other way could we express such facts as in Latin the usages of *ut* or *quod*, or in grammar the function of tense and mode, or such abstract judgments as "π is the ratio of the circumference of a circle to its diameter," or "Virtue is its own reward." In the work of the school the meanings of many nouns, verbs, adjectives, and adverbs, of most prepositions and conjunctions and of all or nearly all pronouns and auxiliary verbs, the logic of arithmetic, grammar (of English and foreign languages), algebra, and geometry, the general laws of geography and other sciences, and the facts of literature and history that concern human motives and moral values are best expressed in words or symbols for words.

Advantages of Expression by the Activities of the Arts and Industries

The advantages of expression by constructive and artistic activities are:

1. Vigor, emphasis, life.
2. Freedom from ambiguity, honesty.
3. Power to express details of shape, color, and arrangement.
4. Appeal to interests in action, in manipulation and in the concrete.

Reality. — Words and figures lack the vividness and emphasis of pictures, models, and other material constructions. They do not so easily stir the emotions or so strongly reinforce the original experience of the object. The boy who says, "A bay is a body of water partly surrounded by land," makes little impression on others and probably adds less to the clearness and permanence of his own ideas than the boy who makes a bay in the mud puddle behind the school.

Honesty. — Construction and art are also more likely to be honest, to tell a clear story of knowledge or ignorance. The boy may define the bay from rote memory and yet not be able to recognize a bay if he should see it or to realize its uses. The repetition of words may express real knowledge or only knowledge of words. The pupil himself also realizes the inadequacy of his knowledge of a fact more fully when he tries to express it in a drawing or model than when he answers questions about it. Although all forms of expression teach the pupil and inform the teacher, the constructive act does so in general better than the verbal.

Special Uses. — In many cases words are relatively powerless. The facts concerning the mouth-parts of a beetle, the location and direction of rivers, the colors of butterflies, or the structure of an engine can only clumsily and inaccurately and inconveniently be expressed in words; their natural handling is through diagrams and drawings. This is commonly the case with facts of shape, proportion, position, and color and is often the case with facts of size.

Interest. — With the introduction into the school of the constructive and artistic activities, there is a great increment of motive power and zeal from the strong interests in the concrete and objective, and in the manipulation of physical things. To write out one's ideas in words is more interesting than to repress them, but the motor process of writing is artificial and difficult and the black marks are so lifeless, so abstract, so remote from the real world that, compared with the other means of expression, writing is a dull affair. Oral language is more attractive because it is less artificial and more associated in experience with interesting acts and events; but drawing pictures, working in sand or clay, acting a part in pantomime and the like, rank far higher in the scale of interest. The interests in action, movement, possession are behind the latter activities and they do not presuppose the capacity for apprehending the abstract.

Since all the forms of motor expression are useful for mental development, it is the privilege of the school to make use of whatever forms best serve its purpose. The monopoly which verbal expression has so long enjoyed should disappear. The sand pile as well as the slate can record thought. A class in geography should recite with chalk and paint brush as well as with lips. Arithmetic should mean measurement and diagraming as well as calculating. To make a pair of scales is often better than to answer questions about the principles of the balance.

DISADVANTAGES OF LANGUAGE AND OF OVERT ACTIVITIES AS FORMS OF EXPRESSIONS

The dangers in the use of verbal expression are : (1) that the pupils' spoken or written words represent only rote memory or, at the most, a misty, inadequate notion ; and (2) that more useful and appropriate motor arts may be neglected.

The dangers in the use of drawing, modeling, constructive work, and the like are : (1) triviality, the ex-

pression of what is not worth while, (2) the expression of
the wrong thing, (3) overemphasis and misapplication
of technique, (4) injustice to those pupils who have the
experience of thought and feeling in question but lack the
technique to express it, and (5) waste of time.

Triviality. — There is a great risk that what is drawn,
modeled, carved or woven will be from the standpoint of
real intellectual advance nonessential. Four hours spent
in weaving a red and blue blanket may be worth while as
motor training but little as a means of increasing appreciation of Indian industry and art. The group of pupils
who at great expense of time constructed an elaborate
cohort of gaily colored clay knights on horseback may
have been well occupied as artists, but so far as concerns
real understanding of and feeling toward the activities of
the medieval warrior they almost wasted their time. It is
not enough to express something; it must be something
worth expressing.

Falsehood. — A still worse error is to mistake the expression of one thing for that of something quite different.
A teacher who took the drawing of an Indian blanket as
a proof of appreciation of Indian life or fancied that the
table full of colored clay figures witnessed a real understanding of the age of chivalry would probably deceive
herself and mislead her class. These constructions probably express ideas of the color and fashion of blankets and
of the dress and armor of the knight, and may express
only remembrance of certain copies seen. An elaborate
drawing of a rabbit may be made by a student utterly
ignorant of the essential facts of its anatomy. It is not
enough to express something; it must be the right thing.

Overtechnique. — *It is a constant temptation to emphasize the workmanship at the expense of the story told
by any art of construction.* The student is encouraged to

spend hours in drawing a sea urchin, putting in spine by spine with extreme care, when a rough sketch would answer the purpose nearly, if not quite, as well. Children are allowed or even required to spend all their spare time for a week at coloring in each state on a map, mixing the colors with the utmost care, making all of each state of exactly the same hue and beginning all over if a drop of New York's green happens to spill on Massachusetts. Technical skill is a desirable thing, but it must not be allowed to appropriate time that belongs to motor expression.

Injustice. — Almost everyone has control of the technique necessary to say and write with ease such words as he knows. But many months of study are required to master the means of presenting objects in perspective or of modeling a fair likeness of the human face in clay or of matching a given color with paints. Lack of capacity and training prevents many boys and girls from ever doing justice to their knowledge and emotions in drawing, painting, and constructive art. Their technique never catches up with their insight; their art is never equal to their emotions. This limitation of artistic expression, however, may be greatly reduced by better training.

Waste of Time. — A final deficiency in drawing, painting, modeling, and construction for the expression of many ideas and feelings is that adequate expression by these means often requires far more time than verbal reports. At the same time, many ideas can be expressed both more quickly and more clearly by a sketch or model than by words. The question of time is one which should be considered along with other advantages and disadvantages.

Choice of Means. — Principles of guidance in this choice are necessarily somewhat vague: the question is almost always one of balancing advantages and disadvantages. Sometimes the choice is fairly sure; *e.g.*, a drawing rather than words to express the structure of the eye, words rather than a model to express the uses of the Latin word *ut*, a model rather than a line-drawing to express the relation of the earth's orbit to the sun. Sometimes it is difficult; *e.g.*, making maps in relief with sand or flat on paper, speech *versus* drawing and painting in the case of history. The teacher will get on best without fixed rules, keeping in mind the facts just given and guarding against:

1. Being overinfluenced by the convenience of words.
2. Being overinfluenced by the attractiveness of manual construction.
3. Relying on words alone to express facts of size, shape, proportion, or color.
4. Relying on words, drawing, and painting alone to express facts of action and change.
5. Confusing two things, (*a*) construction for the sake of motor skill, or power over technique, and (*b*) construction for the sake of general mental development.

The Need of Abundant Experience. — The learning of any fact requires primarily the reaction to many different, realistic situations which contain it. As ability to perceive the fact develops, situations which contain it in more obscure and subtle forms should be introduced.

Only after considerable experience of this type will the child really know what an abstruse fact such as *mass* or the meaning of the *ei- ie* rule is. To know such a fact is to be able to react by realizing the existence of mass in or the application of the rule to appropriate situations encountered. How many situations a child must react to before he knows an abstract fact fully, that is, wherever it appears, depends upon the skill with which his reactions have been guided, upon the variety of the situations which were presented and greatly upon his intelligence. Problems in demonstrating knowledge of abstract rules and abstract facts such as heavy, light, right, left, similarity, difference, pity, charity, revenge, weight, liberty, etc. are among the best indicators of intelligence. The more intelligent person learns with less experience than the duller person to react correctly to such abstract features of situations.

Summary. — The mastery of any fact, then, is the cumulative process of reacting to many situations. The teacher's function consists in arousing readiness, sustaining whole-hearted responses, selecting appropriate situations which tend to elicit the right and sidestep the wrong reactions, encouraging by demonstration, indication, speech, and otherwise, the correct reaction, making it satisfying where it appears and detecting and eliminating the wrong reactions.

Other Educative Influences. — In acquiring the reactions which constitute information, the learning is facilitated by a number of details of classroom management such as by having pleasant but not distracting surroundings, work periods suitably placed in the school day and neither so long as to reduce readiness nor so short as to fail to satisfy interest; by not introducing so many new facts at once as to cause confusion and conflict nor so few as to make repetition monotonous; by taking advantage of the gain secured by an optimum distribution of practice and review; and by utilizing other advantageous methods of classroom management which are now commonly described in texts in educational psychology.

Acquiring Facts during Activities of Reasoning, Constructing Objects, Acquiring Skills, etc. — Thus far we have discussed only certain phases of the process of acquiring facts and extending their significance and usefulness to the learner. We may learn facts and refine their meaning in the course of any type of activity which introduces new demands for the use of information. The activities of reasoning or of solving any kind of problem or of learning to use a new tool or of acquiring a new skill or of advancing an old one or of changing one's conduct or one's tastes or feelings provide the means of acquiring facts and perfecting their use. In turning, then, to these topics we shall still be suggesting means of developing knowledge.

THINKING AND OTHER INTELLECTUAL SKILLS

Varieties of Thinking. — Reflection, creative imagination, reasoning, problem-solving are different forms of thinking which depend more on the situations thought about than upon the nature of the thinking process. We shall be concerned merely with the process and technique of thinking in general. We shall not be concerned with the thinking which is mere reproduction of past experiences as in memory or recollection, nor with idle, uncontrolled thinking as in dreams or reverie, but with the controlled purposeful thinking which one resorts to in solving a particular problem, or in discovering a fact which solves many problems.

Bases of Purposeful Thinking. — This type of purposeful and productive thinking depends primarily upon three things: (1) upon information, or ability to react to the problem-situation with awareness of the facts which it contains; (2) upon sagacity, or intellectual capacity to perceive the serviceable facts and their relations, and (3) upon skills, or techniques of managing the process of thinking. We may say at the outset that education may succeed in improving directly the first and third requirements, but only indirectly can it affect the second which depends primarily upon native intellectual endowment.

Thinking Requires Knowledge. — Thinking can go on only when one can react to the situation by awareness of the facts which it offers. Other things being equal, the fertility and success of thinking is directly proportional to one's knowledge about the elements involved in a problem. Thinking is the manipulation of facts; unless there are facts to manipulate nothing can be done. Present a person with a carburetor and ask him to think out an improvement. Unless he can react richly with facts — the principles involved in the construction and purpose of the appliance as he examines it — his thinking is doomed to failure. Ask a man to solve a problem in medicine, finance, geometry, engineering, or in any other field. Except as the particular problem elicits relevant information, thought is futile. Knowledge about the problem situation, facts that come to mind in the face of that particular situation are absolutely essential to productive reflection.

Increasing Knowledge an Aid to Thinking. — The one thing which education can do best to facilitate thinking is to teach facts which are relevant to the problems which children and adults are likely to need to solve and to teach them in such a way that they will come to mind when the concrete problem is faced. Facts about Latin syntax are unlikely ever to be serviceable in solving a practical mathematical problem nor are facts in geometry, unless they are taught in the right way. For example, merely to learn the verbal proofs of all the propositions about triangles may result in no assistance when the pupil wishes to measure the height of a tree. Knowledge to be useful must be relevant, and acquired as a reaction to a situation which has something in common with the problem situation which calls for further thinking.

The Technique of Using Facts in Thinking. — Thinking purposefully to solve a problem or to achieve a new fact requires the most complex type of manipulation of facts. It requires seeing the promising facts, knowing that they are promising, getting several such facts together, and finally perceiving other facts which should emerge from the group. For example, suppose we ask a person: " Is it better for a person suffering from tuberculosis to live in Southern California or in New York City?" The situation calls, first, for recalling facts about tuberculosis, Southern California, and New York City. About each are many known facts, relevant and irrelevant. To recall that New York is a big city, that it has the tallest buildings in the world, and so on is of little value. The relevant facts concerning the air, sunshine, humidity, and quiet of the two localities must be recalled and the others neglected. Then the facts related to the influences of physical factors on the treatment of tuberculosis must be gotten in mind and thought of in connection with the facts about the two localities. It is the getting together of many facts and the seeing of their relations that leads to a successful culmination of thought. To a considerable extent the vital arts of seeing the facts, getting the right ones together and seeing the relations among them depend upon native intellectual capacity which is little subject to modification. Nevertheless some things may be done in the way of improving the technique of thinking by assisting the child to develop certain habits of procedure.

The Need of Practice in Thinking. — Few people realize exactly how they think. The process is one of the most subtle of all forms of human behavior. For this reason it is difficult for the teacher to establish precedents and models — to show how thinking should be done. This much is certain, however; the child learns to think only by thinking; he learns to solve problems only by practice in problem solving. To improve thinking and problem solving in general, abundant practice must be provided in all school subjects and activities. This fact is gradually being recognized by the schools. They are increasing the amount of problem-solving activities in most subjects. In history and geography and in all the social studies, in science, arithmetic, reading, and literature, thinking is being stimulated increasingly by providing more problems, questions, and exercises which require not mere recall of facts but utilization of information as means of observing new facts and of solving new problems.

Value of an Outline of the Thinking Process. — If convenient guides to fruitful thinking could be provided, as demonstrative performances, slow motion pictures, model results, explanations, and the like are used to demonstrate the simple motor skills, learning would be greatly facilitated. Specialists have sought in all directions for such guides. The skeletons of thinking used in logic, the procedures which comprise the scientific method, the opinions of various thinkers concerning the ways they think have been studied. The opinions of thinkers about their thinking are rarely useful; the outlines of logic are of limited value, the rules of the scientific method are of some service provided they are explained in and applied to the actual activities of thinking in one situation after another. The analysis of the complete act of thought, of which the most notable is that of Dewey, into such steps as " (*i*) a felt difficulty; (*ii*) its location and definition;

(*iii*) suggestion of possible solution; (*iv*) development by reasoning of the bearings of the suggestion; (*v*) further observation and experiment leading to its acceptance or rejection " often serves as a useful guide to the teacher in preparing for the management of thoughtful classroom work; but there is much thinking which cannot be reduced to any series of formal steps like these. Moreover, thinking of the most subtle and important character may go on at every one of these steps, thinking that is too complex and varied to conform to any simple mechanical scheme.

Good and Bad Technique in Thinking. — Progress in thinking is to be achieved best by well-motivated practice in which evidence of the pupil's mental operations is secured and acted upon. In this process, there are a few good habits which the teacher should learn to detect and encourage and a few bad ones which she should discover and eliminate. Some of the good symptoms are: careful apprehension of the main question or problem; constant awareness of the question while thinking goes on; detailed analysis of the elements of the problem-situation with the main question in mind; systematic procedure without overlooking some elements and repeating others; constant effort to raise hypotheses; full consideration of each hypothesis without hasty acceptance or premature dismissal; full formulation of hypotheses; persistence in the inquiry; open-mindedness or willingness to consider other hypotheses; habits of verifying and reconsidering a conclusion believed to be satisfactory by retesting it in the light of the details of the problem itself; habits of trying to discover how the correct solution was reached; habits of comparing one's conclusions and the steps leading thereto with those of other thinkers; habits of considering that the other person's conclusion may be as good as, or better than, one's own ; habits of surveying the field covered during thinking for the most general facts or principles ; habits of applying the results obtained to other situations. The bad habits are the opposites of, or distinct variations from, those in this list.

Individual Differences in Technique. — When children of approximately equal intelligence and preparation are grouped together, classroom discussions provide one of the best means of developing skill in thinking. When they are not so arranged, only a few can fully participate — if the progress of thought suits the bright it mystifies and discourages the dull ; if it fits the dull it bores the bright. It is more difficult to teach the technique of thinking *en masse* than to teach playing the violin. The problem is complicated, too, by the fact that there are different forms of procedures in thinking by means of which good results are attained just as there are different forms or styles of execution among experts in tennis or golf. Indeed, many of the suggestions to be offered presently for developing motor skills may be applied to training in the technique of thinking.

Difficulty *versus* Success as a Motive for Thinking. — It is so frequently stated that thinking starts when a difficulty is encountered that it is sometimes believed that the difficulty itself initiates and sustains thought. While it is true that we usually think when habitual reactions fail us, it is not true that mere difficulty motivates or sustains thinking. Difficulties are annoyances ; we attack a difficulty because we wish to remove it to satisfy some want which it withholds. We do not like difficulties. What we do like is to overcome difficulties successfully. The victory is doubly sweet if we get both the thing we want — the door unlocked, the fact desired — and the satisfaction of success. But success is necessary if thinking is to be encouraged. The continuation of the difficulty — failure to overcome it, in other words — is a most potent inhibition of thinking. We shall learn to prize good thinking and learn to think well only by having it usually eventuate in success. Hence the supreme importance of offering the child problems which his own thinking can usually solve and of increasing their difficulty only enough to permit him successfully to apply his best efforts to them.

Relative Value of School Subjects for Training in Thinking. — One of the most debated problems is the relative value of different school subjects as a medium for developing ability to think. Latin, geometry, mathematics, and science have claimed preëminence as a means of fostering sound thinking because of the rigidity of their procedures and the definiteness with which errors and successes are revealed. Civics, history, literature, sociology, and the social studies generally claim preëminence because of the richness of their content and the practical importance of successful thinking in these fields on the part of the masses. To appraise the merits of these and other claims is a complicated task which will receive our attention in Chapter IX. For the present it may be said that the detailed techniques of thinking in one field are not precisely the same as those in any other field, and even if they were, their establishment in one field will not guarantee their transfer, fully, to another. To develop ability to think with any class of data requires not only knowledge of the data, but successful experience in thinking with them. Since it is desirable to be able to think in all fields in which one may be engaged, it is necessary that experience in thinking be provided in every subject whose content possesses real worth.

1. What objection is there to telling a story to a class before they read it?

2. Criticize the following examples as means of teaching arithmetic to meet real situations in life.

    A. A nail, after being driven through a board, projects $1\frac{5}{7}$ inch on one side and 1.12 inches on the other. The nail was 3.15 inches long. How thick was the board?

    B. If 4 persons can stand on one square yard of land, how many could stand on an acre?

    C. A man bought $\frac{6}{7}$ of a box of candles and having used $\frac{7}{8}$ of them, sold the remainder for $\frac{16}{25}$ of a dollar. How much would a full box cost at the same rate?

3. If a person wishes to learn French in order to read it, which will be more useful, extensive practice in listening to spoken French, extensive practice in speaking French, or extensive practice in reading French? If one learns merely to read French will he be able to understand or speak it well? At all?

4. How would you teach a child to understand more fully the meaning of *weight?*

5. After years of experience and education is it more or less *necessary* for a physician, teacher, or mechanic to reason in order to do his work? Should the *ability* to reason increase or decrease with knowledge and experience?

6. Of the various suggestions offered concerning methods of improving ability to think, which are most useful? Which are least useful?

7. What subjects have been most useful to you as means of improving your ability to think? What characteristics of the subject were most responsible for this effect?

8. What were the several qualities listed as desirable in any means of expression? Which of them are possessed in high degree by drawings? By models? By schematic diagrams? By spoken words? By gestures? By written words?

9. *a.* In which years of school life is the interest in action strongest?
b. In which years is the appreciation of abstract symbols least?
c. In which years will the constructive arts be relatively the most valuable means of expression?

10. Why is language so important in modern life? Which form of

language — gestural, spoken, or written — has been increasing most in value in recent decades? Has any form decreased?

11. Apply the suggestions given in the text to the development of understanding of the meaning of *subject* and *predicate*.

REFERENCES

DEWEY, J., *How We Think*. Heath.

FREEMAN, F. N., *How Children Learn*. Houghton Mifflin.

GATES, A. I., *Psychology for Students of Education*. Macmillan.

KILPATRICK, W. H., *Foundations of Method*. Macmillan.

LaRUE, D. W., *The Child's Mind and the Common Branches*. Macmillan.

PYLE, W. H., *The Psychology of Learning*. Warwick and York.

STARCH, D., *Educational Psychology*. Macmillan.

THORNDIKE, E. L., *The Psychology of Learning*. Teachers College, Bureau of Publications.

THORNDIKE, E. L., *The Psychology of Arithmetic*. Macmillan.

THORNDIKE, E. L., *The Psychology of Algebra*. Macmillan.

See also references for Chapter V.

Chapter VII

THE ACQUISITION OF MOTOR, MORAL, AND APPRECIATIVE REACTIONS

Close Association of Intellectual and Motor Skills. — In the preceding chapter we observed a close connection between motor and intellectual activities. We noted that facts are often best learned and most clearly expressed through bodily activities of manipulating, modeling, drawing, constructing, and the like. In connection with this statement it should be realized that the process of learning by reading, or by observing anything with the eyes, is dependent upon very delicate, acquired motor activities. The only sure indication of the possession of knowledge is the ability to express it, and practically all expressions of thoughts or feelings are motor reactions. Speech and writing are as truly muscular reactions as carving or modeling; a change in facial expression or in pulse or a " lump in the throat " is as truly a motor response as dancing in glee or fighting in a rage. Thinking, as when one is working with a stubborn lock or implement, is dependent upon and enriched by skilled manipulation. Indeed, careful studies have shown that careful, observant manipulation with the hands is often more productive than mere manipulation of ideas " in the head." Even thinking " in the head " usually is accompanied by — and some authorities contend it always is dependent upon — subtle movements in the muscles of the sense organs, vocal apparatus, and other parts of the body. Despite these close associations of knowledge and skill, we can contrast the cases of utilizing motor activities primarily as a means of developing information — a problem discussed in the preceding chapter — and the development of skill for its own sake. In fact, it is important to make this distinction lest motor training as a means of developing techniques and skill be confused with the use of muscular activity primarily as a means of gaining information and furthering insight.

DEVELOPING MOTOR SKILLS

In teaching designed to develop motor or mechanical skills and power over technique, the same general principles previously mentioned should be observed. The need of selecting tasks suitable to the learner's ability at the time and of creating readiness and interest is as acute in motor as in any other form of learning. Arranging the situation so that the right reactions are facilitated and the wrong ones discouraged often offers considerable difficulty. This difficulty is apparent in such skills as singing or speaking in which it is impossible either to show the movements that the learner should make or the movements that he does make. In most complex skills, much of the most subtle and important muscular reactions are similarly obscure. In such cases, the teacher must set up a product of the movement instead of the movement itself as a guide to learning. Thus she speaks the words, sings the notes, or writes a copy for handwriting which the pupil attempts to reproduce. Where the movement involved may be readily shown to a pupil as in the case of fingering the typewriter, managing the breath, or moving the legs as in dancing or swimming, the learner is helped by observing the teacher's performance, or motion pictures, and diagrams, and models of the activities and positions.

Models and Explanations. — Although explanations are sometimes helpful, they should usually be a supplement to rather than a substitute for a demonstration or model. There are so many things in school work that need explanation that teachers get used to talking instead of showing. But young children rarely, if ever, learn well how to hold a pen, or to cut, or to sew by being told how; they have to be shown how and they should be shown model results to reproduce.

Standards and Variations in Form. — A difficulty in teaching skills lies in the fact that in many cases excellent results are obtained by different forms or methods. The forms of execution of the best golfers, tennis players, singers, or artists, differ in many details. Despite these variations, there are in each skill certain essential elements of form. It is a good teacher who knows the essentials from the unessentials and who also knows what variations are suited to each individual pupil. Teachers of skill far too frequently exaggerate the importance of mere form, and by struggling to prevent the child's natural but unimportant variations from the strict standard waste time and kill interest.

Controlling Practice. — In general, the teacher in developing a skill must motivate the work, set up the clearest possible indications of good results or of good form in execution, and then keep alert to detect good and bad variations in the learner's reactions. There is no other way. Efforts to force a child through the movements, as by taking his hand and pushing it through writing movements, or by letting him push his pencil through letter-shaped grooves are not as helpful as reactions under the full control of the child. Tracing a letter in a groove is a very different reaction from writing a letter without any such mechanical aid. Experiments have shown that practicing the one does little to improve the other. Breaking up a total act of skill, such as writing, into its constituent movements and then practicing these elementary movements one at a time is also a wasteful procedure since practicing the parts in not equivalent to practicing the whole. The whole is more than the sum of the parts. The main task in all skills is to get the elementary movements to work together as a unit. It is the working together which needs the practice. Practice, then, should be directed and observed, but it must consist of free reactions aiming at a total execution of the normal act and the production of a model product. The serviceable variations must be noted and made satisfying — the useless and harmful ones observed and eliminated.

Teaching Pupils Self-Criticism. — While to reward good impulses in motor performances is made more difficult to the extent that different individuals may succeed best by somewhat different forms or techniques, it is easier in so far as the success or failure of work is clearer and more emphatic to the pupil than it is in the case of purely mental activities. Children who cannot see that their ideas about geography or history are silly, illogical, or mistaken in fact, may see very well that their handwriting is shaky, that there are blots of ink on the page, that the table legs they have made do not fit into the table top. It is easier to tell whether you have made a right angle correctly than whether you have defined it correctly. One can thus learn a trade by himself more easily than a science.

It is wisdom in teaching the motor arts to make this advantage counterbalance the disadvantage of lack of uniformity in form and product by teaching pupils from the start to be in part their own critics — to feel satisfaction and discomfort themselves at the right times with less and less aid from the teacher. The teacher's " This is right; that is bad," should soon become, " Which is right? What is wrong about this part of the drawing? What do you wish to change in this? Why isn't that just the way you would like it to be? " — in order to encourage habits of searching for and finding merits and defects and their causes.

Information about good products and the reactions which yield them, about good form and how to strive for it and detect it, about erroneous symptoms to avoid, not to mention general information about how long and how often to practice, about the inadvisability of continuing to practice errors when something goes wrong with one's performance, about the futile and disastrous effects of practicing lazily, of losing one's temper, and so on may be immensely useful.

Similarity of Acquiring Facts and Skills. — The acquisitions of facts and skills are achieved in a similar manner. Both are reactions. Both are taught best in manners that differ only in detail. Knowledge and thought cut all the way across the development of skill and the acquisition of facts usually depends upon skills. At the very least, the development of skill requires knowledge of what to do and how to proceed to do it, and at the most, the process may result in increased knowledge of things and events in the world, in improved tastes, in emotional appreciations and controls, in volitional and moral habits. Indeed, it may be said that the possibilities of increasing skill by means of acquiring more knowledge about the skill itself and of increasing knowledge and character through the utilization of motor ex-

periences and expressions have both been greatly underestimated in schools of the past.

RESPONSES OF CONDUCT

Relations of Knowledge, Skill, and Conduct. — Although knowledge, skill, and conduct are intimately related to each other, it is not impossible to distinguish the
three factors. Consider, for example, forms of etiquette
or "manners." Adequate conduct requires knowledge
of what to do and, often, certain skills of execution.
While a child may be so trained as to form habits of mechanically reacting properly to many familiar situations,
without insight, his deficiency in knowledge may become
apparent when he is confronted by a somewhat unusual
condition. To practice good manners in general requires
rather keen intellectual insight into innumerable situations. Otherwise one can scarcely become aware of what
is, for each new occasion, the most appropriate act or re-
mark. In this type of conduct, skill in motor execution
may also be distinguished. In such a conventional exercise as acknowledging an introduction, a wide range of
proficiency is apparent. Thus in developing a familiar
type of general conduct we shall still need to utilize the
principles discussed in connection with acquiring facts
and skills.

Varieties of Conduct. — Reactions of conduct cover a
wide range of adjustments to things and mechanisms,
animals, people in the family, in the social gathering, in
the crowd, to members of the opposite sex, to husbands
or wives, to one's working conditions, employers, and
employees, toward situations in the realms of labor, government, religion, recreation, health, and so on. We can
discuss here but briefly a few samples of conduct with the
assurance that the principles are similar in all other types

and situations. We shall consider chiefly the development of that type of conduct usually termed moral behavior, since for the reasons to be mentioned presently, it offers certain special difficulties to teachers.

Difficulties Confronting Moral Training. — Moral conduct is difficult to develop, in comparison with knowledge and most motor acts precisely because it often involves acts that conflict with strong instinctive cravings. The ten commandments and all moral and ethical codes are aimed at the powerful human tendencies to collect and hoard, to satisfy hunger, thirst, and sex, to seek domination, to attempt to excel our rivals, to hunt, fight, express scorn, and so on. Because of these powerful opposing tendencies, the task of creating readiness, of securing the right reaction and of making it more satisfying than the wrong is especially important, even if unusually difficult.

Limitations Due to School Conditions. — The conditions of school life set several limitations upon the work of the teacher in establishing desirable moral reactions. The first limitation is due to the fact that by the time children enter school they have already formed innumerable habits, some of them desirable, some undesirable. The variation among children will be great and skill is required to determine exactly the particular pattern of habits developed by each one. The second limitation is due partly to the results of preschool habit formations and partly to variations in native endowment, physical abilities and disabilities, emotional propensities, and the like, which produce wide variations in individual needs in a typical class of thirty or more pupils. Some of the pupils need opportunities to exercise their courage while others need to reduce their rashness. The significance of such individual differences will receive detailed consideration in a later chapter. A third limitation is due to the fact that the school has children under its control only part of the time. The life of the home and street may undo the habits and ideals which the teacher tries to establish and form other, undesirable tendencies and ideas which the teacher must correct. The fourth limitation is due to the fact that schools are now required to teach so much information and skill of the academic type that the teacher feels hurried by and restricted to the prescribed curriculum. The fifth limitation is due to the fact that teachers are generally better trained and more skilled in teaching the "fundamental subjects" than in developing conduct.

That the opportunities of the teacher for training in conduct are fewer than are desirable is no excuse for their neglect. On the contrary, efficient teaching requires even greater care than otherwise to utilize those opportunities which do exist and to use them wisely. We shall first suggest some of the general characteristics of effective conduct and then discuss some of the methods of training which lie within the teacher's control.

Establishing Approved Habits and Making Them Satisfying. — The primary requirement is that the child be given exercise in making the approved reaction and that it yield a satisfying result, and, conversely, that, to the extent possible without too much artifice, the child be prevented from making the disapproved reactions and that, when one is made, it result in annoyance. This principle is fundamental although often difficult to apply. Only persistent and skilled application of the principles of exercise and effect will guarantee a high level of morals and manners. It was for this reason that we suggested in a preceding chapter that approved habits of conduct must be cultivated in every school subject and activity, and that much depends upon the skill with which a teacher applies satisfying and annoying effects. The approval and disapproval of the social group may be a strong weapon; the teacher's approval and disapproval may or may not be. If she is morally prim; if she unduly lauds goodness and deplores badness; if she " harps " too much on the subject, her influence is more likely to be diminished than to be increased. A moral taskmaster may only arouse the child's resentment and his desire to outwit an opponent, whereas the pupil's craving for masterly behavior and domination may, by skill, be enlisted to make positive, masterful moral acts satisfying. To put a boy on his mettle, skillfully to approve progress, to meet a fall from grace by mere recognition tinged with disappointment may be better policies than threats, scoldings, or actual punishment. To distract the mind of a six-year-old from the ideas that make him cowardly — to encourage him to be brave by telling him that he *is* brave — may thus be better moral training than arguments about the folly of fear, which he cannot appreciate, or a rebuke for his cowardice which only gives him the idea of being so. To take it for granted that students expect to be honorable — to arouse the virtues of the gentleman and of the lady by behaving as if they already existed — is likely to be more effective than any form of argument or legislation.

Discussing Wrong Acts. — The same principle implies the folly of any extended discussion of wrong acts. Such a discussion is more likely to suggest the act to pupils who would otherwise never have committed it than to prevent it in those who otherwise would. Like the parent's admonition " Do not ever put the fishhooks in your ears," and the teacher's statement, " I hope that no boy in my school will ever cut a live animal open to see its liver," suggestions of wrong acts may do more harm than good except where they refer to actually committed acts in which the undesirable feature is not perceived by the pupil.

Desirable Outcomes of Habit Formation. — Continued application of the principles of exercise and effect should result in increasing the strength of *habits* of reacting to various situations in the approved manner. As the habit becomes stronger it should not only be more certain to function but it should also become increasingly satisfying when it does occur and produce greater annoyance when it is not exercised. Just as a man finds that the more consistently he exercises such a habit as eating at a given hour, or greeting people in a friendly way or paying his debts promptly, the more desirable and necessary it becomes to continue to act in that manner and the more annoying it becomes to do otherwise, so a child finds the moral acts more insistent and satisfying and the unmoral exception more disturbing.

Limitations of Sheer Habit Formation. — Although development of approved moral habits, by application of the general principles of exercise and effect, is fundamental it is not alone sufficient. Mechanical habits are adequate so far as they go, but they often do not go far enough. The world is likely to offer continually to any child situations which differ in great or small degree from those to which his moral reactions have been adjusted. Despite their urgent character, mechanical habits may be inadequate in novel situations. The most effective moral equipment requires knowledge and intellectual insight as well as favorable habits.

The Value of Knowledge and Moral Insight. — Moral conduct requires, in other words, the ability to examine any situation and perceive what the essential fact in it is which should determine action. Before he can act honestly, fairly, courteously, kindly, or loyally, a child must be able to perceive just what act is most appropriate in that situation. To know that, in a given situation, honesty consists in some one act rather than others requires essentially the same type of intellectual reaction as to know that a given situation contains the fact of squareness or weight or smoothness. The ability to perceive the honest, or any other moral element, is built up like the ability to become aware of squareness — by meeting the honest element in many different situations, by seeing it clearly, by contrasting it with dishonesty, by having it emphasized, freed from irrelevant details, and explained. The moral understanding and insight emerges, like knowledge of other subtle facts, from direct experience with realities. While definitions, exhortations, explanations, slogans, and the like may enrich direct experience, they are no substitute for it.

Since the procedure for combining the use of demonstrations, examples, verbal explanations with properly organized experiences as a means of developing moral understanding and insight are the same as those previously described in Chapter VI, we shall not review them here, but confine the discussion to a few additional suggestions especially applicable to the development of conduct.

Value of Habit of Not Acting on First Impulse. — The first suggestion is based upon the fact that most situations, because of their complexity, elicit ideas of several lines of action, the first of which is likely to be motivated by instinctive desires and therefore likely often to be the unmoral one. The policy of thinking twice before you act is, therefore, psychologically sound. In a stirring situation, one should distrust first impulses. The impulse to steal may be sidestepped if the boy stops long enough to consider the consequences. The schoolboys, celebrating an athletic victory, respond to the proposal to tear down Jones's fence by tearing it down if they think only of the aspect " celebrate by a bonfire " but they may refrain if they stop to think of the aspect " destroying the property of a poor old workman who often comes out to see us practice." The teacher should assist pupils to acquire habits of thinking before acting on first impulses.

Value of Habit of Seeking the Proper Meaning of Acts. — Second thoughts may be even more effective if children are gradually led to try to discover specifically the element of the situation which is morally the essential one. To induce them to think of copying another's work as " stealing " may eliminate the practice from the conduct of many pupils who previously thought of it as " what everyone does." Hence to reveal the true significance of copying may be enough to prevent it in some cases. The occasional faults and failures of children who are in general well disposed are often failures to perceive the morally essential element, to put the situation in the proper class, or to call it by the right name. The habit of deliberating for a moment over the meaning of alternative courses of conduct will not only forestall many undesirable acts, but it will also foster the development of keener moral insight and sagacity.

Value of Seeking Motives for Acts. — A final suggestion to the teacher is to seek the motive for an undesirable act. Wrong acts are rarely done without a motive. Careful studies of juvenile delinquencies show that the motives for any given act — theft, cheating, or rudeness — may be very numerous. A child may steal food from the lunch boxes of others because he is insufficiently

fed at home and suffers acute hunger, or because he has
formed habits of " piecemealing " at home, or because he
has a disease which causes a stomach irritation resem-
bling hunger, or because he resents other children having
more and better food, or because he feels that the risk
justifies the act, or because he craves the excitement
which the risk affords, or because he covets the self-es-
teem which results from successful accomplishment of a
risky venture — or for one of many other motives. To
ascertain the motive behind misdemeanor is to accomplish one step toward more effective remedial work. If
the motive reveals ignorance or misunderstanding, a
remedy may be effected by enabling the child to see the
situation in the right light. If it reveals physical deprivations, or disease, the correction of home conditions
or of the physical disorder may be essential. If it reveals peculiarities in native emotional or temperamental
equipment, or distortions in acquired emotional and mental adjustments, it may be advisable to treat the whole
personality rather than merely the tendency to theft,
which is but a particular expression of a more general
difficulty. Since serious and persistent misconduct rarely
exists without some underlying cause which may be the
result of deprivation, weakness, defect, or misunderstanding, unfavorable motives and their sources should be
known by the teacher and in many cases by the pupil as
well.

Main Opportunities for Moral Training in the Schools.
— The opportunities which now exist for moral training
in the schools fall into three groups: (a) opportunities
for developing desirable behavior in the classroom and
in connection with various extracurricular school activities; (b) opportunities for training in moral appreciation and insight through the regular school studies; and

(c) opportunities provided on many special occasions for specific moral instruction.

Opportunities in Classroom and Extracurricular Activities. — Although in fairness to teachers it must be said that the typical school curriculum provides little in the way of assigned or primary means of developing conduct and leaves moral habits mainly to be secured as concomitant learning, the trend is, and should be even more, in the direction of specific provisions for such training. The increasing time and supervision devoted to athletics and sports, social functions, health instruction, excursions, manual and other projects, school banks, self-government, school publications, participation in charitable and relief work, campaigns for bettering the health, government, and physical appearance of the community not only widen the possibilities of training conduct but, by bringing school life closer to out-of-school life, provide the means of wider transfer of good habits.

Opportunities in the " Fundamental Subjects." — The possibilities of developing conduct as concomitant reactions in the work of reading, writing, history, and other school subjects should receive more attention than they now do. Habits of punctuality, honesty, efficiency, emotional control, thoroughness, intelligent deliberation, criticism of one's own ideas and opinions, open-mindedness, " light rather than heat," acting for the future as well as the present, and fitting behavior to reality rather than to foolish fears and hopes are possible concomitants of ordinary school learning which have high moral value.

To obtain this value, however, the aim of school discipline must be made the moral welfare of the pupils rather than the convenience of the teacher. Offenses against other pupils must be considered as objectionable as offenses against the teacher. The success of discipline must be measured by the sum of positive well-doing more than by the absence of bad behavior. The virtues of boyhood and girlhood must not be made subservient to the virtues of the classroom. Obedience and zeal in school duties must not be put on a pinnacle above honor, kindness, justice, and courage in life at large.

Opportunities for Special Moral Instruction. — The development of conduct may be augmented in some measure by the selection of materials in history, literature, science, and other subjects, which describe in concrete, vivid, and intelligible form the characteristics of noble conduct and the satisfactions which it may bring. The problem of appraising the school subjects from this, and from other points of view, will occupy another chapter, but we may here suggest certain warnings concerning oversimplification of the task of selecting materials and unjustified expectations based on the general nature of subject matter and method.

The advocates of each school subject are fond of asserting that it not only gives valuable knowledge and habits of thought, but also strengthens the will and enlightens the conscience. It is asserted that arithmetic makes you truthful; science makes you patient; geography makes you love your neighbors in the Philippines as yourself; history makes you humble and brave and honorable; literature stirs every noble emotion and gives birth to all the virtues. These are extravagant and unjustified opinions.

Some Cautions to Be Observed. — In considering the effects of any subject on conduct, we may bear in mind four facts. (a) The work in a subject may give rise to bad as well as good concomitant reactions; good habits are insured only as the teacher actively applies the principles of learning to secure them with the same definite care with which she applies them to the development of the primary contents and skills. (b) A reaction that is formed in connection with one school subject will not guarantee its appearance elsewhere; it must also be formed in many other situations. We must not base hopes of moral education on the false dogma of formal discipline. (c) There is a fundamental difference between getting ideas of what is good and acquiring habits of being good. To know what is right does not insure ability to do right. A boy may read tales of courage with great emotional satisfaction and still be unable to act courageously; a girl may adore fine manners and virtues in the heroine but be unable to act similarly herself. (d) There is a difference between having knowledge and ability to do the right thing and wanting to do it. The right conduct must not only be known and executed; it must produce a satisfying effect out of which an attitude of readiness, or an ideal — that is, a reaction tendency which brings satisfaction when the apparent course of moral action is followed and annoyance when it is not — may emerge.

With these cautions to prevent us from overestimating the moral values of studies, we may state, on the positive side, that (a) on the basis of their natural moral tendencies and previous moral experiences children can be taught what is right for the same reason that they can be taught what is true; that (b) interests can be aroused in being honorable and just and kind for the same reason that interest can be aroused in being well informed and skillful; and that (c) while nothing save conduct with a satisfying issue can finally determine character, the ideas and insight which specific school instruction in morality can give may be useful stimuli to right conduct.

Reactions of Emotions and Feelings

Types of Emotions. — An emotion is due to a reaction of a complex pattern of internal organs — the glands, blood vessels, stomach, intestines, heart, liver, and various muscles. The emotions may be divided into two groups, the strong or " emergency emotions " which are of service only in physical exigencies and which draw heavily upon the resources of the body, and the milder or constructive emotions which facilitate the upbuilding and storing of bodily resources. In the first group belong anger, rage, vexation, dread, fear, melancholy, sorrow, jealousy, excitement, and the like. In the other group are found the milder joys, mirth, bodily exuberance, or well-being, cheerfulness, hope, confidence, good will, and the milder aesthetic pleasures and satisfactions.

Effects of the Emergency Emotions. — The first group of emotions upset mental balance and poise, disturb delicate skills, disrupt the organic processes, waste the bodily reserves, strain the visceral organs, and tend to release the more violent reactions of original nature. Careful physiological and psychological research justifies an almost unqualified statement that the more these emotions are brought under control and the less they are expressed, the better one's health, morals, and efficiency will be. The strong emotions are elaborate internal preparations or states of readiness for violent, primitive acts — unmoral acts — and their mangement is consequently one of the main tasks of moral training.

The management of the emotional reactions requires the observance of the principles stated for moral training in general. We need add only a few comments.

Controlling Strong Emotions. — It is often stated that repression of the strong emotions is especially dangerous and harmful. This statement is true but likely to be misleading. It is true that efforts to swallow rage or other emotions are harmful partly because they are futile and partly because they provide no outlet for the energy mobilized by an emotion that is now under way. If an emotion once gets started it has already gone too far. Proper management consists in attaching other reactions to emotion-inciting situations so that the violent emotions do not start. If they do get under way the best procedure is not to let them run their course — to cry it out or fume it out — since such expression only strengthens the undesirable connection and makes such expression the more necessary on the next occasion. The best thing to do is to substitute some other vigorous, whole-hearted, if possible engrossing, activity. If you become angry, engage yourself with cheerful companions in a vigorous hike or handball game or sing some pleasant song. If you are subject to grief, play the piano, read an interesting story, or get engrossed in attractive work. This principle, which we use to stop the infant's weeping by getting him to play with the rattle, holds throughout all emotional training. The notion that all strong emotions must have occasional expressions to keep us healthy in body and mind is perverse to the core. In training, attempt to attach a wholesome and satisfying reaction to every situation which tends either by nature or established habit to elicit a strong emotion.

The Mild, Pleasant, and Aesthetic Emotions. — The mild emotions of pleasure, mirth, cheer, confidence, and the like have been shown to affect beneficially digestion, storage of reserves, bodily health and vigor, mental efficiency and skill, and in many other ways to promote the better wants and to increase their satisfaction. To cultivate them and to establish them as concomitant reactions to as many life situations as possible should be an objective of every phase of education. The methods are those already given. Cultivate health, efficiency in work, avoid fatigue and conflict, as a means of keeping them in readiness. So maneuver the situation as to produce these emotions instead of their opposites and to increase in any possible way the fullness of the satisfaction which they bring.

Habits of Emotional Response. — To arouse a desired emotion at a particular time in connection with a particular situation, we may use one of three methods. (a) Ideas that have in the past been connected with the emotion may be aroused. Thus the child nursing a grudge may be restored to a feeling of affection by being induced to think of some of the kindly things done for him by the person concerned. (b) The emotion may be communicated through imitation. If the teacher and half of the class are thrilled with admiration for a member of the class who has honorably confessed his unfairness toward a classmate, the rest of the class will be more likely to admire him also. (c) The bodily response characteristic of the emotion may be aroused. Let the frightened one walk steadily toward the platform, throw back his shoulders and look the crowd in the eye, saying to himself, " I'm not afraid of you " — and fear may be replaced by confidence. If the kindergarten teacher who feels disgust at a dirty, misshapen baby whose face is covered with sores and pimples will treat him just as she would a dainty, red-cheeked picture of health and cleanliness, take him on her lap, pet him, smile at him, and caress him, she will often find disgust giving way to tolerance and even to affection.

The last is indeed the surest way to secure the presence of an emotion. In the long run our feelings grow into harmony with our conduct. Greed cannot live unsupported by greedy acts; the manifestation of love begets affection. Get pupils to act as they would if the emotion were felt and they are likely soon to feel it.

Appreciations and the Aesthetic Feelings

Types of Enjoyment. — By nature and by training, we become able to enjoy many experiences. We may enjoy a prize fight which elicits our unwholesome strong emotions. We may enjoy a drama or story which makes us weep, rage, and exult. Strong emotions may be as enjoyable as they are wasteful. Emotionality may become debauchery and vice as truly as indulgence in food or drink. Youths may enjoy racy stories, magazines portraying nudity because of the stimulation of sex. On the other hand, sports, the drama, music, literature, drawing, and painting may arouse the milder emotions and the so-called aesthetic emotions or feelings. Exactly what organic changes underlie the aesthetic emotions science has not as yet discovered but that they are more closely related to the mild emotions of cheerfulness, mirth, and the like than to the emergency emotions such as anger and fear, and that they have beneficial rather than harmful secondary effects seem highly probable. There is common agreement, therefore, that cultivation of the appreciations and aesthetic reactions is a worthy educational aim which is justified on other grounds as shown earlier (see pp. 52-54).

Cultivating Aesthetic Reactions. — The aesthetic appreciations and emotions, justified by their contribution directly to the satisfaction of the wants of anyone without deprivations of the satisfactions of others and indirectly by increasing health and efficiency, are attained by promoting interest and readiness, cherishing appropriate and nullifying inappropriate responses. Appreciations in any aesthetic field are increased by knowledge about the art and by skill in execution in it. One can appreciate music, to be sure, without knowledge of its elements or without ability to compose, play, or sing, but knowledge and skill increase the range and variety of situations which elicit appreciation and the richness of the appreciative response itself. The inexperienced person may enjoy the general effects of harmony and rhythm of simpler music, but may fail to get the equally keen, or even more satisfying, enjoyment of the more complex classical music. The untrained person may appreciate the general effects but fails to secure the equally genuine appreciation of the technique in the execution of the expert. Knowledge and skill fortify one against monotony by providing for continued growth in effective stimuli and in the level of the appreciative reaction. To illustrate, if one is so untrained as to be unable to appreciate classical music, one of the richest sources of appreciation of music is cut off from him.

Appreciation may be reduced by education that dwells on unessentials or by training on those essentials which are beyond one's power of comprehension and execution. This is one of the greatest faults in instruction in music, literature, and the arts. According to one careful investigation, ninth-grade children are commonly taught to study details of form and meaning in literature which they cannot understand or appreciate even in a general way. Much musical training, because of the unwise choice of periods for practice, unwise selections for execution, and the formal manner of drill, yield more annoyance than appreciation or skill. By unwise training, appreciation may be killed before it is born.

SUMMARY AND CONCLUSIONS

In these last two chapters, we have introduced the reader to the operation of the general principles of learning and teaching in the case of several types of reactions — reactions of knowing and thinking, of muscular skills and general conduct, of feelings, emotions, and appreciations. By so doing, we have sought to clarify the fact that, fundamentally, the processes of teaching and learning are the same in every case. We have tried, too, to show that every learning-situation, every school subject and activity, offers opportunities to establish desirable reactions of knowledge, thought, skill, conduct, emotional control and expression, feeling, and appreciation. It should have been apparent not only that the pupil's response to any situation may embrace reactions of every possible kind, in either desirable or undesirable form, but also that these reactions interact upon each other. The facts observed influence thought, skill, conduct, emotions, and feelings; the emotional response affects all the others, and so on. It is true, furthermore, that to develop the desirable and eliminate the undesirable reactions of any sort, the teacher must be concerned about them. She must consider the influence of everything in the situation upon each phase of the reaction; she must manage the situation to favor the desired and discourage the undesired response; she must be alert to observe the reactions which do appear, so as effectively to apply satisfaction or annoyance as the case may demand. Finally, it should be clear that no desirable reaction of any kind by being established in one situation is sure to become a permanent response in that situation and much less sure in any other. Repetition with effect in many situations is required to influence behavior as a whole.

Character, personality, temperament, efficiency, will, morality, and wisdom are merely the total of all the reactions of conduct, emotion, feeling, appreciation, skill, knowledge, and thought to the situations encountered in everyday life.

The facts presented in the last three chapters indicate, finally, the wisdom of the earlier statements that education is living rather than preparing to live. Living is a complex of reactions; we learn to live by living, by reacting to lifelike situations in a lifelike manner. To learn to live the good life, desirable reactions to real life must be elicited and rewarded. The nearer school life is to real life, the more surely will the good reactions transfer to real life.

Every school subject and activity provides opportunities for securing and fixing desirable reactions of many sorts. While this statement is true, some school subjects and activities offer better facilities than others for establishing certain reactions. In the next chapter, we shall consider the relative values of different subjects and activities which are or may be placed in the school curriculum.

QUESTIONS AND EXERCISES

1. Do some of the instinctive tendencies, mentioned in Chapter IV, lead a child toward undesirable conduct? Consider the Ten Commandments in connection with native tendencies.

2. Give some instances in which children of good intent acted wrongly because of lack of knowledge or insight.

3. What will be the probable effects on pupils of the following practices?

   a. Putting children on their honor and expecting each child to report at the end of the day any infraction of the rules he made during the day.

   b. Having a daily reading lesson on some phase of the nature and value of honesty, obedience, etc.

    c. Reading stories of the dire effects asserted to befall persons who lie, steal, etc.

    d. Requiring children to learn such slogans as "Honesty is the best policy."

    e. Letting children participate fully in punishing any form of unbecoming behavior committed by a member of the class.

    f. Making good behavior a partial determinant of marks in the school subjects.

    g. Treating undesirable conduct more as if it were an accident or misfortune, like a sprain or a cold, than as if it were a sin or willful meanness.

4. In what respects, if any, should undesirable conduct be treated like a difficulty in reading or dancing?

5. In treating drunkenness Dr. Richard Cabot states that the most important matter is to discover the *motive* which drove a person to drink and then to find a better outlet for that motive or, this failing, to build up another motive which is stronger. Would this doctrine be applicable to misbehavior in school? Illustrate.

6. If a person feels sad should he have a good cry and "get it out of his system"; if he feels angry, should he permit himself to rage it out? If he does either of these things, is he practicing a desirable habit? Will it be more or less necessary to give the emotion full expression on the next occasion of grief or anger?

7. What undesirable bodily and mental effects does indulgence in fear, anger, worry, etc. have?

8. How would you help a child to overcome fear of thunder? Spells of temper? Timidity in the presence of strangers?

9. If the emergency emotions are of so little value to-day, when and how could they ever have been of value to the race?

10. To develop aesthetic appreciations of color and form, which of the following devices would you use in the elementary school? Add to this list what you consider to be better methods.

    a. Tell pupils why some of the classic paintings are so highly prized.

    b. Ask them to try to copy some of the fine paintings.

    c. Give them lectures on the principles of color harmony.

    d. Let them decorate, draw, and paint things as they like and show them with few words how to make improvements.

11. To develop desirable feelings in first-grade children toward

animals which of the following devices would you use? Why? Add other methods.

    a. Read to the class such poems as the following by Stevenson:

> The friendly cow all red and white,
>   I love with all my heart:
> She gives me cream with all her might,
>   To eat with apple tart.

    b. Have pupils memorize such poems.

    c. Read many stories about animal life.

    d. Have at school such pets as goldfish, rabbits, canaries, which the class may feed and care for.

12. What are the essential features of a good plan for developing among pupils an interest in and appreciation of music?

References

James, W., *Talks to Teachers on Psychology.* Holt.

Kilpatrick, W. H., *Foundations of Method.* Macmillan.

Lewis, M. H., *An Adventure with Children.* Macmillan.

Rugg, H. O., and Shumaker, A., *The Child Centered School.* World Book Company.

Sisson, E. O., *Educating for Freedom.* Macmillan.

Strayer, G. D., and Norsworthy, N., *How to Teach.* Macmillan.

Symonds, P. M., *The Nature of Conduct.* Macmillan.

Thorndike, E. L., *Principles of Teaching.* Seiler. Chapters XI, XII, XV.

See also references for Chapters V and VI.

Chapter VIII

THE CHOICE OF SUBJECTS AND ACTIVITIES

Purpose of the Chapter. — We have before us for consideration two problems: the choice of subjects for the curriculum and the choice of particular methods of instruction. To make choices either of material or methods requires careful scrutiny of all the facts previously presented and others yet to be offered. Subjects and methods must both be selected to contribute to the fulfillment of the aims of education which were discussed in the first three chapters. They must be selected to harmonize with and influence favorably the fundamental human wants and capacities sketched in general terms in Chapter IV. They must be chosen so as to make possible the most fruitful utilization of the factors which control the learning process. In this chapter we shall try to bring together all of these general facts and apply them to the choice of subjects. The value of different methods will be similarly appraised in later chapters.

Material, Method, and Pupil Closely Related. — At the outset, emphasis must be placed upon the fact that subject matter and other materials of education cannot be fully considered separately from the individual pupil or the particular method. Actually the subject, the child, and the method are but three parts of an integral whole. The whole is an experience or activity. The subject, which may take the form of printed paragraphs, teacher's words and actions, pictures on the blackboard, apparatus, and so on, is the situation to which the child reacts. Any change made in the child is in the form of modifications of reactions which he makes to the learning situation. His reactions are determined partly by the situation, partly by his own nature, and partly by the teaching method — by the means employed by the teacher to influence reactions by controlling the materials and directing the child. The distinction between materials and method is less important than the reciprocal relation of the two which we shall discuss later in the chapters on method. For the present, it is sufficient to note that the means of education, including materials and methods, become meaningful only as they are considered as means of influencing the reactions of a particular child and that they are effective only as they do provoke and control desirable responses.

Value Equals Value as Studied. — The first fact to consider in judging the worth of a study or activity, then, is that its value, as a means or instrument of education, depends on how the teacher teaches it and what the pupil learns from it, not upon what the study or activity is, in and of itself. English literature has little value as a means of refining taste, broadening sympathy, and deepening insight, if the teacher makes it a system of petty gossip about Carlyle's dyspepsia and Shelley's eccentricities. Geometry does little for the reasoning powers of a pupil who learns it by rote.

Two of the greatest sources of misleading arguments about the value of studies are the false assumptions that by merely putting a subject in the course of study we can put its value into the lives of the children, and that the value which a subject may have when pursued with zeal by an expert will be realized when it is studied by young students. For example, it might seem that, since psychology is the science of human nature and behavior, and since to learn to control oneself and live well with other human beings is man's greatest work, psychology should be a leading subject in schools for all. But, as it was taught in certain high schools, psychology did not have any such superior value although by superior treatment it might have had. So, also, expert lovers of a study are likely to feel sure that, since it does so much for them, it should be studied by all. They learn their error if they observe the actual results of teaching the subject to typical people.

The Main Criterion of a Subject's Value

A Subject or Activity Is Valuable to the Extent That It Promotes Adjustment to the Major Phases of Life and Cultivates the Major Personal Resources. — To appraise the value of a subject, then, we must ask to what extent the outcomes of information, skills, attitudes, appreciations, and ideals actually acquired by children contribute to the realization of the major aims of education. Thus in terms of the ultimate aims of education, we must measure the service of each subject or activity in making man's wants better and in making him more able to satisfy them. Or, in terms of the more tangible aims of education of the present day, we must appraise the contributions of each subject or activity to the improvement of adjustments to the physical world, to family, social, economic, and civic situations and the effects of each in increasing bodily and mental health and balance and the recreational, ethical, and intellectual resources. The main criterion of the worth of any experience is, indeed, the degree to which it promotes these general objectives of education. In putting this criterion into effect, difficulties are encountered which require subordinate considerations, and to these the remainder of the chapter will be devoted.

General Value Is the Sum of Many Different Values. — The first difficulty is due to the fact that the value of any subject or activity is complex; it is the resultant of several different sorts of value. Thus the study of history aims primarily to foster some of the major needs of life while manual training and physical culture attempt primarily to meet other demands. It is hard to balance ten per cent improvement in health against four per cent improvement in moral conduct or eight per cent advance in intellectual resources. The general value of an activity, then, is the total of several particular values. But to secure a reliable sum of several types of worth we must have some means of weighting the several particular values. At the present time we can do so only in a very general way because scientific data concerning the comparative values of the several desirable outcomes of education are not yet adequate. We may, however, suggest certain considerations that may be taken into account in attempting to arrange the most desirable total school curriculum.

WEIGHTING VALUES TO SECURE PROPER BALANCE

Weighting Values to Secure Balanced Growth. — The first suggestion is that all school subjects and activities should be appraised in order to provide a reasonably well-balanced curriculum. We must tentatively assume the importance of adjustments to the physical world, to economic, family, social, and civic situations and of physical and mental health balance, of recreational, ethical, religious, and intellectual resources and then attempt to see which, if any, of these demands is getting relatively little or great attention. Subjects and activities must then be rearranged to secure a more even balance until more knowledge is available concerning the relative values of each of these phases of life in promoting the interests of life as a whole. We may therefore state as a general criterion of the worth of any subject or activity in the curriculum the following : Other things being equal, choose that activity which contributes the most to a well-balanced development of the major adjustments to life and the major personal resources.

CORRELATING SCHOOL AND OTHER EDUCATIVE INFLUENCES

In order to select the subjects, materials, and activities essential for the school curriculum, we must take into account the means utilized by other agencies and the results secured by their use since it will be unwise and wasteful to duplicate the teaching of desirable information, skill, conduct, and appreciations adequately handled elsewhere and to overlook the formation of undesirable reactions acquired in other places. In their out-of-school life children come under the influence of educational factors in the home, church, theatre, street, playground, and elsewhere. Natural objects, plants, animals, hills, and all of the material creations of civilized life exert educative influences. But, in general, the greater influences are exerted by human beings. The school teacher and her work provide only a fraction of the human means of education. Playmates and parents are perhaps surer means; public speakers and writers are often more weighty; and the vague sum of behavior which is called public opinion, custom, or the *mores*, is more widespread.

There can be no doubt, however, that the teacher, the school, and school materials are rapidly becoming a more potent and far-reaching influence. With the exception of religious education, the school has been rapidly assuming more and more responsibility for all the major aims of education. The school is taking charge of children earlier, even in infancy in some of the large cities, and keeping them longer than ever before. Although in general the influence of education in the school is increasing, the educative effects of other agencies are still great and in many cases are also increasing. New developments in the character of activities in the church; improvements in public playgrounds, libraries, and museums; the multiplication of movies and radios; the increased ease of travel by automobile; the development of the Boy Scouts and other juvenile organizations; the enlargement of provision for education by industries; and the increase in the publication of informative materials cannot be disregarded in organizing the work of the school. If the school is to establish leadership in determining the direction of education in general and in facilitating other agencies in carrying out the functions they can best perform, it must arrange its own work to articulate with and facilitate the activities of the other institutions. The school should not disregard or duplicate the education otherwise satisfactorily provided. It should assume the responsibilities not discharged by other agencies and organize its curriculum as a phase of life fully integrated with life as a whole. The school program, then, must not merely be an intrinsically balanced unity but a body of experiences arranged to give proper range and proportion to the totality of educative influence which school life and out-of-school activities together provide.

To summarize the preceding discussion, we may say that, in arranging the school curriculum, we should, other things being equal, favor those subjects and activities which are not fully or properly provided by other agencies and arrange them so as to provide, in combination with outside education, a well-balanced emphasis upon the several major objectives of education in general.

The problem of organizing the school curriculum, then, requires evaluation of the degree to which the various activities round out the educational program of life as a whole in promoting adjustments to the physical world, to family, social, economic, and civic situations and in increasing bodily and mental health, recreational, ethical and religious, and intellectual resources. In judging the relative values of different subjects and activities, certain further suggestions should be taken into account.

Comparing Primary and Concomitant Learning

Primary or Assigned Learnings Easier to Evaluate Than Unassigned or Concomitant Learnings. — The first suggestion grows out of the distinction between primary or assigned learnings and concomitant or incidental learnings. It is based on two facts. The first is that the pupil tends to be more likely to acquire, and to learn more fully, the reactions that are *assigned* than those that are not specifically set up as objectives. He may, in fact, be totally unaware of the kinds and values of simultaneous or concomitant learnings. He learns, first and primarily, the things he is told to learn. While he cannot fail to learn other reactions, he is likely to learn unfavorable instead of favorable ones to the extent that they are not assigned and controlled. The second fact is that teachers are more likely to teach, encourge, manage, demand, and reward the things that are assigned and primary. In general, then, we can estimate a subject's value at present more reliably on the basis of the assigned learnings than on the basis of the concomitant values. Could we assume that teachers would usually take advantage of the possibilities each subject offers for simultaneous learnings, we might reach very different judgments concerning the subject's total value from those based on the assumption that the primary results are well obtained whereas the others more often go willy-nilly. But at present, this assumption is not warranted. We shall at present secure more reliable results, therefore, by appraising the immediate, primary, or assigned reactions than by judging the possible concomitant learnings which a subject may provide.

Evaluating Assigned Learnings in Terms of the Main Demands of Present Life. — The first step in appraising a school subject, then, is to ask whether the primary or assigned learnings — information, skill, ways of thinking or handling data, forms of conduct, or taste — are of direct value in promoting adjustments to the physical world, or to economic, family, social, and civic requirements, or in increasing physical and mental health or recreational, ethical, and mental resources. In the light of this criterion, it is obvious that learning to read English fluently is superior to learning Latin as a means of promoting all of the main purposes of education. It is, perhaps, nearly as obvious that learning the fact that diseases are caused by air-borne germs which are sprayed into the air by coughing, and of acquiring the habit of covering the cough is of more value than learning what the Least Common Multiple is and how to compute it, for the reason that the first fact and habit will certainly have utility in promoting health, whereas the second is unlikely to be valuable for promoting appreciably any immediate demand of life. It is probable for similar reasons that learning the common business and social usages of arithmetic is more useful than learning geometry; that learning some of the facts about the growth, transportation, and care of food is better than learning facts about the solar system or that information about the government of the local community is more useful than knowledge of the government of ancient Egypt.

The first criterion is that those subjects are most useful which provide knowledge, skill, or other apparent reactions which are directly and obviously applicable to situations encountered in the more important phases of modern life previously mentioned. The general criterion may be helpfully broken up for more refined appraisals.

The Wider the Range of a Subject's Utility, the Greater Its Value. — Learnings in a subject are of value, other things being equal, in proportion to the number of situations to which they apply in actual life. This principle is important not only because its observance results in teaching the more widely applicable primary or assigned reactions, but also because it provides for the widest transfer of all concomitant learnings. Any concomitant reaction tends to recur when the primary reactions with which it was acquired is revived. The more frequently the primary response is called for in life the more frequently and fully one's conduct will be characterized by the type of concomitants learned. Thus, if training in common business and social usages of arithmetic is as fruitful as training in higher mathematics for eliciting desirable reactions of intellect, morality, efficiency, emotional control and appreciation, the former will affect one's whole behavior more extensively because the primary information and skills, which tend to reinstate the concomitants, are more frequently exercised. The more the primary values get into life, other things being equal, the more the associated, concomitant values will also get into life.

Scientific Methods of Determining Frequency of Use. —
In appraising a subject or activity on the basis of the
principles just enumerated, objective methods can be
utilized to a considerable degree. Since such assigned
learnings as solving " $1826 \times 3.5 = $ " or spelling
haughty or writing 60 letters per minute at Quality 9 on
the Thorndike Handwriting Scale or learning the duties
of the President and the like are fairly definite, statistical surveys of the frequency with which such abilities
or facts are called for in the lives of representative people
and the purposes for which they are used can be determined. Thus extensive investigations have been made
of the words which people most frequently write at
different ages in childhood and in different vocations in
adult life; of words most frequently needed to read
various types of literature; of the arithmetic and algebra
most commonly required in business and social intercourse; of historical and other data most frequently
referred to in current newspapers and other printed
materials. The results of such investigations are clearly
superior to personal opinions concerning the frequency
with which facts and skills are needed in various phases
and stages of life.

The criterion of frequency of use is alone a sufficient
measure of the value of a study only when all other things
are equal. Certain " other things " may be quite un-
equal, and these we must consider.

Evaluating Concomitant or Transfer Values

**Subjects May Differ in Fostering Concomitant Learn-
ings.** — If subjects develop equally important and
equally useful primary facts and skills, they may be of
different value on the whole because one obviously provides a more fertile field for developing certain concomi-

tant habits, techniques, or reactions than the other. As stated above, the value of a subject for producing concomitants must be obvious — must be demonstrated before much weight can be given to it. We must not be influenced now by such extravagant claims of the general, or concomitant, or disciplinary values of subjects as the following, which have been and still are defended on *a priori* grounds :

The pursuit of mathematics gives command of the attention. . . . The man or woman who has been drilled by means of mathematics is the better able to select from a number of possible lines which may be suggested that which is easiest or most direct to attain a desired end. The second purpose of this study is . . . the strengthening and training of the reasoning powers.

By means of experimental and observational work in science . . . the attention will be excited, the power of observation . . . much strengthened, and the senses exercised and disciplined.

Correct use of the foriegn language . . . makes concentration imperative and serves in an eminent degree as a discipline of the will . . . . Practice in the use of a foreign language cultivates the imagination.

Will-power and attention are educated by physical training. When developed by any special act, they are developed for all acts.

Alleged Values of the Exact Subjects in Developing Ability to Think. — A conflict still rages over the degree to which different subjects facilitate the development of one or another or many of the desirable intellectual, moral, volitional, appreciative, and other reactions as incidentals of the primary facts and skills taught. Latin, higher mathematics, geometry, much of physics and chemistry as taught in high schools, much of traditional history and geography, formal gymnastics, grammar, the analytic treatment of English, and many other parts of subjects which cannot easily show the frequency or importance of the use of the specific facts and skills in everyday life have mainly to defend themselves on the basis of formal or procedure value as means of developing concomitant habits. Specialists in education who know the general principles of transfer and who have no bias for or against these subjects disagree about their possible values for concomitant learnings. Thus Chapman and Counts[1] seem to favor the idea that the languages, mathematics, and exact sciences are of maximum value for developing ability to think because of the ease and clearness with which errors in thinking are brought to light. " The student who fails to solve a problem in geometry is cognizant of his own shortcomings — in such clear-cut fields there is no ' shuffling.' Lax procedure and lax thinking fail to yield the product desired, and nobody is more clearly aware of the fact than the student himself. The same student in other subjects, which are more speculative and less exact (such as the social studies) indulges in equally loose thinking, but from the very nature of the subject, he is not so painfully conscious of the lacunae in the process."

Possible Limitations of Training in the Exact Subjects. — On the other hand, it may be argued that the very fact that geometry reveals so easily and clearly the errors of thinking may mean that it fails to give experience in evaluating the process of thought in dealing with problems concerned with civic, family, social, economic, ethical, and recreational experiences in which final and objective standards of right and wrong are not so numerous or obvious. The argument fails to take into account adequately the high probability that habits of thinking, however well established in the content of geometry, mathematics, and the exact, abstract sciences, are not precisely suited to reasoning in the other fields, and even if they were, the transfer to problems of such very different

[1] *Principles of Education,* pp. 390–392.

content would be small at best. Finally, the argument fails to weigh, adequately, the relative infrequency and unimportance of the use of the factual data from geometry and similar exact disciplines in solving problems which face the majority of people in their everyday lives.

Facts Concerning Transfer Must Be Determined by Experiment. — Since opinions differ concerning the degree and kind of transfer from even the common subjects, the facts must be determined by scientific study. Groups of pupils equivalent to each other in every respect must be secured and then treated identically in every respect except that one follows subject A, another B, another C, and so on for a length of time sufficient to reveal the effects of each special study. Then the effects of the study upon every phase of adjustment and upon all types of individual resources must be determined. The most valid information now available concerning the transfer value of certain subjects is to be found in reports of studies conducted in this manner.

Typical Facts Concerning Transfer Values Obtained from Experiments. — In one study it was found that even in tasks with verbal and mathematical material the improvement from a year's study of foreign languages and mathematics in high school is not much greater than the improvement from a year's study of typewriting and sewing or from a year of ordinary work in the world.

In an experiment with about fourteen thousand pupils in high school in which their ability at intellectual tasks with verbal material, numerical material, and spatial material was measured before and after a year of school work, the amounts of gains made were compared with the studies taken. For example, we may compare the average gain of pupils who took English, history, Latin, and geometry with that of pupils who took English, history, cooking, and sewing.

When pupils of equal ability at the start are compared, the differences in improvement accompanying differences in studies taken are real. Science, mathematics, and Latin do have larger concomitant results in the way of improvement in the tests than the commercial or manual subjects have. But the differences are small. They depend more on what the person is than on what he studies. The most intellectual person would gain more with no schooling than the average person from the most disciplinary program.

The influence of any study is also specialized. Pupils who study mathematics gain much more in the numerical tests and much less in the verbal tests than pupils who study Latin. The superiority in gain of pupils who study mathematics or languages over pupils who study manual training and shop work is almost entirely confined to the verbal and numerical tests. If the tests with spatial material had been the only ones used, the effects of the study of algebra, Latin, and the manual arts would have been practically indistinguishable.

The Need of Further Experiments. — Many more such experiments need to be made before we can apply the criterion of concomitant or transfer values with validity. Our present difficulty in applying the test of concomitant values does not, however, destroy the validity of the criterion itself. To determine the relative richness of the concomitant learnings in various school activities is, indeed, one of the most crucial educational needs. When differences in concomitant values are demonstrated, we should immediately favor those which — other things being equal — possess superiority in this respect.

Evaluating Present and Future Values

Knowledge of the Past *versus* Knowledge of the Present and the Future. — Another principle of guidance in the choice of subjects is that knowledge and skills connected with the present and future, which predict and prepare for thought and action in connection with oncoming events are of more worth than knowledge of the past and skill in reacting to past events, and also more valuable than materials which reflect an artificial or temporary present interest. History may be and often is a dead record of those past events which have few implications concerning present problems or concerning new issues which the future may provide. Yet there are vast amounts of historical data which bear directly on present trends and which afford useful preparation for oncoming problems and emergencies. Not only in history, but in other subjects, due to the tendency of experts to round out their subject as a whole, much is taught to every pupil that is useful only to specialists in the subject. The school itself thus places in wide circulation many mathematical symbols and procedures, many technical details, many historical incidents, scientific conceptions, and artificial problems that are of little vital significance. Since we tend to use those facts and abilities which we have learned and since newspapers and other agencies of public expression attempt to appeal to us in terms of the knowledge and interests that we have, many trivial matters are perpetuated. Statistical studies of the frequency with which certain facts, skills, and interests are used by representative adults, therefore, need to be corrected not only to avoid the effects of mere temporary enthusiasm in particular topics or activities, but also to avoid giving undue emphasis to trivial matters which the school and other agencies keep alive. Subjects, then, should be tested to distinguish between what is merely of temporary value and what will be useful for considerable time and between what persists by artificial pressure and what is really necessary for a constructive attitude toward trends or problems that will continue into the future. Other things being equal, we should favor those subjects and activities which not only meet present demands, but which also prepare for oncoming problems or emergencies rather than those which merely satisfy temporary, immediate interests or perpetuate academic interests resulting primarily from past teachings of the school itself.

Means of Predicting Future Needs. — What facts and skills will be most useful in dealing with future events is not easily determined by objective methods.   The method most widely used at present depends upon opinion. Although opinions are themselves subjective they may be treated objectively.   In securing opinions, the first step is to find those persons whose judgments are most likely to be sound.   Thus in attempting to determine the most vital social problems immediately before us, the predictions of the leading authorities should be sought.   Experts in viewing social issues from different angles should be employed in sufficient number, moreover, to obtain breadth of view and to make possible a statistically reliable consensus of opinion.   While such a consensus of expert opinions cannot be counted upon to yield perfect predictions of the gravest needs of the immediate future, it will give more reliable results, on the whole, than any other method now available.   Opinions of experts upon the relative importance of different materials within their own field in the light of impending changes and forthcoming issues and needs will serve also to check the perpetuation of trivial matters which tend to be continually taught merely because they always have been.

Evaluating the Influence of Interest

The Criterion of Interest. — A final criterion is interest. Other things being equal, we should select the school subjects and activities that are most appealing to the child's interest. By interest, we mean ease of securing readiness, eagerness, whole-heartedness in the activities of learning. The criterion is based both on the fact that the greater the interest in the work the greater the happiness which results from it and on the fact that the greater the zeal, the more abundant the results of learning. Although important, the criterion of interest is one of the most difficult to apply. It is difficult to apply to a subject or activity as a whole or even to a particular topic or exercise because it depends so greatly upon *how* the subject is taught or *how* the activity is conducted. Interest depends tremendously, as suggested earlier, on adjusting the task nicely to the individual so that by enlisting his best efforts, the pupil succeeds in mastering the tasks assigned. It depends greatly on the skill of the teacher in enlisting the elements of movement, competition, demonstration, and recognition of progress, proper distribution of practice and review, proper time and length of the period of work, and so on. The usefulness of a fact and skill in everyday life is a powerful influence on interest. Children are exceedingly practical-minded and enjoy not only using what they learn but learning what they can use. As a matter of fact, if a subject or activity satisfies the other criteria — if it proves useful in the affairs of the family, social, recreational, and other phases of life, or in adjustment to the physical world or other people, if it provides useful mental resources or approved conduct and if it is also adjusted to the individual's capacity and managed with skillful observance of the principles of teaching — it is practically certain to be interesting. Examine any school work reported as uninteresting and you will almost always find that it was either baffling in its difficulty or trivial in its ease, or that it required reactions of little applicability outside the recitation period, or that it was taught — like multiplication tables — in such a manner as not to reveal or establish its usefulness, or that the teacher unwisely hampered physical and mental expression, refused to reward achievement effectively, or otherwise failed to teach properly. Interest is the natural symptom of *effective* management of the acquisition of reactions which are intelligible and useful in ordinary life. This being the case there should be no subjects or activities in the curriculum which are without interest.

Limitations of Interest as a Sole Criterion. — Although all subjects and activities should possess intrinsic interest, some are likely to be more interesting than others. The pupil then prefers some and wishes to neglect the others. The wisdom of young children, especially, is insufficient to overcome this tendency. The child's own interest is not a perfect guide in the choice of subjects any more than it is in the selection of foods. It is necessary, therefore, that teachers should assist the child to circumvent the tendency to follow slavishly the lead of interest. The extreme position of those who would give the child complete freedom to follow his interests is probably due mainly to the justified resentment against teachers' failures to realize the importance of interest as a symptom of capacity and successful learning and the disastrous results which often come from the crude use of coercion and authority to secure work in the less attractive subjects. Coercion is never the alternative except as a final resort like a surgical operation, and, like the latter, it should be used with caution and applied with skill.

The problem of whether pupils should be given much leeway in the choice of subjects is, of course, closely tied up with the whole question of the elective system *versus* the prescription of studies. The solution of this problem will differ according to the advancement of the pupil. In general the more advanced the pupils are, scholastically and intellectually, the safer and more advisable it is to rely upon their interests. Other things such as the nature of individual differences in capacity must also be taken into account, and these we shall have to consider in later chapters. At this time we can say merely that children's interest in a subject constitutes an important criterion of the subject's worth but not the *sole* criterion. And in applying this criterion it is necessary to observe the conditions under which it is valid and to distinguish between genuine interest in a subject and the child's feelings about a subject before he has really tested his interest.

Facts Needed to Apply the Criterion of Interest. — The criterion of interest, it should be recalled, was stated in the following form : *Other things being equal*, choose that subject matter or activity which is most interesting to the child. If several subjects are equal in all other values, there is much to be gained by choosing the most interesting. Thus, if several different selections for primary reading work are equally valuable when measured by all other criteria, but differ in their appeal to children's interest, the most interesting ones should be used. If several different ways of presenting the essential materials concerning the colonization of America satisfy equally well other standards of value, but one is more attractive and gripping than the others, it should be selected. Or if physics and chemistry were, for a given group of pupils, equally valuable in general and only one could be taken, by all means give them the one which would be more interesting. In all of these cases, the criterion of interest can be safely applied only when other things are equal and when one can reasonably be sure which material or subject will really be more satisfying.

As a rule a pupil cannot tell which selection or subject he will like best until he has tried all of those from which he can choose. For this reason, it is usually better and safer to be guided by the results of careful scientific studies of the interests which children have shown in different materials, activities, or subjects than to rely on the child's guess concerning which he will like best. To apply this criterion of interest, then, we need first really to know the interest values of different materials and then to guide the child so that he will be able to enjoy those activities which will be most interesting to him.

The discussion of interest may be summarized by drawing attention to three facts: (*a*) that guidance is very different from coercion, (*b*) that genuine interest in a subject is not guaranteed by a child's notions about how he will like it before he has tried it, and (*c*) that consequently, the criterion of interest is not likely to be applied so effectively by giving the child complete freedom to choose as by guiding him into those studies and activities, found, by scientific studies, to be most absorbing.

The Need of Scientific Investigations

In discussing the relative values of different subjects and activities for the curriculum, it has been necessary to stress the need of scientific investigations. In fact, not one of the principles suggested can be satisfactorily applied without the results of extensive and objective investigations. The relative frequency with which different facts and skills are required in life, the relative importance of these facts and skills in promoting the major needs of life at the time, their relative values in connection with the most probable forthcoming issues and needs, the degree to which they are satisfactorily taught by other agencies, the extent to which they make possible the cultivation of concomitants over and above the assigned learnings, the strength of their appeal to the interests of pupils, can be accurately determined only by direct investigations. In research of this type, investigators are needed who are equipped with all of the available technical tools for scientific work and with an unprejudiced attitude toward the various studies. Fortunately there is now a great and increasing activity in this field of research. The work is extremely intricate and the best that can be done in an elementary treatise to suggest its character is to mention the general criteria that are used in evaluating content for the curriculum. In closing the chapter, these criteria may be briefly stated.

Summary of the Main Principles of Selection of Studies. — In selecting subjects and activities for the curriculum, we should be guided by the following principles :

1. Subjects and activities should be given preference which develop information, skills, habits, attitudes, appreciations, and other reactions that improve adjustments to the physical world, to family, social, economic, and civic situations and that increase bodily and mental health and balance and recreational, ethical, religious, and intellectual resources. This is the fundamental criterion to which all the others to be listed are subordinate.

2. Other things being equal, those subjects and activities should be favored for the school curriculum which are least likely to be provided satisfactorily by other agencies such as the church, theatre, Boy Scouts, and the like.

3. Other things being equal, subjects and activities should be selected for the school curriculum which will give proper range and proportion to the totality of educative influences when school and out of school experiences are combined. Only thus will a properly balanced general education be secured.

4. In general, the value of subjects and activities should be judged more on the basis of primary or assigned learnings than on the basis of secondary or concomitant learnings since the former usually receive greater emphasis, are more surely achieved, and are easier to appraise.

5. In general, the more directly a fact, skill, or habit meets a genuine life demand the more valuable it is in itself and the more surely and fully the concomitant learnings will function in life.

6. Other things being equal, the more widely a primary fact, habit, or skill may be employed in life the more valuable it is both in itself and as a carrier of concomitant learnings.

7. Other things being equal, favor the subject matter and activities which are the most effective means of fostering such desirable concomitants as improvement in ability to think, originality, sociability, initiative, trustworthiness, and the like whenever reliable experimental evidence is available.

8. Other things being equal, favor the subject matter and activities which not only meet present demands but which also prepare for forthcoming problems

or emergencies rather than those which merely record the past, or reflect temporary, immediate interests or perpetuate academic interests resulting from the past teachings of the school itself.

9. Other things being equal, favor the subject matter and activities which are most interesting to pupils at the time.

QUESTIONS AND EXERCISES

1. Give some illustrations of the educative influence, for good or bad, of public opinion, customs, conventions, and superstitions.

2. What native tendencies tend to make the influence of companions even greater than that of parents or teachers?

3. Why are more and more of the responsibilities of education in the future likely to be placed upon the school? What are the main advantages and disadvantages of such an increase in the function of the school?

4. Why is it hard to say, in general, whether Latin is a better subject than French or physics?

5. Did you ever encounter a teacher of a particular subject who would admit that that subject was relatively unimportant? Why is such an admission very rare?

6. Take some subject whose value you believe to be very high and another whose merit you place low and appraise each in terms of the various criteria set up in the chapter. What difficulties, if any, do you have in consolidating the results of the various separate appraisals?

7. Should all the criteria be weighted equally? If not, arrange them in an order of importance. Compare and discuss your arrangement with those made by other students.

8. What criteria of the value of a school activity would you add to those given in the chapter?

9. Dewey says: "An activity or project must be within the range of the experience of pupils and connected with their needs — which is very far from being identical with any likes or desires which they consciously express." How does this statement harmonize with the belief of those who would make a child's interest the sole criterion of choice of subject matter? How does it harmonize with the statements made in the chapter?

10. If you should agree with Dewey that "a social order different in quality and direction from the present is desirable and that schools should strive to educate with social change in view by producing individuals not complacent about what already exists, and equipped with desires and abilities to assist in transforming it," to which of the criteria listed in the chapter would you give greater weight and to which ones less weight?

11. Which subjects do you believe are more useful — other things, such as the teacher's skills, etc., being equal — for developing ability to think, the more rigid and exact sciences, such as mathematics, physics, etc., or the less exact social sciences? Prepare a defense for your views.

12. Do any of the considerations in the chapter offer a defense for the view that certain subjects because of their difficulty should be included to discipline the mind or to develop habits of doing hard and difficult work or of securing satisfaction from overcoming difficult obstacles or otherwise developing character?

13. Which do you think would be more useful for developing accuracy of observation: practice in observing and recalling (a) small geometrical drawings, etc., or (b) such weather signs as the color of the sky, character of clouds, direction of wind, etc.? Would training in either appreciably influence one's ability to observe the behavior of children in the classroom?

14. Criticize the belief of the authors that the value of school subjects and activities can be adequately determined only by means of scientific study.

15. Draw up a list of types of experiments that should be performed to determine the best selection of materials in arithmetic to teach in the first six grades.

REFERENCES

BOBBITT, F., *The Curriculum*. Houghton Mifflin.

BOBBITT, F., *How to Make a Curriculum*. Houghton Mifflin.

BONSER, F. G., *The Elementary School Curriculum*. Macmillan.

BRIGGS, T. H., *Curriculum Problems*. Macmillan.

CHARTERS, W. W., *Curriculum Construction*. Macmillan.

Cox, P. W. L., *Curriculum—Adjustment in the Secondary School*. Lippincott.

DEWEY, J., *The Child and the Curriculum*. University of Chicago Press.

HARAP, H., *The Technique of Curriculum Making*. Macmillan.

KILPATRICK, W. H., *Education for a Changing Civilization*.   Macmillan.

RUGG, H. O., and Others, "Curriculum Making: Past and Present";
    Twenty-sixth Yearbook of the National Society for the Study of Education, Part I; and "The Foundations of Curriculum Making";
    Twenty-sixth Yearbook of the National Society for the Study of Education, Part II.   Public School Publishing Company.

See also references for Chapter XIV.

Chapter IX

THE INFLUENCE OF AGE AND MATURITY

The capacities of a human being pass through a period of growth and development to a stage of maturity which is followed by a period of decline. The interests, behavior, and proficiency of each individual are affected by the inevitable ebb and flow of a multitude of special capacities and functions. Almost every problem in education is affected in some manner by the facts concerning the growth, maturity, and decline of human traits. Long based, necessarily, on rather general speculations concerning the biological significance of infancy, adolescence, adulthood, and senility, educational principles may shortly be guided more adequately by the results of detailed, scientific studies of the life history of different human traits. Already a considerable body of knowledge concerning the changes from year to year in height, weight, strength, agility, speed of movement, sensory capacities, intelligence, special capacities to learn, recreational interests, emotional propensities, and the like has been accumulated. But it is not within the province of this book to treat these details. We shall be able merely to mention some of the more general facts and a few of their implications.

REASONS FOR EMPHASIZING EDUCATION IN INFANCY

Commonly Accepted Characteristics of Infancy. — The two characteristics of infancy most emphasized have been the helplessness and the plasticity of individuals from birth. It is commonly assumed that the helplessness and plasticity of an individual are greatest at birth and that they decrease gradually as time goes on until a maturity is reached at which the individual attains a stage of near or quite complete independence and fixity. From these assumptions it is commonly concluded that the period of infancy extending from birth to maturity is biologically designated for education. It is frequently assumed that the younger the child is the more fruitful his education will be and that all really effective learning must be completed before biological maturity is reached. Since both truth and falsehood lurk in these assumptions, they must be examined critically.

Differences in Infancy of Different Species. — It is true that the human infant, compared to other animal infants, is relatively helpless at birth and remains so for a longer period. This helplessness is due partly to the slow maturation of the skeleton, muscles, and other bodily organs and partly to the very wealth of reaction tendencies which the human infant inherits. The bee or chick, as compared to a human being, even under primitive conditions, requires and makes during its entire lifetime relatively few types of reactions. Organisms of these species, born with their reactions relatively fixed, have a temporary advantage over those more helpless at birth. By natural selection, these species have come to be composed of those individuals whose few reactions are inherited in relatively definite and unmodifiable form and which achieve functional capacity early in life.

The result of this mode of inheritance is relatively effective adjustment so long as the environment into which the animal is born and in which it lives is very similar to the one to which it is adapted by nature. But if the environment changes greatly as the result of drought, fires, floods, or human influences, or the invasions of other species of animals, birds, insects, etc., the fixed, limited, slightly modifiable reactions prove futile and the species perishes.

The Significance of Helplessness and Plasticity of the Human Infant. — Although the human infant is more helpless because his reactions are not fixed hard and fast by heredity, he is nevertheless more modifiable, more adaptable to changes in the conditions of life. To any given situation the human infant may respond in a far greater number of different ways and in far more complex combinations of these elemental reactions than any other infant. Slight variations in the situation result in more marked variations in the reaction. These variations in the total pattern of response give the appearance of lack of uniformity — often of aimless, random, uncoördinated, futile adaptations — that is, of helplessness. Futile and uncoördinated the human infant's reactions often are; but they are also versatile. They fall more readily into new patterns as the result of each experience; they may develop into more satisfactory and refined adjustments because they are more complex wholes of more intricate parts. Like a kite, the young bee or chick is a simple machine which functions well only when the environment is favorable. The human being is like an airplane which, because of its greater complexity, is more independent of the environment and more adaptable to it. The acts of the latter are no less definite than those of the former; they are merely more complex, versatile, adaptable to, and independent of, outside conditions. But the refinement of the adaptation requires time and experience. The cost of greater versatility and refinement of adjustment is a longer period of trial-and-error development out of a period of apparent helplessness. The human infant is more helpless because of the number and variety of his tendencies to reaction, but he is more plastic because of the possibility of forming a greater number and variety of patterns of reaction to any situation than the young of other species.

The Importance of the First Learnings. — The helplessness and plasticity are both evidence that from a biological point of view infancy is the period for learning, for education, for perfecting adaptation to the environment. The initial impossibility and later difficulty which infants experience in taking care of themselves and the wastefulness of their unguided methods of learning are both evidence that children need more than mere opportunity to learn; they need to be taught. Education is a crucial need of infancy not only because of its plasticity, in the sense of capacity to learn, but also in the sense of its being free to learn, of being unincumbered by habits already fixed. The younger the child is, the less his acquisitions of knowledge, skills, conduct, tastes, emotional attachments are influenced by other acquired habits of reaction. Habits, which are rapidly formed from the time of birth, come to exert an increasing influence upon a child's further learning. New acquisitions emerge from the old; new hierarchies of habit develop out of those already formed. Thus, in considerable degree, the habits formed first become the basal structure of the edifice of mind, character, efficiency, and personality. Not only because infants are helpless, unable to care well for themselves or contribute productively to the care of others, but also because they are active and capable of learning and because first learnings may assume great importance as the materials upon which later acquisitions depend, infancy is properly a period for education.

Things Learned Early May Be Used Longer. — Concentration of education in the early years may be defended by the fact that, other things being equal, the earlier a fact or habit or skill is acquired, the longer, and consequently the greater, the use that may be made of it. If a person is to learn to read, other things being equal, it would be better to do so at six than at twenty, since, by learning earlier, the total service of reading in a lifetime is greatly increased.

Children Are More Docile When Young Than Later. — Due to their dependence upon adults for food, shelter, and other needs, children are usually more obedient and docile when young than they will be later. The young learn to submit; they learn to do what they are told to do. In the sense of being more obedient, more submissive to direction, people may be said to be more *teachable* when young. This type of teachableness is often assumed to make childhood a more appropriate time for being educated.

Labor Relatively Dangerous and Unfruitful. — The relative helplessness, inefficiency, and docility of children makes their earning power relatively slight and the danger of placing them under the control of commercial interests relatively great. For these reasons, it seems better to concentrate on education during the early years in schools which have no interests to serve other than the interests of their pupils.

Conclusions. — The helplessness, docility, dependence, economic incompetence, and other characteristics of children as well as the value of first learning as means of establishing desirable and avoiding undesirable basal habits and of providing many facts, habits, and skills for the longest possible use sufficiently justify the provision of guardianship for children during infancy and childhood, that is from birth to approximately fourteen, and the devotion of children's working time during this period primarily to education. Whether it is desirable to provide education and guardianship for later years is the next problem for consideration.

EDUCATION AND GUARDIANSHIP DURING AND AFTER ADOLESCENCE

In attempting to appraise the need and capacity for education and the value of guardianship after the age of fourteen, we shall first consider the educability of persons after this age. We shall take this approach for the reason that certain facts which will be thereby revealed have a direct bearing on the problem of the need both for prolonged education and for protection.

Greater Independence and Initiative. — The relative helplessness, docility, and dependence of the early ages, while indicating the need of careful nurture, at the same time suggest deficiencies in educability. The fact that young children will patiently study the most uninteresting and futile materials, that they will uncomplainingly memorize poems they do not understand, master facts and skills that are of no value to them at the time, and struggle with detailed work and accept assertions that do them actual harm reveals weakness in the plasticity of childhood. Docility and dependence alone are an insufficient equipment for most effective learning. Among the other requirements are such traits as self-assurance, general power, self-initiative, self-expression, self-determination, all of which should normally increase with age until twenty or later. As these traits increase, other things being equal, learning should be more effective and abundant.

Early Acquisitions May Facilitate as Well as Interfere with Later Learnings. — The ability to learn increases with age after fourteen for another reason. Previously formed habits may facilitate as well as interfere with the formation of new, desirable habits. The early establishment of desirable emotional responses or desirable tastes facilitates the acquisition of additional and more refined emotional and appreciative reactions. Every fact that is learned increases the ease of learning related facts. Every act of skill established, although it may interfere with learning some motor responses, will facilitate the learning of others. Later education, then, may be very fruitful precisely because it utilizes facts, habits, and skills established earlier.

Many Learning Capacities Increase after Fourteen. — Almost every capacity utilized in learning, such as motor speed, steadiness and control, physical power and endurance, intellectual power and insight, as well as the acquired techniques of studying, thinking, managing oneself and the tools of intellectual work, increase with age after fourteen. The pertinent facts of growth revealed by recent studies may be briefly surveyed at this point.

Characteristics of Growth. — In general, the growth of physical and mental capacities proceeds at a steady and uniform, rather than spasmodic, rate from birth to a maturity between the middle teens and the early twenties. The skeleton reaches its maximum length in the middle teens and persists with little change until death. Bodily strength and endurance, though much subject to environmental influences, reach a maximum in the vicinity of twenty, remain relatively stationary for ˉabout ten years, and then gradually decline. Speed and flexibility show a similar curve of growth and decline. The ease and speed with which most forms of information and intellectual skills may be acquired and the permanence with which they are retained increases at a rather steady pace and reaches a maximum, probably, between 18 and 22, for most persons, and maintains approximately the same level for several years, thereafter declining gradually perhaps by one per cent per year until old age.   Thus while infancy is most plastic in the sense that the young child is eager to learn along lines of childish interest, is most submissive to guidance in learning, and is, so to speak, most wide open to the influence of experience, and, perhaps, most fundamentally affected by what he does learn, it is, nevertheless, not the most plastic period in the sense of *ability to learn* quickly.   Indeed, the zenith of power to acquire most forms of information and skill appears after the eighteenth year.   Sheer capacity to learn is appreciably greater in the period from 14 to 28 than from birth to 14.

Having established the fact that the power to learn after fourteen is relatively high, we may next question whether the *need* of general education during this later period is great.

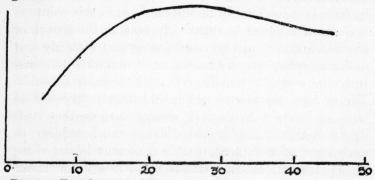

FIG. 1. — THE GENERAL FORM OF THE CURVE OF ABILITY TO LEARN IN RELATION TO AGE

The figures on the base line indicate the age in years, from zero (birth) to 50.   The height of the curve above the base line indicates the degree of ability to learn.   (From E. L. THORNDIKE and Others, *Adult Learning*, p. 127, by permission of The Macmillan Company.)

Significance of Maturity of Essential Biological Functions. — Among many primitive peoples, maturity of the biological functions of sex is assumed as the time for formal education and guardianship to cease and for self-support and self-direction to begin. For the civilized white races in America, the sex functions mature between 12 and 18, slightly earlier for females than for males, and for the majority of both sexes before 16. In every civilized country, moreover, a considerable percentage of youths have shown the ability to maintain themselves economically in their early teens and more would do so were they not prohibited by the compulsion of parents and society.

The Amount of Learning Now Advisable Greater Than Heretofore. — It must be recognized, however, that our biological equipment, including the sexual functions, provides an adjustment to the simplest of primitive conditions and not to a complex modern civilization. If we were still living the simple roving life of the jungle, we might safely heed the implications of the early maturation of the essential biological functions and the demonstrable ability of persons in the early teens to make a living, to relinquish the education of youth by fourteen. But, under present conditions, there is so much to be learned that few youths can be adequately prepared to advance the best interests of society as a whole by this age if reared under anything like present methods of education. The future, moreover, promises to increase rather than to decrease the amount of learning required for constructive participation in the life of the community.

Modern Society Demands Learnings Too Difficult for the Early Teens. — Even if the *amount* which the majority of people must learn to participate effectively in various essential phases of modern life could be compressed into the period before fourteen, the sheer *difficulty* of much of the necessary knowledge and skill makes this abbreviation difficult if not impossible. Not only are many of the most important facts and experiences essential to thinking concerning family, social, civic, religious, economic, cultural, and other problems beyond the intellectual grasp of the average youth of twelve — after which he would have but two years before fourteen — but they are also alien to his interest, and unsupported by his emotional propensities. Even if better earlier education should increase his intellectual facilities considerably, the average twelve- to fourteen-year-old youth lacks the maturity of instinctive and emotional equipment to react with the feeling, the emotional concern, the volitional interest that the complete education in many vital problems demands. The full effects of sex education can hardly be realized before the mature sex impulses are experienced; a full concern about economic and industrial problems can scarcely be achieved until the youth has reached a maturity where the need and difficulties of earning a living have been actually felt. Serious consideration of religious and moral issues is rarely possible before the complex emotional life which characterizes adolescence has been awakened. Lacking the emotional and volitional responsiveness to the stresses and strains, the obligations and deprivations, the expressed passions and conflicts, the racial, social, and economic clashes and rivalries, the preadolescent pupil will fail fully to appreciate much of the significance of literature, history, sociology, and other basal social studies.

The Importance of Careful Education during Adolescence. — On earlier pages we have stressed the futility of attempting to educate children for the life that lies years ahead of them. To be effective, education must conform to the intellectual capacities, the interests, emotions, and feelings of the pupils at the time. If education would touch real out-of-school life in its fullness, it cannot be completed until these capacities and propensities have approximately reached maturity, as few of them do before 18. Because of the greater ease and fullness of intellectual grasp, because of the rate and permanence of learning, because of the volitional and emotional congruity with the affairs of independent life in a modern society, not to mention the need of education in its own perplexing problems, the adolescent period, roughly from 14 to 18, offers highly important educational needs and possibilities in a democracy.

The Importance of Post-Adolescent and Post-Adult Education. — Nor is adolescence the latest, or necessarily the most important of postchildhood periods for education in our present society. Indeed, the point we wish to make, with great emphasis, is that the facts concerning human abilities to learn and those concerning the needs of society both *indicate great, in fact, nearly equally great possibilities and importance for learning at every age from birth to senility.* One function of education is to teach human beings as early as possible to educate themselves as fully and as long as possible. As truly as education cannot begin too early it cannot continue too long. Life should be one continuous process of learning. The more effective the learning the richer life will be.

Since both the need for education beyond the age of fourteen and the relatively great intellectual capacity to profit by it have been shown, it will be advisable next to consider the form which such prolonged education should take. We shall first consider the effects which prolonged full-time education under guardianship may have.

VALUES AND LIMITATIONS OF PROLONGED FULL-TIME EDUCATION

During the past half century there has been a rapid increase in the proportion of children remaining in school beyond their twelfth year. The age of compulsory attendance has increased until in 1925 all but one state had laws

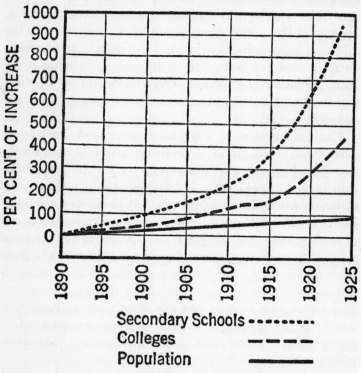

FIG. 2. — INCREASES IN ENROLLMENTS IN COLLEGES AND SECONDARY SCHOOLS IN COMPARISON WITH INCREASE IN GENERAL POPULATION SINCE 1890

Figures for 1890 are taken as a basis. The percentages of increase are least for the general population, greater for secondary schools, and greatest for the colleges. (From E. D. GRIZZELL, *Education: Principles and Practices*, p. 119, by permission of the author and The Macmillan Company.)

requiring attendance until at least fourteen; forty-one states until at least sixteen; and five states until eighteen. Although the attendance laws admit of many exceptions to avoid working financial or physical hardships upon pupils and parents, the enrollment of students over fourteen years of age has increased tremendously, and is apparently still growing. Figure 2 shows graphically how much greater the increase in enrollment in the secondary schools and colleges has been than the increase in the total population. In 1926 there were nearly twelve times as many pupils in the secondary schools as there were in 1890. Convinced of the economic and social values of higher education, parents are voluntarily providing the means for sending still larger proportions of youths through high school and college. The consequences of such a striking tendency to increase the period of full-time school attendance merits careful consideration.

Increase of Expense and Decrease of the Period of Economic Productivity. — An increase in the school period will not only increase the financial burden upon society of maintaining schools and teachers, and of supporting the pupils, but also decrease the proportion of life that will be devoted to labor directly productive. Whether the returns for this expenditure in education will be repaid with substantial interest by the increase in the social and economic efficiency of those who received the prolonged education and support is a difficult but important question.

Danger of Loss of Contact with Real Life. — Prolongation of full-time education increases the chances of isolating youth from contact with real life. There is the danger that the school, as a distinct institution, may become too much of a cloister and rear youth, as it is prone to train children, to live not in the world at large but in an artificial environment. Since the beginning of public schools in America, the distinction of school and society has been too great. After the age of sixteen, a failure of the school to articulate closely with life would be especially disastrous.

Dangers of Docility, Indoctrination, and Stagnation of Thought. — Prolonged education while the child is dependent upon parents and society and forced to submit to the rule of home and school incurs the dangers of forming bad as well as good habits and of fostering stagnation as well as growth of mind and character. Both parents and teachers are likely to force docility, sometimes to the point of stifling initiative. In the realm of opinion and belief concerning matters of religion, morality, politics, sociology, and other social subjects, the danger of indoctrination is grave even during the adolescent period. Despite the best of intentions, teachers are likely, moreover, to fail to keep abreast with the times, with the result that the substance taught fails to touch the most vital present and oncoming issues. This is notoriously true of teachers in primary and secondary schools in which the burden of teaching is so heavy as to make difficult continued study and fresh outlooks, as the result of the reconstruction of their own experience.

The present system of mass education, a product of the demand for fiscal economy rather than for teaching efficiency, tends to decrease greatly the possibility of recognizing individual talents and defects and of treating each pupil according to his needs and possibilities. It favors memorizing instead of thinking, prescribed duties instead of self-initiated projects, textbooks instead of activities, uniform methods and results instead of individual procedure and unique outcomes, conformity of thought instead of individual expression. Such uniformity tends to cramp action, efficiency, and individuality.

Danger of Developing Social and Economic Irresponsibility. — To sweep the pupil's life of all economic pressure and responsibility invites undesirable habits and attitudes. If students are relieved entirely of the need of earning a livelihood or of contributing to the support of others, and if they can leave immediate problems of food, shelter, savings, markets, competition, cut prices, and the like to their parents, it may become more difficult to bring these issues firmly home to them. The incentives for forming desirable habits and attitudes of thrift, conservation, productiveness, economic foresight, and dependability are reduced. Continued full-time schooling may thus tend to foster habits of dependence and extravagance; it may tend to breed social parasitism with its indifference and impracticality.

Mitigating the Danger and Increasing the Effectiveness of Education. — However grave the dangers of prolonged guardianship and institutional education may be, it is possible to mitigate them greatly. Better teachers may be secured; better training and greater opportunity to keep abreast of developments in all phases of life may be provided for them. School subjects and activities may be more closely related to out-of-school life than they now are. The resources of the school may be more effectively directed to the determination and cultivation of individual talents and to the increase of personal resourcefulness and responsibility. Instead of dutiful memorizing and complaisant acceptance of authority, independent thinking and enterprise may be fostered. Practical projects, creative enterprises, work that is economically valuable as well as educative may be introduced, as will be suggested later. In these and other ways, the school may mitigate the dangers and increase the effectiveness of full-time education and guardianship of youth.

Prolonging Education into Adult Life

Until the school changes its character greatly and integrates its activities much more fully with life, graduation will produce a sharp change from learning to working. Under present types — indeed, even under vastly improved types — of schooling, there is much to be said in favor of a plan which provides for a gradual transition from life in the school to life outside and from a condition of complete support by others to complete self-support. Instead of compressing education wholly into a few years of full-time work after fourteen, it could be extended by devoting a decreasing portion of each year to school work and the remaining portion to outside work, or by alternating periods of work and schooling until well into adult life. While the proper form of distribution of time between work and education is yet to be determined, we may at least consider some of the advantages of the general policy of extending education into adult life instead of concentrating the last several years wholly in the middle teens with the resulting sharp break between school and work.

Full Time for School after Fourteen Often Proves Irksome. — It is common opinion that the continuation of full-time schooling for several years after fourteen proves irksome to vigorous youths. After the age of fourteen or thereabout, a craving develops for sharing in adult enterprises, and for engaging in activities for which society is willing to pay. To be self-supporting, in whole or part, may then seem as natural and desirable as to be supported by others earlier. To assume responsibility may then seem as proper and satisfying as to enjoy freedom for play in childhood. Sharing in adult enterprises, assuming responsibility and maintaining himself in part, is likely to be a stimulus to development for a person during his teens. Such a procedure might also help to produce a better correlation of the affairs of in- and out-of-school life, and by enabling a youth to put the results of education to demonstrable use, breed greater respect for, and interest in, further education.

Greater Capacity to Learn after Fourteen. — The concentration of education into the earliest ages possible, instead of scattering it into adult life, has been due in large measure to the belief that the capacity to learn rapidly decreases with age, especially after the middle teens. People believe that they must compel their offspring to learn when young because of the fear that they will soon be unable to learn. Of first importance, then, is the fact, previously mentioned, that learning ability actually increases after fourteen to a zenith in the vicinity of twenty, a maximum which persists until twenty-five or later and thereafter declines very slowly. During the decade from twenty to thirty, ability to learn is at a higher average than during any other decade in life. Even from forty to fifty, capacity to learn is as high as it is at the age of fourteen or fifteen. If adults after the age of twenty should continue systematic learning, their abilities would probably be greater than they now commonly are because the techniques of learning would be kept in better working order and the prevalent fear that they are "getting too old to learn" would be proved to be groundless. If adults could be shown that they *can* continue to learn after thirty nearly as well as before, they would perhaps be more willing and able to learn. Thus continued schooling in some measure would tend to keep alive both the inclination and ability to learn.

Better Adjustment of Material and Methods. — If

schooling were spread over a longer period, instead of being concentrated into the fewest years possible, a much better adjustment of content and methods to the needs, interests, and aptitudes of learners could be arranged. Other things being equal, the best time to learn a thing is when it is needed or just before. Things learned when they are needed are learned better because they can be more fully applied to practical purposes. Things learned long before they are required are likely not only to be less well learned but largely forgotten before they are used. Again, learning things when they are needed is likely to prove more interesting and to be pursued with greater vigor. Education may then conform to the Dewey-Kilpatrick doctrine: " First the felt need, then the knowledge or technique to satisfy the need." When systematic education is extended into adult life, it may also be better adjusted to native capacities and to the emotional tastes and incentives which augment interest. Thus instead of studying politics and government chiefly in the seventh grade, one may study these subjects with greater zest and insight nearer the time when one is ready to vote, with less time for forgetting and more opportunity for extending knowledge by applying it. Similarly a woman may profit more by studying certain phases of domestic science nearer the time of establishing a home of her own than ten or more years before.

Keeping Pace with Arts and Sciences. — Only by continuing education into adult life can the citizens keep pace with new advances in the arts, sciences, culture, and philosophy which make possible greater contributions to society and better adjustments to the conditions of life at each stage. At the present time, the majority of people on leaving school begin rapidly to fall behind the advance of knowledge and culture. In part, the lack of mutual respect and understanding between offspring and parents is due to the failure of adults to maintain familiarity with the scientific information, artistic standards, social and religious convictions which young people, in school, are finding to be in highest repute. A progressive development of the sciences and arts requires continuous education. The advance of education especially would be greatly facilitated if adults would continue to familiarize themselves with the efforts of the school to improve its methods of promoting human welfare. No better means of securing such an understanding could be devised than to have adults continue to enjoy the direct benefits of school education.

Increasing Respect for Productive Labor. — Another consideration in favor of extending education into adult life by combining it with other work is the possibility of mitigating the present attitude of condescension or even scorn toward many forms of productive labor and the disposition of many persons to regard education as a means of escape from work. If such an attitude is not corrected there " is a very real danger that schooling may unfit a community to produce by itself its own necessities, and lead it to depend on industrial mercenaries imported to do all the dirty work. As a psychologist, considering the intricate hierarchies of customs and traditions and checks and balances by which the instinctive tendencies of man are directed into the operations of modern industry and trade, the writer wonders that the whole apparatus does not crack with the strains to which it is subjected or explode from the passions which it harbors in its vitals. He feels most devout thanks for his daily bread. So he looks with favor on a mixture of schooling and productive labor, and is unwilling to assume that the latter is a curse to be postponed as long as possible. He sees hope in adult schooling as a means of social health, and is ready to exchange early schooling for it nearly at par." [1]

Providing for Education According to Individual Needs. — The present method of distributing schooling is indiscriminate. It requires that everybody go to school for a certain number of early years (usually until 16) and leaves later schooling entirely to individual choice and volition. The educational needs of individuals are not identical. For some the required amount of concentrated schooling is too much; for others too little. The continuation of nearly full-time education of some individuals until twenty, twenty-five, or even later may be so useful to society that it should be assured. The continuation of various schools into adult life is a promising means of gaining the flexibility required to take care of the varied needs of different individuals.

PLACEMENT AND ORGANIZATION OF MATERIALS AND METHODS IN ACCORDANCE WITH THE DEVELOPMENTAL STATUS OF LEARNERS

The facts which have been reviewed concerning differences in intellectual, emotional, volitional, physical, and other traits, in interests and attitudes, in acquired equipment for work and in power of self-direction from year to year demand a careful adjustment of materials and methods to the pupil's nature at each step in the education ladder. This is one of the reasons why we found it difficult, in the preceding chapter, to make definite statements concerning the relative values of different subjects and activities. A study which is interesting and useful at one stage will be dull and futile at another. In the development of the average child there is an optimum

[1] E. L. THORNDIKE, *Adult Learning*, New York; Macmillan, 1928, pp. 193 f.

time for beginning reading, writing, drawing, music, handwork, arithmetic, algebra, history. Since most of these subjects and others include a great many facts and skills which require several years in the learning, the problem embraces not only the placement of materials at the optimum step but the arrangement of facts and skills in an optimum order.

The Main Principles. — The chief principles concerned in the optimum placement of a fact or skill have been presented or suggested in the preceding discussion of the distribution of schooling. They may be summarized as follows:

1. Other things being equal, introduce a fact or skill at the time or just before the time when it can be used in some serviceable way. This is the criterion of *need*.

2. Other things being equal, introduce a fact or skill at the time when the learner is conscious of the need for it as a means of satisfying some useful purpose. This may be called the criterion of the *felt need*.

3. Other things being equal, introduce a fact or skill when it is most suited in difficulty to the ability of the learner. The optimum degree of difficulty is one which challenges the learner to enlist his best efforts but which is not so hard as to lead to failure or serious errors. A person's ability will depend both upon the level of maturity reached through inner growth and upon the facts and skills acquired by means of previous experience. This is the criterion of *difficulty*.

4. Other things being equal, introduce a fact or skill when it will harmonize most fully with the level and type of emotions, tastes, instinctive and volitional dispositions most active at the time. This may be called the criterion of *temperamental compatibility*.

5. Other things being equal, introduce a fact or skill

when it is most fully facilitated by immediately preceding learnings and when it will most fully facilitate learnings which are to follow shortly. This is the criterion of *facilitation*.

Illustrations from Content Subjects. — Proper application of these principles to the organization of the curriculum will result frequently in perceptible departures from the sequential arrangements of subjects which, until recently, have prevailed in schools. The sharp divisions of material into the subjects — geography, history, sociology, political science, etc. — which adult specialists find convenient are likely to give way frequently to less artificial groupings in which facts related to each other and to the real and felt needs, the abilities and temperamental dispositions, are taught together instead of separately and at different times. Chronological organizations as in history, logical organizations as in arithmetic or geometry, and other schematic sequences which prove most useful to the expert who already knows more of the subject than the average person will ever learn, rarely harmonize with the five criteria just set up. Thus in history it may be found that the story of the voyage of the parents of some pupil in the class should precede that of the voyage of Columbus. The date when some building in the town was built, what was there before it and what was there in the boyhood of the grandfather of some child in the class should perhaps be studied before the dates of the first colonies and the complex political and other factors which caused colonization. Thus in arithmetic, fractions and decimals, although they come late in the internal logic of the subject, will be introduced early in school in connection with quarters of pies, quarts, etc., and in connection with cents and dimes and other decimal parts of dollars.

An Illustration from the Skills — Drawing. — The teaching of skills, like that of information, may be guided by the same principles, which may be briefly illustrated in the case of drawing.

Drawing is a means of telling facts as in a picture of a fight, a map, or the floor plan of a house. A drawing may merely *represent* objects, giving to the eyes something more or less like the impression that the objects themselves would give. A drawing may be made to give a purely aesthetic effect as in the case of designs on book covers, wall papers, friezes, and the like. These three features of drawing may be termed informing, duplicating, and beautifying; or illustration, representation, and decoration.

By far the commonest, earliest, and most potent of the corresponding interests in drawing is that in informing or telling facts by it. Drawing is to children first of all a language. Children's first drawings tell stories. Children at first show little concern about representing the objects as they would appear to the eye or producing anything beautiful. This story-telling drawing leads naturally, with improvement, to map making, mechanical drawing, and schematic illustrations in science; but it leads to representative drawing only in consequence of the special need of identifying an object very exactly, as in portraits, by giving to the eye the impression the object would give; and it leads to artistic drawing only in consequence of the need of giving the observer a sense of beauty.

The promising arrangement of a course in drawing in the elementary schools is then to begin with the " natural," fact-telling drawing; to develop it along such lines as drawing maps, plans, illustrations of the facts learned in elementary science, history, and the like; and to introduce representative drawing by first showing the need for it — as when a series of objects one back of another at various distances needs perspective drawing to explain it, or as when a disk is meant to represent a ball and needs shading to tell the story. The artistic drawing or creation of beauty with the pencil would begin with simple designs to decorate real objects which the pupils wish to have beautiful. Each element of technique would be taught similarly when the effective telling of the story made the need for added techniques realizable.

The traditional arrangement in drawing neglected or even went dead against interest and nature, forcing the pupil to copy cubes, cylinders, cups and saucers in representative drawing at the very beginning, compelling exactness of outline when what the children cared to tell with the pencil did not in the least require it, putting illustrative, schematic, and mechanical drawing after, instead of before, representative and decorative drawing, and teaching formal technique before — often long before — the pupil felt any need for it. As a result, children who might have become fair draughtsmen with a permanent interest in the use of the pencil, drew painfully sad-looking chairs, buttercups, and vases while they were in school, and nothing at all thereafter.

Developmental Organization Methods. — Methods, as well as subject matter and activities, must be adapted to the status of the child. While we shall treat this topic later, it may be said here that, in general, the implication of the facts of growth are that the child should become gradually more capable of selecting, initiating, and managing his own learning. The neglect of developing competence to select one's own projects, to manage one's own affairs, to appraise one's own strengths and weakness and to be wisely influenced thereby, and to acquire the many particular skills in learning, studying, and planning is one of the most conspicuous and serious deficiencies in the present educational system. Conscious of these defects, many educators have hastily resorted to extreme methods in which the child is thrown upon his own responsibilities before he is ready to assume them. Instead of being wisely guided when his powers are undeveloped and his abilities immature he is forced to flounder in wasteful trial and error. Independence, initiative, and efficiency, like other traits, are achieved most surely and rapidly through education conducted according to the principles of learning and the process of growth. They should be fostered by education and not left to chance. They cannot be realized suddenly at any time; they should emerge gradually and be adequately exercised and justly rewarded as they appear.

QUESTIONS AND EXERCISES

1. Do the facts concerning growth presented in this chapter support the old theory that a child during development passes through several distinct periods or epochs such as the hunting age, the fighting age, etc., or through periods corresponding to the characteristics of various animals in the biological series? Explain.

2. Do the facts in the chapter support the theory that the child passes through several stages such as the motor stage, the sensory stage, the memory stage, the reasoning stage, and so on? Explain.

3. Do the facts presented in the chapter support the widespread belief that young children can memorize more readily and retain better than older children or adults? Is it probable that young children memorize more than older ones because they are less capable of acquiring ideas by other means such as reasoning or because they have less effective and varied study techniques?

4. Will children between 6 and 10 or youths between 14 and 18 be more able to learn each of the following? Give reason for your answer.

    a. To use a typewriter
    b. To dance
    c. To understand a foreign language

  d. To drive an automobile

  e. To understand Lincoln's Gettysburg Address

  f. To repeat the multiplication tables

  g. To learn not to say "He don't."

5. To what extent, and in what manner, will previous learnings affect the answer to each question in (4)?

6. At what age will a large proportion of direct experience with things and events in the immediate environment be most advisable? Why?

7. At what period between 6 and 16 can children most readily understand descriptions of things and events distant in time or space?

8. Enumerate some of the emotional dispositions and interests formed in adolescence that are weaker or absent in childhood. Some that are prominent in childhood which are inconspicuous in adolescence.

9. What are some of the main dangers of prolonged guardianship? How may they be mitigated?

10. Suppose that the average child were to be allowed the equivalent of 12 years of 9 months each for schooling. Distribute this time as you think best for the interests of the individual and society. Consider the question of beginning full-time or part-time work outside of school and other matters that seem to you important.

11. Would you advise the same program for dull, average, and very bright children? Explain.

12. What are the advantages and disadvantages of beginning to do vocational work in the school compared to beginning such work outside?

13. What means would most effectively foster the continuation of education into adult life?

14. Consider the merits and limitations of a plan of extending the school day considerably in order to enable average children to complete their required education at an earlier age. Consider extending the school year to eleven months. Consider extending both the day and the year.

15. Compare the advantage of teaching civics between 18 and 20 with teaching it between 10 and 12. Make the same comparison for a course in the fundamentals of health.

16. How may instruction in history be made to correspond most adequately to the abilities, needs, interests, emotional dispositions, etc. of pupils at different ages?

17. Recall some instances in your own experience in which materials were not taught in accordance with one or more of the criteria listed in this chapter.

REFERENCES

FISKE, J., *The Meaning of Infancy*. Houghton Mifflin.

GESELL, A., *Infancy and Human Growth*. Macmillan.

GESELL, A., *The Mental Growth of the Pre-School Child*. Macmillan.

GESELL, A., *The Pre-School Child*. Houghton Mifflin.

HOLLINGWORTH, H. L., *Mental Growth and Decline*. Appleton.

HOLLINGWORTH, L. S., *The Psychology of the Adolescent*. Appleton.

NORSWORTHY, N., and WHITLEY, M. T., *The Psychology of Childhood*. Macmillan.

PECHSTEIN, L. A., and JENKINS, F., *Psychology of the Kindergarten-Primary Child*. Houghton Mifflin.

PECHSTEIN, L. A., and MCGREGOR, A. L., *Psychology of the Junior High School Pupil*. Houghton Mifflin.

THORNDIKE, E. L., *Adult Learning*. Macmillan.

THORNDIKE, E. L., *Educational Psychology*, Vol. III. Teachers College Bureau of Publications.

See also references for Chapter I.

Chapter X

THE INFLUENCE OF INDIVIDUAL
DIFFERENCES

In the preceding chapter, we observed that an individual from the beginning of life goes through a series of changes which depend in part on education and experience and in part upon the innate development of muscles, glands, nervous system, intelligence, capacities for special types of learning, emotional tendencies, feelings, and other traits. These changes are so numerous, so great, and so complexly interrelated that the interests and abilities of children show such marked differences from year to year that great skill must be exercised to make the materials and methods of education conform to them at each moment. To adapt every aspect of education to the developmental status of children becomes an essential requirement of education.

Individual Differences in Personality. — Although all normal children — normal in the sense that their development is not blighted by disease or by native and acquired defects — pass through a cycle of growth and decline, the growth of different persons in any trait proceeds at various rates and reaches different levels at maturity. The consequence is that, at any given age, children are far from identical in any particular trait and are even more diversified in the total combinations or pattern of their traits. They differ greatly in each minute trait and more markedly in total personality. These individual differences among children similar in age or in grade placement in school have been subjected to careful, scientific study since 1900. To the facts revealed by these studies and their implications the present chapter will be devoted.

Nature of Individual Differences in Single Traits

Variations Are Continuous. — The individual differences of children at any given age in any one trait take the form of variations up and down from the average of all children in that trait. Individual differences, in other words, are variations from the middle or average or *typical* individual. The average represents the type — the typical characteristics — of that age. From the middle or typical amount of a trait, individual variations in both directions, downward to smaller and upward to greater amounts, are continuous. There are no gaps from one extreme to the other. There are no big steps. From the least to the greatest amount of the trait, individuals are found at steps imperceptibly minute. The number of individuals is greatest at the middle or average and becomes systematically, but not uniformly, smaller as either extreme is approached. The rate of the falling off of the number of individuals as the amount of the trait approaches either extreme cannot easily be expressed in words although it can be designated by a mathematical formula and pictured in a diagram. The diagram or graph, which is shown in Figure 3, is called the Normal Curve or Normal Surface of Distribution of a human trait.

The Normal Curve of Distribution. — This bell-shaped curve or surface shows a base line which varies from the least to the greatest amount of the trait. The height of the curved line above the base line indicates the number of individuals at any point on the base line. The num-

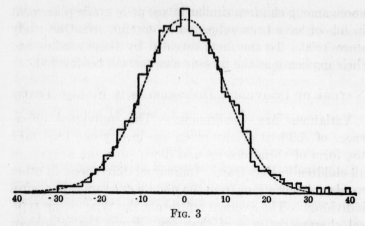

Fig. 3

The Normal Curve of Distribution is indicated by the dotted line. The solid lines show the actual distribution of the scores in mental tests of 1656 pupils in Grade IX. Note how closely the curve based on actual scores approximates the theoretical curve. (From E. L. THORNDIKE, *Journal of Educational Research*, November, 1924.)

ber is greatest at the average and decreases first rapidly, then more slowly as the extremes are approached. This curve indicates the approximate nature of the distribution of the pupils of any age in any trait. What is equally important for our purposes, this curve depicts at the present time, approximately, the distribution of pupils in any one school grade in any one trait.

Children Not Divided into a Few "Types." — Before turning to a consideration of the magnitude of the differences between children at the two extremes, it should be noted that the children of a given age or in a given class do not fall into two or more separate groups in any ability. When the teacher says : " I have two kinds of children, good and bad " ; or " I have three kinds of workers, quick and careless, average workers, and the slow and sure " ; or when the psychologist, after applying an intelligence test, divides the kindergarten children into idiots, imbeciles, morons, the dull, the average, the superior, and the geniuses, they are misstating the facts. These divisions, which do not exist in nature, are artificial classes — mere matters of definition. They are justified by convenience of expression when one fully realizes the fact that in each trait or combination of traits there is only one type — the average — from which individuals vary by steps imperceptibly minute.

Differences between Extremes of a Given Age or Grade. — The amount of the difference between the extremes in any one age or grade is much greater than was realized until recently. Measure a thousand ten-year-old boys and you will probably find one whose intelligence is only equal to that of the average child of six years and another who equals the average youth of fourteen — a difference of eight years of average intellectual development. Among a thousand fourth-grade children the range may be from a mentality of seven and a half or eight to thirteen and a half. The range of ability among school children of the same age is such that, in a majority of capacities, the most gifted child will, in comparison with the least gifted child of the same age, do over six times as much in the same time or do the same amount with less than a sixth as many errors. School grading reduces the differences in a class considerably, but by no means fully. Roughly speaking, the teacher of a class, even in a school graded as closely as is possible in large cities where two classes are provided in each building for each grade and where promotion occurs every six months, will find in the case of any kind of school work that the best pupil can do from two to five times as much in a given time or do the same amount with only twenty to fifty per cent as many errors as the poorest pupil. In manual dexterity, musical talent, emotionality, aggressiveness, kindness, endurance, perseverance, and all other traits differences among children in the same class, although not easily measured or stated in quantitative terms, are probably equally great.

INDIVIDUAL DIFFERENCES IN COMBINATIONS OF TRAITS

Every Personality Unique. — Scarcely any school task is dependent upon a single human trait or characteristic. A particular lesson or project in reading, writing, painting, music, appreciation, moral adjustment, group control, or what not depends in various degrees upon intelligence, special motor and intellectual aptitudes, bodily size, appearance, speed, vigor, determination, interest, and many other factors. Actual achievement in any line, then, depends upon a combination of traits. When we think of an individual as possessing each of every trait in some degree, we can realize that no two can be alike. Think of the almost innumerable different tastes or colors. All tastes also result from combining some amount of only four taste qualities — sweet, salt, bitter, and sour; and all colors come from combinations of but four psychologically primary colors — red, green, blue, and yellow. A human being comprised of an exceedingly large number of different traits, each present in some amount, appears in an almost infinite number of total combinations and patterns. It is highly unlikely that any teacher during her lifetime will ever encounter two identical children. Every child is unique.

Theory of Compensation. — Before discussing the significance of individual differences we must consider the way in which traits tend to be combined. According to one theory, children are, for practical purposes in education along the fundamental lines, more alike than the picture of variations in single traits tends to indicate. The theory is that strength in any one trait tends to be compensated for by weakness in others, and vice versa. The effect of this tendency for strength to be balanced by weakness and weakness by strength would be to make individuals approach an average — become more alike — in general fitness. To illustrate, suppose that arithmetic ability depends upon the total effect of intelligence, a special arithmetic capacity, emotional stability, volitional perseveration, and manual dexterity. According to the theory of compensation, a child high in some of these traits, such as intelligence and special capacity, would tend to be low in the others and vice versa. The result would be that, despite wide differences among pupils in each single trait, the average or combined equipment for learning arithmetic would tend toward equality. Thus, from the point of view of practical competence, pupils would not differ so greatly.

Theory of Correlation. — The results of many careful studies of the interrelations of traits have not been in harmony with this view of compensation. The fact is that correlation or correspondence among desirable traits, rather than compensation, is the rule. If a child has a high degree of intelligence (or any other trait) which contributes to efficiency in learning arithmetic he is more likely instead of less likely to be superior in the other traits than are other children who have low intelligence. Strength in one trait tends to go with strength in others; mediocrity in one with mediocrity in others; weakness in one with weakness in others. The facts, then, tend to emphasize the significance of individual differences in combinations of traits rather than to minimize them. There is a tendency toward a high, average, or low level in general.

Need to Detect Special Strengths and Weaknesses. — Although each individual tends to be high, average, or low in the sum of all desirable traits, each may vary considerably in particular traits above and below the average of his own traits. Indeed, although among children of low abstract intelligence high degrees of other talents are relatively rare, we find *some* who are above the average of the bright children in strength, manual dexterity, emotional control, and other desirable traits. The children of poor artistic or musical sense, while averaging a little lower in all other traits than those of fine aptitudes in artistic and musical lines, may nevertheless be distributed over almost the entire range of abilities in other traits. Thus we may expect to find children inept in learning arithmetic who are of slow, average or very high competence in music, drawing, athletics, carpentry, and other fields less closely related to abstract intellect. This is due to the fact that, while all correlations between desirable traits tend to be positive, some are very small. Despite the *general* tendency to positive correlation, each individual is a highly specialized organization. Each has his special strengths and weaknesses which education should find and take into account.

In sum, we must deal with each person as an individual, but, in so doing, we should not consider each of his traits in isolation from others, but study the combination. Vocational choice, teaching methods, and materials should be determined by the character of the total pattern of abilities revealed. Although the varieties of combinations of human traits are many, the possible vocations, teaching methods, and materials are also numerous and any individual is likely to be better fitted to some than to others.

With the facts of individual differences now before us we may proceed to discuss their significance.

EDUCATIONAL SIGNIFICANCE OF INDIVIDUAL DIFFERENCES

Adaptation of Aims of Education to the Individual. — The facts of individual differences affect the application of all the principles of education which have been previously stated and which will be mentioned later. They affect, in the first place, the carrying out of the immediate aims of education. They require the adaptation of the curriculum to the talents and limitations of each pupil. The particular facts and habits required to promote the physical and mental health, the specific adjustments to the physical surroundings, the optimum development of intellectual resources, the special needs for a wholesome sexual and family life, the most significant adjustments to other people, the best equipment for participation in civic, religious, and economic life, the most favorable preparation for vocational and recreational activities will vary from person to person. To enable each person simultaneously to satisfy most fully the wants of himself and of all others, it is necessary to explore the equipment of every pupil and promote his development along the lines in which he is most richly endowed and to the extent that his capacities justify. In order to provide satisfactorily this differential education, the school must assume and inculcate in others a new and broader attitude of respect and appreciation of individual talents and limitations.

Need to Recognize Value in the Less Abstract Studies and Capacities. — Schools have been developed to reward most fully those who excel in abstract intelligence. It is a fixed tradition of schools that the teaching of reading, spelling, composition, history, mathematics, and other abstract and linguistic subjects is the main objective.

It has, until recently, left for shops, trades, athletics, picnics, public meetings, and other institutions the task of providing much of the education for other phases of life. Moreover, teachers, because of the acceptance of the scholastic tradition, are likely to look down on the children who do not do well in the typical school studies, however great their artistic, social, moral, or practical talents may be. The pupil highly endowed with abstract intelligence enjoys mental gymnastics for their own sake in the same way that others enjoy mere movement or color, mechanical operations, or " tinkering " for their own sakes. The former, however, get sheer enjoyment out of following the teacher's excursions into formal grammar or mathematics or geometry, while those less gifted are confused or bored. The abstract intellect is likely to be the pride of the teacher and the recipient of the school's greatest honors. While intelligence of this type can be counted second to no talent in practical importance, the world needs achievement in hand work, mechanics, art, relief work, and other lines in which talents other than abstract intelligences are a necessary or main element. The school should provide for many types of useful talents; the teacher should esteem them all. If the ultimate aims of education, set forth in earlier chapters, are to be realized, the school must greatly broaden its scope and, still more, its sympathies.

Need of Provision for Different Rates of Progress. — The facts of individual differences affect the adaptation of the aims and methods and materials to the developmental status of the pupils. Individuals grow at different rates and reach different levels at maturity. Individual differences in ability to learn those school functions which require the management of general and abstract ideas, for example, show a constant increase from year to year until the maximum development has been reached. Students, in other words, differ most when the limits of their intellectual capacities have been attained. Among a thousand unselected children born to-day, perhaps two will be unable at their maturity to learn more than the simplest forms of manual activities, ten will be unable to do the present academic work beyond grade 3, and fifty more will be unable to do the work beyond grade 6. At the other extreme are a dozen who could, by the age of sixteen, successfully do college work and who could richly repay society for giving them several years of the most highly advanced instruction. Individual differences, then, demand a longitudinal as well as a horizontal specialization. Different rates of progress and different lines of study are both required to fit differences in capacity and to harmonize with the different vocational, recreational, social, civic, and other duties which will characterize adult life.

Need of Providing and Inculcating Respect for Many Lines of Study. — In addition to determining the aptitudes and weakness of pupils and planning the length and type of the entire school career in advance, education should devote itself to the establishment of a new point of view concerning individuality and its consequences. Already the danger of snobbishness of those who fortunately have demonstrated their capacity to complete the work of college is felt and the personal, social, and moral virtues of the less educated underestimated. Vocational " levels " are freely assumed; the aristocracy of all sorts of " white-collar trades " over manual trades is asserted; even recreations are graded into " highbrow " and " low-brow." As a consequence, parents struggle, too often in vain, to push their children through the liberal arts schools at any cost. The failure of pupils, endowed often with real possibilities in other lines, is a blight upon themselves and their parents and the cause of dangerous resentments. By their zealousness for intellectual advancement the schools have themselves fostered this difficulty. The remedy is education — broader education. Not only must the schools provide for natures not preëminently intellectual in abstract and linguistic lines, it must also develop respect for other types of achievement.

Means of Fostering Practical Studies. — Merely to introduce into the schools a number of much needed practical, aesthetic, social, dramatic, and other subjects and give them the dignity and respect now accorded mathematics, literature, or Latin will be a first great step in the right direction. To provide for a wider participation in such subjects — which may be justified on other grounds — is one means of distributing more widely the satisfaction of mastery now largely confined to the intellectually superior. For the latter to find themselves not supreme in every line will also have wholesome effects. Finally, the school must strive to abolish unwholesome notions concerning the relative dignity and value of different vocational pursuits and the different school curricula which are preparatory to them. As we now consider the fat to be different from but not necessarily superior to the thin, or the big and strong not to be superior *in general* to the small and weak so we must come to regard intellectual, motor, mechanical, artistic, and other aptitudes and editorial work, surgery, carpentry, painting, and other productive labor as equally dignified and essential, and therefore equally important.

Equalizing Rewards by Means of the Accomplishment-Quotient Technique. — Since desirable traits tend somewhat to go together and undesirable ones also tend to appear together, there is no escape from the fact that some individuals are superior to others in general. One of the most promising ideas for offsetting the ill effects of such total differences is found in a recent invention of educational psychology — the Accomplishment-Quotient technique. The purpose of this device is to make it possible to reward not only absolute achievement along any line but also attainment in proportion to the capacity of the individual for productivity in that line. It provides a tangible goal and a functioning incentive for every person, namely to achieve a result that lies within his powers. It provides a universally applicable standard of comparison — namely the amount of achievement in comparison with capacity. It provides a new and just basis for competition and reward. The prize should go to him whose accomplishment, whatever its absolute amount may be, is highest in proportion to his aptitude. The dullest or clumsiest pupil in a class may win the prize by making of his limited talents the most productive use. Thus the pupil who with a capacity of 10 achieves a result of 15 is rewarded in preference to the pupil whose achievement is 20 but whose capacity is 25. Although perfect methods of application are not yet worked out, the idea of the Accomplishment Quotient is sound and wholesome.

Need for Better Instruction of the Most Gifted. — Past applications of the Accomplishment-Quotient idea in somewhat defective form have revealed some highly significant facts concerning the adjustment of the school to individual differences. It has shown that, probably, the pupils of the highest talents are most poorly educated. Teachers are most determined and able, and the school is best equipped, to take care of the average and lower talents. Although usually leading the others in absolute achievements the most talented pupils lag farthest behind their possibilities. The system of inflexible promotion, the narrow range of materials, the scheme of definite assignments, the use of unvaried teaching devices are all designed to retard the development of those of highest endowment.

This unfortunate situation springs in part from the social pressure brought upon the school to realize " normal " progress for every pupil. People, including teachers, are more impressed by the needs and weaknesses of a particular individual than by the needs and sufferings of society as a whole. This humanitarian attitude has led to vast expenditures for caring for the blind, the feeble-minded, the crippled, and otherwise defective, although superior care for these unfortunates can little advance the interests of society as a whole. A strict observance of the ultimate aims of education, to do those things which do the most good for the most people, plainly demands equal or even greater attention to the most talented. To give the best possible training to the most gifted is one of the surest means of advancing most fully the interests of all — including those of the least gifted.

Need of Attention to Differences in Emotionality and Other Traits. — Individuals differ not only in capacities to learn but in the relative strength of the fundamental wants and interests outlined in Chapter IV. All individuals possess the same types of wants, but they possess them in different amounts. Some, compared to others, show a stronger craving for physical activity, for mental activity, for domination, for novelty and change, for collecting and hoarding, for social approval. Some are more emotional in general or more timid, fearful, pugnacious, courageous, or joyful in particular situations than others. In all instinctive, emotional, temperamental, and volitional tendencies differences are found. In all these traits we find extreme cases — the extremely timid and overly aggressive; the emotionally unstable and the emotionally callous; the hyperactive and the extremely sluggish in movement; the weak and vacillating and the persistent and stubborn wills; the melancholic and the frivolous temperaments. All of these extremes require special management.

Need of Adapting Materials and Methods of Instruction in the Common Subjects to Individual Differences. — Finally, a practical consequence of the facts of individual differences is that every general law of teaching has to be applied with consideration of the particular person in question. Every stimulus must be given not to men or children in general, but to a particular individual or at least to a group characterized by certain known peculiarities. The responses of children to any stimulus will not be invariable like the responses of atoms of hydrogen or of filings of iron, but will vary with their individual capacities, interests, and previous education.

Ideally, instruction should be individualized. Incentives, materials, and methods should be adapted to personal needs. This statement does not mean that instruction should be individual in the sense that each child should be taught in isolation. The presence and activities of a group, preferably as homogeneous as possible in the capacities for the particular work at hand and unlike in one or another or several other respects, offer too rich possibilities for the development of social habits needed in modern society to be dispensed with even were such a change a possibility. But within the limitations of group work, instruction can be largely adapted to individual differences. Different amounts and kinds of content can be used to teach reading, writing, arithmetic, and most other subjects; applications and illustrations

of different degrees and types may be arranged; methods
differing in rate of movement, in degree of detail, in the
amount and distribution of practice and review, in the
type of activity used as a medium — much or little physical action, much or little abstract language, much or little
self-management, etc. — can be selected or developed to
meet a large range of individual demands. In fact, one
criterion which we shall apply to all the specific methods
to be described in the following chapters is: To what
extent does this method provide for adjustment to
individual differences?

Some False Assumptions concerning Individual Differences

Now that some of the important applications of the
facts of individual differences have been made, we may
consider briefly a few errors in practice due either to the
disregard or misinterpretation of the facts of individuality.

Error of Neglect. — The first error of teachers with
respect to individual differences is to neglect them, to
form one set of fixed habits for dealing with all children,
to teach " the child " instead of markedly different living
individuals. To realize the varieties of human nature,
the nature and amount of mental differences, is to be protected against many fallacies of teaching.

**Assumption That Children Are or Should Be Like Our-
selves.** — A second error from which all of us suffer is to
credit our students with natures like our own. We think
of them as duplicates more or less of ourselves. If we
are quick learners, we expect too much of them; if we
have sensible, matter-of-fact minds, we have no patience
with their sentimentalities and sensitiveness; if we are
precise and neat and systematic, we fail to understand
how intolerable it is for some of them to lead a regular,

orderly existence. Teachers need to add to the maxim, " See ourselves as others see us," the still more important one, " See others as they are."

Assumption That Individual Differences Are Inconsistent with General Aims and Principles in Education. — The third error is the belief that the diversity of the patterns of human nature and the need of widespread adaptation of the aims, materials, methods, and other phases of education to individual differences nullify the value of general principles, aims, and procedures. They do not. The principles of intellectual growth are true though children develop mentally at different rates; the principles of readiness and effect are sound though children have different interests and inclinations. Nor should the differences among children blind us to their likenesses. Similarity in general features is as truly a fact as differences in details. Children differ greatly in their likes and dislikes, but almost all children like action and novelty. Some children like action more than others, but almost all children like it very much. Children differ greatly in their capacities, but it is safe to expect that in the great majority of cases the capacity for concrete thought will be stronger than that for abstract thought. It is folly to give up the attempt to get rational principles for teaching because the teacher's task varies with the individual to be taught. So also does the task of medicine depend on the individual to be cured, the task of agriculture on the particular crop to be raised. In all three professions we need sagacious application of general principles to individual problems.

Assumption That Individual Differences Are Hostile to Selection and Organization of Subject Matter. — The fourth error concerning individual differences is to assume that they are incompatible with efforts to select material and activities and to organize them into a unified curriculum. Since the doctrines of Dewey have sometimes been misinterpreted in support of this false assumption, it will be well to read what he himself has to say on the problem.

Progressive schools set store by individuality, and sometimes it seems to be thought that orderly organization of subject matter is hostile to the needs of students in their individual character.... It is quite possible for teachers to make such a fuss over individual children, worrying about their peculiarities, their likes and dislikes, their weaknesses and failures, so that they miss perception of real individuality and indeed tend to adopt methods which show no faith in the power of individuality. A child's individuality cannot be found in what he does or in what he consciously likes at a given moment; it can be found only in the connected course of his actions. Consciousness of desire and purpose can be genuinely attained only toward the close of some fairly prolonged sequence of activities. Consequently some organization of subject matter reached through a serial or consecutive course of doings, held together within the unity of progressively growing occupation or project, is the only means which corresponds to real individuality. So far is organization from being hostile to the principle of individuality . . . that much of the energy that sometimes goes to thinking about individual children might better be devoted to discovering some worth-while activity and to arranging the conditions under which it can be carried forward.[1]

QUESTIONS AND EXERCISES

1. Theoretically should all pupils take the same studies? Should all pupils take the same amount of any study? Should all pupils require the same time to master any assignment?

2. Theoretically should all pupils receive a common minimum of education with respect to adjustment to the physical world, to economic, social, civic situations, etc.?

3. If the brighter pupils learn more rapidly and have greater

[1] From a reprint of *Progressive Education and the Science of Education*, an address made at the Eighth Annual Conference of the Progressive Education Association, March, 1928.

ability to adapt themselves intellectually to new situations, should they not be given less education than the dull, instead of more?

4. Should not pupils who learn more in a course be given more credit for their work, say, by giving 4 points for an A, 3 for a B, 2 for C, 1 for D, and 0 for F? On the other hand, since bright children learn more easily, should not credit be given for effort, say, by giving, for a given amount of ability, 5 points to the dullest 20 per cent, 4 to the next 20 per cent, and so on to one point for the brightest 20 per cent in a class?

5. Should the school aim to make pupils become more alike or should it attempt to emphasize the differences that are natural? In particular should the school aim more at strengthening a child along the line of the intellectual deficiencies or at making the most of his special talents?

6. Does the classification of children into several sections according to intellectual ability benefit the bright any more than the average or dull? Is dullness or brightness made more or less conspicuous by placing each together with others of the same kind or by combining dull, average, and bright in one group?

7. What would be the propriety and value of fostering the idea that differences in intelligence should be regarded with no more emotionality than differences in height, weight, color of the hair, or speed in running? Why is there now more sensitivity about one's intelligence than about one's health?

8. Defend one or the other side of this thesis: Persons who have enjoyed good health and who have regularly attended school until the age of 16 and have by that time, due to inferior intellect, been unable to complete the work of the sixth grade, should be deprived of the privilege of voting when they reach the age of suffrage.

9. Has the school itself, to any considerable extent, been responsible for the unfortunate comparisons of "high-brow" and "low-brow" interests, vocations, etc.? Give evidence.

10. Do the facts of individual differences harmonize with the present practice of making school attendance compulsory for all children up to a given age? If not, what practicable improvement would you suggest?

11. As pupils grow older, do the differences among them, in so far as they are due to inner growth, tend to become more or less conspicuous and important? Compare the cases of intelligence and height.

12. One writer has stated that it is far more important to educate

the one brightest child in each thousand to the limits of his capacity than to train similarly the hundred dullest. Defend or oppose this view.

REFERENCES

GATES, A. I., *Elementary Psychology*. Macmillan.

HOLLINGWORTH, L. S., *Gifted Children*. Macmillan.

HOLLINGWORTH, L. S., *The Psychology of Subnormal Children*. Macmillan.

HOLLINGWORTH, L. S., *Special Talents and Defects*. Macmillan.

HORN, J. L., *The Education of Exceptional Children*. Century.

JONES, A. J., *Education and the Individual*. Century.

KITSON, H. D., *Psychology of Vocational Adjustment*. Lippincott.

MORT, P. R., *The Individual Pupil in the Management of Class and School*. American Book Company.

THORNDIKE, E. L., *Educational Psychology*, Vol. III. Teachers College Bureau of Publications.

THORNDIKE, E. L., *Individuality*. Houghton Mifflin.

Twenty-fourth Year-book of the National Society for the Study of Education. Part II, ADAPTING THE SCHOOL TO INDIVIDUAL DIFFERENCES.

Chapter XI

METHODS OF TEACHING

Value of Method in Sciences and Arts. — Every kind of work involves a method of employing some material. Successful work at farming requires not only zeal, industry, and a personality adapted to a farmer's life, but also the use of good methods. Much time and pains are devoted in medical schools to teaching the best methods of surgery. A student of mining who knew the facts about geology, metallurgy, and the like, but nothing concerning methods of mining and testing ores would not be given a degree as a mining engineer. A master of any trade or profession will be familiar not only with his tools and materials, but also with the best methods of work.

Value of Method in Education. — Strange to say, many persons have declared the work of education to be the one exception to the universal rule. Some would say that a teacher need know only his subjects; some would add knowledge of the child to mastery of the subject but refuse to countenance method, declaring, in fact, that there *is* no method or that methods do not matter or that a teacher intuitively acquires the best method. Such ignorance and egotism fortunately have been too rare to retard the development of methods in education any more than they have in bricklaying, surgery, or science. And in education, as in other fields, observation and scientific study of techniques have made possible great increases in efficiency. Like the bricklayer, surgeon, or scientist, the

235

teacher must study and practice to make fruitful use of the various methods now available.

Meaning of Method. — By a method in education is meant the way in which a teacher puts educative agents and means to work upon human nature so as to produce some desired result. Thus a book may be used as material to be understood, or to be understood and remembered, or to be merely memorized without understanding, or to be understood, remembered, and used in the solution of problems. Thus, to produce the result — knowledge of certain facts in chemistry — the teacher may describe the facts orally, or have students read printed descriptions of them in a textbook, or demonstrate the facts by experiments, or get the students themselves to perform the experiments.

The variety of methods which one may use to attain even any one result is often very great, since in the last analysis every difference in the teacher's facial expression or voice, or in the wording of his statements and questions, is a difference in method. The variety possible in connection with all the different results which education seeks is practically infinite. It is, indeed, the task of the science of education to know the effect of everything that any teacher can do upon every person to whom anything can be done. But of the total possible facts only a few can be presented in this volume.

TEN CRITERIA OF METHOD PREVIOUSLY MENTIONED

In earlier chapters we have discussed characteristics which are essential to any method. Some of these may be summarized as an introduction to this chapter.

1. The method should facilitate the establishment of readiness for the activity in order to secure vigorous, whole-hearted activity.

2. The method should facilitate the production of the desired reactions and, as far as possible, reduce the undesired reactions.

3. The method should make as obvious as possible to the pupil or teacher or to both the appearance of suitable and unsuitable reactions.

4. The method should provide for the effective association of satisfaction with the desired and annoyance with the undesired reactions.

5. The method should establish the desired reactions in such a way as to provide for the widest transfer or application to the situations which normal life presents.

6. The method should, as far as possible, provide for the development of desirable concomitant reactions of intellectual, emotional, volitional, appreciative, and other types.

7. The method should, as far as possible, utilize the activities and conditions — such as clear objectives, natural activities and dispositions, successful mastery of difficulties, reasonable rivalry, etc. — which arouse interest and zeal and which enlist the most whole-hearted coöperation of the pupil.

8. The method should, in particular, be adaptable to the individual differences in capacity and interest of the pupils taught together.

9. The method should be adaptable to the requirements for progressive adjustment to the growth of the child in knowledge, ability, capacity for self-management, intellectual power, range and types of interests, emotional and volitional dispositions, and other aspects of his personality. The method should, in other words, be so adjusted to the character of growth as most effectively to perpetuate and stimulate further growth.

10. The method should be adaptable to the most fruit-

ful utilization of various principles of economy such as the optimum length of practice periods, the prevention of over and under learning, the optimum distribution of practice and review, effective integration of old and new reactions by review, and the like.

Classification of Methods

It would be instructive to appraise all of the representative types of teaching in the light of these ten criteria. Experience and research have produced such a wealth of teaching techniques that a detailed analysis must be left largely to the initiative of the reader. We shall be able merely to consider some of the special advantages and limitations of a few methods rather arbitrarily grouped under a few general types. The following nine types have been selected as representative.

1. The method of book study.
2. The method of discussion.
3. The lecture method.
4. The practice or drill method.
5. The demonstration method.
6. The laboratory or experimental method.
7. The project method.
8. The method of dramatic expression.
9. The method of self-activity.

In connection with several of the methods in this list, we face the general problems of the relative merits of learning by reading a book on the one hand and listening to the spoken word on the other. In comparing the method of book study with the lecture method, the merits of learning by reading and by listening comprise the main problems. Since other methods such as the drill or demonstration may be modified to take advantage of the better form of presentation, it will be advisable to discuss the merits of voice and print at the beginning.

BOOK TEACHING *versus* ORAL TEACHING

The Value of Speech, Facial Expression, and Gesture. — Personal teaching is commonly largely oral; textbook teaching appeals to the eye alone. Oral instruction has the advantage, in the case of little children, of relief from the work of interpreting the little-known visual symbols and of the stronger appeal of words heard, over black marks seen. Instruction through books has the advantage that each pupil can think at his own rate, get the fact over and over again as he needs, test himself point by point as he goes along, and make notes of his difficulties for later use in questioning the teacher. Book teaching gains in relative value as students, by more training, become used to getting ideas from print. If the same selection were to be read aloud monotonously and given in print, there can be little doubt that second-grade children would profit more by having it given by speech and college students by having it in print.

The intonation, facial expression, and gesture, and the illustrative actions which are accompaniments of oral teaching, commonly add interest and excite to useful mental activity, the more so the younger the children are and the less gifted at reading. These human accessories, even when unpleasant to see and hear, still win attention from most men as books do not. It is only the especially facile reader, who also is intellectually beyond the need of another's intonation and bodily expression, that prefers to read rather than hear a story, and to read men's books rather than hear them talk.

Detail and Consequent Length. — But teachers and textbooks rarely do give anything like the same treatment of a topic. The teacher's personally managed treatment is almost always longer, easier, more determined by special exigencies of the occasion, and characterized by a selection and treatment of facts such as no textbook displays.

Length is an impressive difference. The actual facts, principles, and applications given in a college course of ninety hours can often be printed in a book that a capable reader could get through in nine hours. The extra eighty hours must have a value equal to eighty hours of such study, experiment, problem-solving, and the like as could be guided by printed directions, if it is to be justifiable. One reason why children seem to learn so much better from personal teaching than from books is that many of them spend much time in class-meetings and little time upon books.

Comprehensibility. — The same teacher would almost never make up a textbook with so easy questions, so much repetition, so many illustrations, and so full explanations as he gives personally to a class. He would, for one thing, be ashamed to do so, for the conventional book, even for little children, is a rather dignified affair. Moreover, the book would be very, very long. And it is unconventional to print a book, say of 300,000 words, for an eighth-grade class in history, in addition to all the regular historical reading prescribed. Finally, the book would be full of directions to *do* this and that, to work out this or that problem, to write out such and such an outline; and it is unconventional to print such a mixture. These conventions are unfortunate, for easy courses in print are needed. There is no wisdom in the notion that a textbook is to give the subject matter of a course, but in so difficult a form that every teacher must illustrate and explain it at great length!

Adaptability. — Textbooks, if written by experts in

education, are likely to be the result of thorough consideration of the general facts of the learning process in the case of the subject in question, and so to be better adapted to the general run of pupils than all save exceptionally gifted personal teaching. Personally managed treatment of a subject is, in the nature of the case, more sensitive to the special situations presented by a given group of pupils — their previous knowledge of it and of related facts, their varying abilities, and other individual characteristics. This feature may result in either gain or loss in efficiency, according to whether the teacher adapts the treatment to the special exigencies without neglecting fundamental matters, or, on the contrary, sacrifices general facts in favor of local and temporary interests, neglects the majority of the class in favor of the specially able or specially deficient, or sacrifices the proper balance of training in favor of special discipline to fit his own whims.

Guidance in Habit-Formation and Reasoning. — Textbooks often state what habits are to be formed without giving the reader exercises in forming them, but this is not a necessary feature of printed matter. Textbooks in geography, history, spelling, English composition, grammar, economics, philosophy, or sociology could, by the exercise of enough ingenuity, provide for the actual formation of habits in the same way as do books of examples to be performed in arithmetic, or sentences to be translated in Latin, or experiments to be done in chemistry.

Textbooks still less often guide the pupil to think out conclusions by himself as far as he can. They commonly give the results of reasoning, and perhaps problems demanding reasoning, but they do not so manage the latter that the pupil is at each stage helped just enough to lead him to help himself as much as is economically possible.

They do not, that is, usually get the full value of the questioning, problem, project, discussional, and experimental methods of teaching to be considered presently. Nor do they usually give work in deductive thinking so arranged as to stimulate the pupil to make and test inferences himself.

This fact is partly due to conventional customs. But there is also a real difficulty, due to the fact that some pupils cannot be trusted to follow directions. Books could be written giving detailed data, full directions for experiments and problems, and questions about the inferences. The student could be instructed to read each helping piece of information, suggestive question, and the like only after he had spent a certain time in trying to do for himself what he was directed to do. Such books might be more effective than all but the best tenth of personal teaching, if students would faithfully try as directed before reading ahead for the helps given. If, by a miracle of mechanical ingenuity, a book could be so arranged that only to him who had done what was directed on page one would page two become visible, and so on, much that now requires personal instruction could be managed by print. Books to be given out in loose sheets, a page or so at a time, and books arranged so that the student only suffers if he misuses them, can be worked out in many subjects. Children can be taught, moreover, to use materials in the manner that will be most useful in the long run. Even under the limitation of the natural tendency of children to get results in the easiest way, a textbook can do much more than be on the one hand a mere statement of the results of reasoning such as an ordinary geography or German grammar is, or on the other hand a mere statement of problems, such as the ordinary arithmetic or German reader is.

Interest. — From the point of view of interest in work, personal teaching is usually more sociable, but the difference between it and textbook teaching in this particular could be reduced by skill in organizing the latter.

The evils of rote-memorizing or merely absorptive study on the part of pupils, and of lack of progress on the part of teachers, which are attributed to textbooks, are not at all necessary consequences of their use. It is easy to make it more satisfying to pupils to understand than to memorize, and to think than merely to read. A lazy or stupid teacher will not be cured so well by being deprived of all textbook aids in teaching a subject as by being given a dozen such and required to show that he uses them all well.

The Misuse of Textbooks. — Finally, many of the evils attributed to the overuse of textbooks are really due to misunderstanding and misuse of them. In the case of a good textbook there is a reason for every item and for its position in the whole. Too few teachers know the exact purpose of the textbooks they use. Too often a teacher uses a section of a book much as a savage might use a coat to cover his legs; or as a child uses a saw to cut a string, scissors to cut a board, and a padlock as a bracelet.

Conclusions. — On the whole, the improvement of printed directions, statements of facts, exercise books and the like is as important as the improvement of the powers of teachers themselves to diagnose the condition of pupils and to guide their activities by personal means. Great economies are possible by printed aids, and personal comment and question should be saved to do what only it can do. A human being should not be wasted in doing what forty sheets of paper, a phonograph, or a motion picture machine can do. Just because personal teaching is precious and can do what books and apparatus cannot, it should be saved for its unique work. The best teacher uses books and appliances as well as his own insight, sympathy, and magnetism.

The books that we study are of very different types. Some provide many guides to study in the forms of directions, such as " Read this hastily," " Memorize these facts," or in the form of questions, problems, suggested experiments, applications, references for further reading. Others offer no such aids. Some books, such as texts in arithmetic, provide practice exercises, applications, reviews, tables and graphs, and other mechanical devices to make learning economical and productive. Others make these provisions poorly or not at all. Since there are many types of books, an objective of education is to improve the character of printed texts and an objective of teaching is to teach children how to study books.

METHODS OF BOOK STUDY

Teaching Pupils to Study. — Books and printed materials justly become increasingly used as the student advances through school. From lectures, which also become more prominent, the student records what he can and these notes may be studied like books. It requires considerable time and much guidance to develop skill in learning from books. Many university students of the present generation have amazingly little skill. It therefore becomes highly desirable to teach pupils how to study all types of books and recorded matter. While specific techniques of study will vary widely from subject to subject, the ability to study efficiently — to educate oneself well — will be facilitated by the following habits and skills:

1. Various skills in reading, such as reading rapidly to get the main idea, skimming to review, reading selectively to find the answer to a question, reading precisely to master directions, etc.

2. The habit of studying with some aim in view.

3. The habit of evaluating material and assigning relative values to facts within the material.

4. The habit of recalling from time to time the important facts previously covered and relating them to the present material.

5. The habit of reviewing material at increasing intervals and so relating larger and larger units.

6. The habit of judging what facts, figures, definitions, principles, formulae, etc. should be thoroughly learned and of learning them by economical practice methods.

7. The habit of putting questions to oneself.

8. The habit of problem-solving, of finding and bringing to bear on any problem the relevant facts.

9. The habit of searching in various references for related information.

10. The habit of criticizing, evaluating, testing the relation of facts to the solution of problems.

11. The habit of thinking of possible application of new facts and principles to various fields.

12. The habit of recording in useful form facts acquired during reading and study.

To these should be added suggestions given earlier in our discussion of learning, especially of thinking, and several to be given later in connection with other forms of teaching.

It is, in general, true that methods of teaching which help pupils to learn well and make good use of what they learn will also help them to study well. In order for good habits of learning practiced in the classroom during discussions, experiments, projects, and the like to transfer to book work, the teacher must not only provide the opportunity for, but offer guidance in the individual work. Even gifted teachers often, in commendable zeal for interest and economy of time, prepare pupils in advance for every chapter to be read by outlining it, eliminating all difficulties, and accepting the ability to give the substance of the material as all that the pupils are to do. Too much help is as faulty as too little.

THE METHOD OF DISCUSSION

Because of the opportunity it provides the teacher to stimulate interest and to guide the pupils' activities into desirable channels, the method of discussion has become a basal method in the elementary school. It has become a favorite method of teaching children how to find, use, express, and apply knowledge and how to work together in a social group. Properly used, the discussional method also provides opportunities for encouraging and testing the results of work with books, lectures, and other materials. It can be directed to securing the expression of information, the debating of issues, the testing of assertions and opinions, and the solution of problems. But a method which may be put to many uses is easily subjected to many abuses. Because of the flexibility and indefiniteness of the discussional procedure, great skill is required to put it to fruitful use.

Varieties of Discussion. — Discussion may, of course, take many forms. It may be an aimless series of remarks, miscellaneous comments by teacher and pupil, or it may be systematic and developmental. The teacher may do most of the discussing, or the pupils may take the lead, or both may participate. In general, it may be said that in any case the discussion should assume a definitely progressive course in each lesson. The teacher should seek to promote effective learning and thinking by inquiring into the results of study and leading the pupils to the fullest utilization of what has been learned. The teacher, furthermore, should follow a plan from lesson to lesson designed to throw increasing responsibility on the pupils' self-activity.

Herbart's Five Steps in Studying. — Various efforts have been made to systematize the series of events involved in learning and fully using organized information. The most famous of these efforts is that of Herbart, who arranged the " Five Formal Steps." Although most forms of actual thinking do not follow any simple series of steps, chronologically, but on the contrary, dart hither and yon, following this, discarding that, returning to another suggestion, the formal steps may, nevertheless, be considered as essential phases of the whole study-learn-apply process of handling informative materials. They may serve, therefore, as a helpful outline of the procedure to be followed in classroom discussion.

The five steps of the Herbartian system may be denoted as follows: (1) Preparation, (2) Presentation, (3) Comparison and Association, (4) Generalization, and (5) Application. In conducting a class discussion, all of these phases of acquiring and using information may be represented.

Preparation. — Preparation means securing a proper orientation toward the facts to be learned and used or the problem to be solved. The issue or problem should be clearly established both by offering suggestions to the pupils and by questioning them. The questions may be designed to connect the problem with information already at the pupil's command and with his present interests in order to motivate the work. By questions or statements, the proper materials, references, and points of view for use in solving the problem may also be suggested. In general, then, preparation involves making the issue clear, calling known facts to mind, and thereby putting the pupils in a position to work effectively. Skillfully used, the preparatory discussion will also increase the pupil's eagerness to attack the problem. Preparation includes getting the pupils into a favorable mental set toward the lesson.

Presentation. — Presentation involves giving the pupils necessary particular facts and arranging these facts conveniently for study and for the solution of the problem. The means of presenting the facts will vary with the nature of the subjects and the ability of the pupils. If the necessary facts are partly known by the pupils, the teacher may sometimes draw them out by well-directed questions and suggestions. If the facts are unfamiliar, they should, to avoid waste of time and the risk of dulling pupils' interests by emphasizing their empty-mindedness, be carefully presented by lecture, demonstration, or reading without great indirection. As the facts are elicited from the pupils or presented by the teacher, they should be related and arranged. In this phase of the work, pupils may be encouraged to participate freely and thus learn how to arrange facts for the purpose of solving a problem. As the facts are gradually marshalled they should be related to each other and to the point at issue so that the solution of the problem is finally achieved successfully. This work of relating facts is designated as the next formal step, namely, comparison and association.

Comparison and Association. — This phase of the work consists in connecting the new materials and problems with other facts, problems, and situations. The purpose is to enrich the significance of the material by enlarging the associative connections with facts and issues previously mastered and with interests and situations active at the time or likely to be active in the near future, as well as to organize the data so that a solution of the main problem will be achieved. In this process, contrasts as well as similarities should be emphasized for reasons earlier discussed in connection with the acquisition of complex ideas. (See page 119.) In these ways, the new materials are not left in isolation but woven into the pupils' wider experience.

Generalization. — Generalization is the culmination of the proper understanding, arrangement, association, and contrast of the particular facts with others. It is achieved gradually. It means seeing relatively fully the significance of a fact or several facts or of a principle, definition, axiom, or rule. It means seeing through the lesson or proposition as a whole. By skillful questioning and discussion the significant ideas may be assisted to emerge and may be clarified thereafter. Leading the pupils to summarize the facts in systematic form or to contrive a rule or definition are means of crystallizing the essential facts brought out in a discussion. Another means is the application of the essential facts to other situations, which is included as the last of the Herbartian formal steps.

Application. — Application follows the same general procedure described under comparison and association except that the general conclusion, principle, or formula is used instead of the particular facts. Application is the one sure test of understanding or of ability to generalize. The pupil may recall the steps leading to the conclusion and be able to state the conclusion without understanding it fully. The fuller his comprehension is, the better he will be able to perceive other situations to which the conclusions apply and to show the application to situations presented by the teacher. The teacher should, therefore, ask for voluntary applications and propose situations herself in order thoroughly to test the pupil's ability to apply his knowledge. To be able to apply facts is to be able to transfer experience. And every successful act of applying a principle or of seeing clearly its inapplicability is a potent means, not only of making facts more widely useful, but of making them richer in meaning. The process of application is, therefore, of exceedingly great importance. By comments, questions, and the presentation of new problems, the teacher must see that the whole process has this richest issue.

The Steps Overlap in Practice. — In actual practice, the five " steps " do and should overlap. The last three are especially hard to distinguish in practice. At any moment the teacher may find it advisable to recall and clarify the general issue or problem, or to present new facts or bring in a contrasting or similar element, or attempt a preliminary summary and definition, or propose a generalization, or suggest an application of a partially understood principle. The five steps indicate merely the total range of activities which must be covered to make an intellectual experience most meaningful and far-reaching. Slavish adherence to a step-by-step procedure will often cramp the development of understanding and power.

Discussion Should Facilitate and Not Inhibit Independent Thinking. — The various essentials of the process of teaching have been outlined under the method of discussion for the reason that by mere reading, mere lecturing, or even by following orders, the pupil cannot surely be led to participate actively and consequently to achieve full mastery of the information. Only by questions, suggestions, and problem solving can the pupils be led to participate and to reveal their strength and weakness. The aim of such work should be gradually to enable the pupil to follow a similar procedure in his own work — to set up problems, gather materials, relate, criticize, apply, and generalize his knowledge and to utilize the other means of study outlined on page 245. To promote power in independent work, the teacher must leave more and more of it to the pupil, gradually reducing the discussion to tests of generalization and application. Discussion, in other words, should gradually give way to individual listening, reading, and experimentation except in certain cases, as in the social studies, in which the experiences of expressing and defending one's own ideas, of having them criticized and attacked and of evaluating and criticizing the opinions of others are the primary objectives. Even in the social studies, as in others, much of the preparatory work may be done in individual study after the pupils have acquired some degree of ability. The individual study may be facilitated by printed suggestions, questions, problems, tests of recall and application, and the like made to accompany the textual materials. Thus, the discussion may be confined chiefly to the final stages of the work in which general ideas, conclusions, and applications are compared, debated, tested, and refined.

Merits of Discussion Revealed by Common Errors. — Although the method of discussion may be most profitably used in most subjects rich in factual content, it requires great skill and judgment to use it fruitfully and progressively. Discussion is often too rambling and irrelevant to the main topic. It is often too drawn out, and results in wasting pupils' time and dulling their interest as when the teacher "beats about the bush" presumably to kindle interest or to elicit information children do not have. Too frequently, discussion degenerates to mere oral recitation in which the teacher demands recall of particular facts. Instead of becoming a method of promoting interesting ideas, it may become an embarrassing inquisition. It is difficult, furthermore, to adjust the discussional method to individual differences among the pupils. It is too often dominated by the comments and questions of the aggressive pupils, or swept forward too rapidly by the bright or retarded by the dull. In group discussion the greatest skill is required to keep thirty or forty pupils of vastly different capacities, interests, and experiences actively participating. Among more mature students, the discussion may, by interrupting the most promising lines of individual thought, discourage rather than facilitate productive thinking. As students mature, class discussion may well give way, therefore, to individual study followed by occasional discussions by small groups of students who can move at a similar pace but contribute different ideas and represent different points of view. So great, however, are the possibilities of discussion in promoting habits of calmness, fairness, impartiality, and alertness in a social situation in which personalities, prejudices, and opinions differ and are likely to clash, that the discussion method deserves some share of the students' time at all levels of schooling. It is a method fraught with opportunities in the hands of the skilled teacher, but subject to descent to the depths of futility in the hands of the unsagacious leader.

The Lecture Method

The lecture method should be distinguished from oral methods in general which were compared with the textbook method and from the discussional method just mentioned. By the lecture method we shall here mean an oral presentation without discussion or pupil participation to any considerable extent. The students hear and take notes — or do otherwise as their natures dictate.

The advantages of oral presentation due to the stimulus of voice, gestures, facial expression, the personality and enthusiasm of the speaker or of his acting, drawing, etc., we shall not repeat except to state that in many cases what a teacher does, as well as what he says, is important. Excluding from the lecture the use of questions, problems, demonstrations, discussions, and dramatizations, it may be said that extensive use of this method is mainly suited only for the work of advanced students who seek information that is not easily available in print. Its exclusive use is predominantly a method for advanced work.

The great economy of time which the lecture makes possible, in comparison with the question, discussion, demonstration, and experimental methods, is an important advantage. Although the strict lecture method is quite inappropriate to the elementary schools, proper training in note taking and other habits of study should make it feasible during the senior high school at least. While merely telling a pupil facts does not guarantee that he will learn them, much less that he will use them and think about them, the fact is that pupils advanced enough seriously to want the facts and trained in methods of using them may find new facts more provocative of further thought along lines of special interest and importance to him than class questions, problems, and discussions which can rarely be of equal interest or value to every student. The direct presentation of facts by the lecture, compared to discussional procedures, provides more time than otherwise for further individual study, thought, application, group discussion, and other uses.

Although to confine work to lectures or even to offer long lectures frequently would be unwise in the lower schools, it would be equally foolish to attempt to avoid all use of the method. In the midst of a discussion, study, demonstration, experiment, dramatization, or project, a brief oral presentation may often be most illuminating, stimulating, and helpful. Indeed, the good teacher in every class exercise has something worth while to contribute directly. To know when and how to tell things is as important a part of the teacher's technique as to know how and when to elicit discussion or to test information.

QUESTIONS AND EXERCISES

1. Is an expert football player, musician, or author necessarily a good coach or teacher in his own line of work? Can you cite examples of excellent coaches or teachers who were not remarkable players, musicians, or writers?

2. Are the most profound scholars invariably good teachers? Are excellent college teachers always the most scholarly?

3. What are some of the characteristics of the methods employed by good teachers which are not used by poor teachers?

4. In your own schooling, where did you receive the best teaching — in the lower elementary, upper elementary, junior high, or senior high school, or in college? Is your situation typical? If so, how do you explain it?

5. Are the advantages of reading and listening the same in the sixth grade as in college? What subjects in high school are more profitably learned by being heard than by being read?

6. What are some of the concomitant learnings which may be more readily fostered by the method of discussion than by the lecture method?

7. How do the facts of individual differences influence the choice of methods? Are any of the methods discussed in this chapter more suitable to dull children than to bright?

8. Are any of the methods treated in this chapter more suitable for young than for older children?

9. Which method places the greatest responsibility upon the

student's own initiative? Which method is most useful for developing ability to educate oneself?

10. Illustrate how you would teach history during the elementary school in order gradually to develop power to acquire and use historical data.

11. What is the peculiar value of the problem in teaching? What are the main differences in educative import of solving problems presented by others and creating problems by yourself? Between solving another's problem and solving problems which you have raised?

12. Is the problem method equally useful in spelling, music, history, and civics?

13. In what respects, if any, should a textbook in history for grade 4 differ from one for the high school?

14. In your present work, which is of more concern to you, the quality of the textbook or the ability of the instructor? Why? Did you hold the same opinion when you were in the fifth grade?

REFERENCES

BAGLEY, W. C., *Classroom Management*. Macmillan.

BARR, A. S., and BURTON, W. H., *The Supervision of Instruction*. Appleton.

BETTS, B. H., *Classroom Method and Management*. Bobbs Merrill.

BODE, B. H., *Modern Educational Theories*. Macmillan.

BURTON, W. H., *Supervision and Improvement of Teaching*. Appleton.

CHARTERS, W. W., *Methods of Teaching*. Row, Peterson.

DEWEY, J., *How We Think*. Heath.

DOUGLASS, H. R., *Modern Methods in High School Teaching*. Houghton Mifflin.

EARHART, L., *Types of Teaching*. Houghton Mifflin.

HALL-QUEST, A. L., *Supervised Study in the Elementary School*. Macmillan.

KILPATRICK, W. H., *Foundations of Method*. Macmillan.

McMURRY, F. M., *How to Study and Teaching How to Study*. Houghton Mifflin.

MINOR, R., *Principles of Teaching Practically Applied*. Houghton Mifflin.

MIRICK, G. A., *Progressive Education*. Houghton Mifflin.

NUTT, H. W., *Principles of Teaching High School Pupils*. Century.

PARKER, S. C., *Types of Elementary Teaching and Learning*. Ginn.

SEARS, J. B., *Classroom Organization and Control*. Houghton Mifflin.

STORMZAND, M. J., *Progressive Methods of Teaching*. Houghton Mifflin.

STRAYER, G. D., and ENGELHART, N. L., *The Classroom Teacher*. American Book.

WILSON, H. B., KYTE, G. C., and LULL, H. C., *Modern Methods in Teaching*. Silver Burdett.

WYNNE, J. P., *Principles of Educational Method*. Globe.

CHAPTER XII

METHODS OF TEACHING (*continued*)

In the preceding chapter were considered certain general requirements of all methods of teaching and the particular merits and limitations of such special procedures as the book-study method, the lecture method, and the discussional method. In this chapter will be treated the following:

The Practice or Drill Method.
The Demonstration Method.
The Laboratory or Experimental Method.
The Project Method.
The Method of Dramatic Expression.
The Method of Self-Activity.

THE PRACTICE OR DRILL METHOD

Drill Overused and Misused in the Past. — The method of direct practice or drill has seen so much abuse that to many progressive teachers the very word " drill " is odious. The really open-minded teacher will attempt, however, to distinguish abuse from use. Systematic practice has fallen into considerable disrepute, not because it lacks intrinsic merit, but because it has been overused and wrongly used. Twenty years ago it was employed where discussion, projects, experiments, wide reading, problem solving, and other devices were more useful. It was overused. It was also misused by requiring drill upon materials that were trivial and uninteresting or arranged in such barren form as to prevent understanding or use outside of the learning situation. It was often so arranged as to facilitate undesirable rather than desirable concomitants. It was misused by neglecting individual differences, intellectual insight, economical principles of the distribution of practice, and other criteria. As a result, the method of direct practice was dull, tedious, narrow, unfruitful.

Special Merits of the Practice Exercise. — In the development of skill, as in reading, writing, singing, typewriting, etc., and in the acquisition of facts desired for relatively permanent retention such as the letter combinations which spell certain words, the products of certain numbers, various mathematical formulae, and other rules and procedures, and for learning definitely arranged facts *after their significance is known*, the method of practice, especially that form known as the practice exercise, is the most economical method of learning yet invented. Its use is highly productive where a high degree of proficiency — speed, accuracy, facility, definiteness, or precision — in certain reactions, especially those which constitute tool skills, is needed.

Illustrated by a Study of Reading. — The value of systematic practice may be illustrated in the case of reading. When reading is taught and extensively used in connection with all other subjects, speed and accuracy of comprehension show a curve of development, in the case of the average pupil, as indicated by the solid line in Figure 4. In an experiment performed upon pupils taught in this manner, practice exercises in an important type in reading were utilized for from 10 to 20 minutes, depending on the grade, each school day for six weeks.

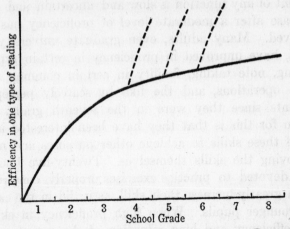

FIG. 4. — INCREASE IN EFFICIENCY IN A TYPE OF READING

The solid curve shows the increase in efficiency through the grades as the result of ordinary reading. The dotted curves indicate the rapid increase in efficiency brought about by making efficiency a specific objective of the use of the practice exercise. See text for discussion.

The results of this practice were improvements in rate and accuracy of comprehension in every case, in amounts varying from 10 to over 100 per cent. On the average, the gains obtained from 300 to 600 minutes of training of the practice-exercise type were more than would have resulted from several years of regular reading in history, geography, and all other work or recreations in school and out. The additional proficiency in this case was most desirable. A twenty-five per cent gain in fluency and fullness of comprehension in any important type of reading saves enormous amounts of time and greatly increases efficiency in nearly every other phase of school work.

When to Use the Practice Exercise. — Experiments have demonstrated repeatedly that the incidental development of any function is slow and uncertain and prone to cease after a moderate level of proficiency has been achieved. Many adults, even graduate university students, have improved in proficiency in certain types of reading, note taking, facility in certain common arithmetic operations, and the like by scarcely perceptible amounts since they were in the seventh grade. The reason for this is that they have been interested in the use of these skills to achieve other purposes and not in improving the skills themselves. Twenty-five hours of time devoted to practice exercises properly constructed would greatly increase their skill, as it did in the case of the younger pupils. When high proficiency in skill or high efficiency and long retention of the use of certain facts or operations is required, the method of the practice exercise is supremely useful.

Desirable Mechanical Features of the Practice Exercise. — To be most effective, the practice exercise should possess the following characteristics:

1. The practice should be conducted under definitely controlled or standardized conditions so that results obtained in one period may be compared with those obtained in others.

2. The purpose of the practice, *e.g.* to increase speed, accuracy, complexity, or quality, etc. of a performance, should be made clear.

3. The results of each period of practice should be measurable in intelligible — if possible in objective — form.

4. The results of each period of practice should be noted and their relations to appropriate and inappropriate techniques discovered.

5. The results of successive practice periods should

be displayed in such a way as to reveal the improvement.

6. Appropriate lengths of practice periods, of intervals between periods, and other mechanical aids to learning should be adopted.

7. Practice materials should be so prepared that the pupil can himself manage the whole learning process. Such materials increase interest and economy; they are adjustable to individual differences; and they enable a pupil to develop initiative in educating himself.

The general method permits many variations. For example, the time feature which tends to emphasize speed and exertion should not be emphasized in the case of first- and second-grade children, or others of unduly excitable natures. Instead of emphasizing speed, it is possible to make a main objective of accuracy, or quality (as in drawing, etc.), range (as in acquiring facts in history), or other features of work.

The Learner's Attitude during Practice. — In addition to arranging for the proper set-up of the materials and the administration of practice, the teacher should encourage the most constructive attitudes toward the work. As means to this end, the following general maxims should be observed.

First, in the words of James, " In the acquisition of a new habit or the leaving off of an old one, we must take care to launch ourselves with as strong and decided initiative as possible." When one attempts to increase his fluency in reading, it is necessary both to break off old and establish new reactions. As suggested earlier, a person must plunge with full energy and zeal to break through the low-level habit and reëstablish himself on a new level or hierarchy. Temporary disturbance and discomfort will be experienced. Indeed, that is one reason why one tends to remain at a mediocre level. One must go at things with a will.

Second, as James puts it, " Never suffer an exception to occur till the new habit is securely rooted in your life." The practice exercise provides the conditions which develop the higher level of performance. In some cases, as in reading, the development of the new habits is retarded if one slumps back to the old lower order of reading at other times.

The third maxim is the positive aspect of the fact stated negatively in the second : " Give the habit exercise." Seize the very first possible opportunity and every opportunity and make other opportunities to act in accordance with the new habit. While the practice exercises are being taken daily, the development of greater proficiency and its independent use, as in reading, are greatly facilitated by consciously reading, not only during the exercise period, but at all other times, at the same high level until its use becomes habituated to all sorts of materials and tasks.

Practice Exercises Useful Only for Certain Purposes. — The practice method should find some use in every subject, but it should not be used exclusively in any subject. Its function is limited ; but when applied properly to appropriate data, its use is most productive. In particular, when a pupil knows just what he is trying to learn and is eager to learn it, he may well use the practice method with properly arranged individual or group exercises, until the desired knowledge, habit, power, or skill is attained. On the whole its more rigorous features should be applied sparingly to young children and gradually more freely. Children should systematically be encouraged to discover for themselves both when and how

— in the midst of the studying of a book, or the carrying out of a project, etc. — to set up material in such exercises for rigorous application in order to economize time and increase efficiency in their later work.

THE DEMONSTRATION METHOD

After the experts in science discovered that it was far more profitable to examine real things and observe how they actually worked rather than merely to speculate and argue about them, and that it was unsafe to trust the authority of any man's opinion without testing it, leaders in education also began to advocate teaching by the direct study of things and the experimental verification of opinions. The demonstration method is a method of *showing* which may be contrasted on the one hand with methods of *telling* by spoken or printed words and on the other hand with methods of *doing* as in the case of the experiment or project. Since in Chapter VI the relative values and limitations of being told and being shown were discussed in some detail, only a brief review of these points need be given here.

Demonstration Often Superior to Verbal Descriptions. — To hear or read that an island is *a body of land entirely surrounded by water*, or that the subjunctive mood in Latin is used to express an *exhortation, concession, or command, or a wish, or a question of doubt or deliberation, or purpose, result, characteristic*, and so on, is not to be taught what an island is or what Latin subjunctives do. Words about things may or may not produce the desired tendencies to respond correctly to the things themselves. There are certain elements of knowledge, certain tendencies to response which can be got only by direct experience with real things, qualities, events, and relations. This fact may, and should, now seem axiomatic, but many teachers in practice forget it. The increased use of methods whereby the realities are examined and experimented with, as well as talked about, enormously improved the teaching of mathematics, science, history, and even language.

Demonstrations Sometimes Inferior to Other Presentations. — The wise advocate of realistic methods would not, however, assert that verbal methods are always wrong or that one should always provide a pupil as nearly as possible with the direct experience of the reality itself. Different degrees of reality may be desirable — the actual thing, a model of it, a set of sections of it, a photograph of it, a rough sketch or map of it, a sketch showing one feature of it — according to the previous experience of the pupil to be taught and the result in him that the teacher intends to secure. It would be absurd to teach the meaning of $\frac{1}{3}$, $\frac{1}{4}$, $\frac{1}{5}$, $\frac{1}{8}$, $\frac{2}{3}$, $\frac{3}{4}$ and $\frac{2}{5}$ without real objects and groups to be really divided, but it would be equally absurd to teach the meaning of .6542 by dividing real objects and groups each into ten thousand parts and counting out six thousand five hundred forty-two of them.

Demonstrations Often Better than Experiments. — The demonstration method is often used in connection with practice, lectures, discussions, and experiments. In handwriting, swimming, or pole vaulting the teacher may demonstrate an act of skill; in carpentry, weaving, or cooking, she may show a product; in science and most practical arts she may show the operation of apparatus, tools, machinery, chemical reactions, etc. by means of real objects or by models, moving pictures, or other reproductions. Such demonstrations are often more effective than words as means of illustrating more fully and accurately and in shorter time certain facts, apparatus, activities, or techniques. Demonstrations, moreover, are often superior to actual experimentation except where some technique must be acquired by actual practice.

The Laboratory or Experimental Method

The so-called laboratory methods of teaching represent the combination of the realistic presentation of facts with the observation and verification of principles by the pupil's own experimentation. A laboratory is a place in which to work with things as well as with opinion; experimental methods of teaching are methods of discovery and verification by instructive questioning of nature itself. To make the laboratory and experimental methods productive, it is necessary to give as much care and to exercise as much ingenuity in providing instructive experiences with things as in providing instructive verbal accounts of them. It is essential to direct carefully what the pupil does as well as what he hears and sees and says. It is especially necessary to teach him to extend, criticize, and refine his ideas by appeals to fact as well as to some accepted opinion.

Laboratory or experimental methods of teaching depend less upon extensive equipment of instruments and complicated arrangements for controlling nature in experiments than upon the attitude of open-mindedness and sincere curiosity. A teacher may be as prejudiced, dogmatic, and pedantic with a thousand dollars' worth of brass instruments as with a textbook; and a scientific teacher can make a pail of water, a hot-air stove, and a school yard the means of first-rate experiments. Indeed, the instructiveness of an experiment is commonly in a rough proportion to the simplicity of the apparatus used.

Misuse of Laboratory Methods. — Like any reform in

education, the laboratory method has suffered at the hands of its friends, by being used indiscriminately and by being overused. It is not scientific to spend two hours in learning by the manipulation of instruments something which could be better learned in two minutes by thought, by reading, or by a skillful demonstration performed by an expert. Washing bottles, connecting electric wires, and putting away test tubes, though doubtless useful tasks in connection with scientific housewifery, are not magical sources of intellectual growth. Nor is it safe to disregard what is taught, so long as it is taught as an exercise in scientific method. A laboratory should teach facts important in themselves. It is disastrous to scientific habits in the young for them to find repeatedly that elaborate experimental work brings at the end some trivial or meaningless result. If descriptions, verbal, diagrammatic, or pictorial, will do as well to clarify valuable facts, both time and expense will be saved and respect for experimentation increased. In more complicated matters, a smooth-working demonstration often produces better effects and reduces the cost for apparatus and materials enormously. For each pupil to do the experiment in detail may add little of educational value, except when the mechanical activities are essential to develop some technique of demonstrable later usefulness.

The Project Method

Meaning of the Term. — The term " project " has come to be nearly meaningless because it has been used to mean so many different things. We shall use the term, first, in what is sometimes called the " narrower sense," to mean the planning and carrying out of some practical accomplishment, or, as Snedden originally used the term, " to describe a unit of educative work in which the most prominent feature is some form of positive and concrete achievement." The baking of a loaf of bread, the making of a shirtwaist, the raising of a bushel of corn, the conducting of a campaign to clean the streets, the dramatizing of an event in history are typical projects in this sense. The project thus involves a practical problem and the arrangement and execution of plans to solve it.

In doing some projects, as in conducting the typical experiment, the pupil is provided with apparatus, materials, and directions. The difference between this type of project and the laboratory experiment is chiefly in the nature of the product. In the case of the project the outcome is a practical product such as a boat, a garden, a model of a bridge, entertainment, etc., whereas in the experiment the issue is a predictable natural event such as a chemical reaction or a physical phenomenon.

For a second type of project few or no detailed instructions for procedure or ready-made materials are provided. Although the general nature of the outcome desired may be suggested by the teacher, the pupils are required to select the materials, plan methods of procedure, and put them into operation.

A third type of project differs from the second merely by the fact that the product sought is suggested by the pupil instead of the teacher.

It should be observed that there are intermediate stages between these three types of projects. The directions provided may be very detailed and definite or only general and suggestive. During the course of the work the teacher may offer many and definite suggestions or few and vague ones. The choice of the project in the first place may have been entirely independent of the teacher's influence or wholly determined by her prescription or due in some degree to her suggestion. In appraising the values of project methods, then, we must keep in mind these differences.

Merits of the Project Method. — Some of the chief values of the project method may be briefly summarized as follows:

1. The method encourages the application of previously acquired facts and skills to new situations and thereby extends their significance. The project method, consequently, emphasizes the practical values of school learning. Projects afford opportunity for learnings to function in realistic enterprises.

2. Anticipation of a practical and tangible issue of the activities tends to increase interest in the work as a whole. This is true, however, only to the extent that the issue of the project appeals to the child as significant and worthy of effort.

3. Projects which do not provide ready-made directions and materials give the pupil experience in developing plans and selecting materials before the work is undertaken. If the project is not too easy or too difficult, experience in selecting materials and tools and formulating plans may foster habits basal to foresight, initiative, and originality.

4. The project should create a need for new facts and materials and, thereby, encourage independent search and study in books, magazines, etc. In so far as a project requires particular skills such as drawing, writing, craftsmanship, computing, etc., it provides a felt need for the mastery of such skills.

5. The method provides experience in applying practical criteria to a series of related activities. It requires not only deciding upon the fitness of each step as a means to a delayed end, but persistence in putting into execution one step after another. It may cultivate patient

and systematic procedure and ability to labor for a postponed reward.

6. Group projects provide an opportunity for cultivating various habits such as coöperating, leading or following, dividing up labor according to fitness, deciding disputes by appeal to authority or practical test, etc., which are essential to any coöperative enterprise.

7. The method may be managed to breed respect for the difficulties and values of constructive labor.

Some Limitations of the Method. — The method, in sum, provides opportunities for realizing most of the valuable results of typical experimental methods, described above, and some additional ones. But at the same time it is subject to many of the same limitations and some others. It is likely to be expensive and time-consuming. The indefinite character of the directions provides opportunity for training in fitting means to ends, but it also allows for more fumbling and uneducative errors. The danger both of mere busyness and mere routine labor is greater.

Limitations Due to Incidental Learning. — In particular, the function of the typical project as a means of effecting economical learning of new facts and skills may be overemphasized. The child's interest is centered on completing a practical project. If he lacks certain facts, skills, or materials to pursue his course, the child is, to be sure, zealous to secure them. But his zeal is, fundamentally, concerned with promoting the project, and this interest tends to result in the quickest possible means to this end. The learning of things needed along the way is not primary; it is instrumental or incidental. The pupil's purpose is not primarily to learn certain facts or operations, but to get ahead with making a dress, building a radio, or putting on a play, as the case may be. Perhaps a more detailed illustration will be helpful to clarify this point. A student one time secured a position as a reporter for a daily paper. While the publishers would accept longhand, they preferred typewritten copy. The project of writing news inciting a desire to learn to use a typewriter, which, together with a treatise on the best method of learning to use the machine, was procured. The zeal in writing the news truly motivated work with the typewriter, but the same zeal to achieve the practical end led to the neglect of the recommended " form " in typewriting with the result that inefficient habits were formed which the student has never been able to break. Thus the zeal in a practical end may lead one to slur practice and to neglect the procedures more fruitful in the long run for methods more expeditious in producing the immediate results demanded by the project.

Project Method Requires Supplementation by Others. — This difficulty, common to all types of incidental learning, is not an objection to the project method. It merely suggests the need of guidance and of supplementation by other methods. The pupil may be taught, even against his inclination, to learn thoroughly those things that would repay careful study or to practice at other times in correct form those skills that have high practical value. In fact, the pursuit of projects provides an excellent test of what facts or skills are worthy of exact and high-level mastery, and it should, therefore, motivate work to achieve high proficiency when it is needed.

Difficulties in Organization of Materials by Projects. — At the present time, danger lurks in the justifiable enthusiasm for the use of projects of these types. The danger is overuse of the method as an educational panacea to the neglect of other methods. Several enthusiasts favor organizing all school work on the basis of projects.

It would be difficult to organize a series of really natural projects which led to the learning of all facts and skills needed in life as a whole in the most fruitful developmental order and to the optimum degree. The advantages of leading from one fact to another, or from one stage of skill to a higher one in the most favorable sequences and of securing the rich returns from the optimum distribution of practice and reviews, and from systematic surveys of accumulated information, would be difficult to realize. Learning limited to projects is likely to be too disjointed, too scattered and haphazard in arrangement to give the necessary continuous development and integration needed for a well-balanced mastery of fundamentals and a broad perspective of the subject, which are necessary for the deepest understanding and widest application. Although it is not advisable to teach a subject in its logical outline, it is advisable to teach it in a gradual developmental sequence. Good teaching requires systematic association of new information not only with the practical demands of life — *application* — but with the related information already covered and next to be undertaken — *integration*. When used exclusively, the project method is likely to stress the immediate usefulness of knowledge at the expense of breadth and thoroughness of understanding.

We may say, in summary, that projects are rich in possibilities for teaching when combined with direct learning, with systematic study, with discussional development of subject matter, with demonstration and experiments. All these devices should be organized into a well-knit unit, each assuming the phase of education to which it is peculiarly adapted, each being integrated with the others to secure the greatest mutual facilitation.

Project Method in the Broader Sense. — The project method in the narrower sense of a definite technique as just discussed should not be confused with the project method as it is used in a broader sense by Kilpatrick, Bonser, and others. To some of these writers, the " project method " is a caption under which the outstanding characteristics of the learner-teacher-subject matter situation are conveniently summarized. These writers wish to suggest that each educative experience should *project* — it should point toward something, it should lead somewhere, satisfy some need, contribute to some purpose, facilitate some activity, provide for some utility *beyond the momentary task*. They wish to suggest, furthermore, that the pupil's activities should project; that is, they should have some significance beyond themselves, they should illuminate other activities, should promise to satisfy some need, or to facilitate some purpose. Thus in this broader sense, the project method requires that education satisfy needs which life, aside from the artificial requirement of the school, sets up; that as far as possible these needs be felt; that the situation be arranged to facilitate the emergence of learnings which most effectively and broadly serve to satisfy felt needs. Define needs to be fostered in terms of the social criterion which, as we found in Chapter II, will eventually enable each person to satisfy the most wants most richly, and the project method suggests a point of view substantially in harmony with the educative implications of our studies of the general aims of education, the nature of the child, the process of learning, the choice of subjects and activities, and the requirements of efficiency in method.—

The direct learning of a poem or multiplication table; the observation of a demonstration; the effort to dramatize a story or song; the participation in a class discussion; the reading and review of a chapter in a history text; the carrying out of a practice exercise in writing; the conducting of an experiment in physics according to definite directions; or the endeavor to execute without directions or guidance such a practical " project " as building a model of a bridge — any of these activities might be a project in this broader sense.

Project in this sense does not refer to a definite teaching device or technique such as those to which the present two chapters are devoted. It is a word used to suggest the spirit of good education method in general. On the other hand, under certain circumstances any one of these activities might fail to satisfy the implication of project. If any activity merely satisfies a momentary interest, and does not cause the experience as the dictionary says in defining *project* — " to extend forward "; if it is a task unrelated to real needs or other activities immediately in the offing, so that its effects can scarcely be projected into them, it would not satisfy the requirements of a fruitful educative method.

Since the project method in this broader sense is not a procedure which can be described in terms of its structure, as other special methods now under discussion can, it will not be discussed further. Our purpose in mentioning it in this chapter is merely to suggest that such a broad conception of the principles of method be not confused with particular forms of teaching which have been denoted by the same term.

THE METHOD OF DRAMATIC EXPRESSION

Values of Dramatic Expression. — In discussing the value of motor activities on earlier pages (Chapter VI) we drew attention to the wider educational significance of expression by bodily movement. The original fundamen-

tal form of learning, in the child and in the animal king-
dom, is by reacting with the body as a whole to the
situations which life offers. Merely to say " yes " is a
sort of short circuiting of a complex adjustment of
approval; to say or think " I am going to a party " is a
curtailment, brought about by social pressure, of shouting, clapping the hands and dancing with glee; to say
" it was a big bear " is a less full feeling and expression
of the idea than shouting the words, growling, stretching
to tiptoes, swinging the arms, and looking fierce. Children are naturally disposed to dramatic or full bodily
expressions. Some forms of expression have instinctive
roots, based on native tendencies, some are acquired by
virtue of trial and error learning guided by the observed
effects of the reactions on others, and some are due to
the acquired habits of imitating the expressions used by
other people.[1] The method of dramatic expression is
justified by its naturalness and the consequent satisfaction to children. It is justified by the value of bodily
movement, bodily postures, facial expression, gesture,
vocal intonation, etc., in enriching social life, and by the
fact that full bodily expression is a means of influencing
one's own understanding and conduct.[2]

Using the Method. — To employ the dramatic method
to the best advantage, discretion must be used to avoid
overexpression as well as underexpression. Expressive
reactions may be wasteful as well as helpful; they may
disturb and mislead others as well as facilitate their understanding and emotional congruity. The fact that
thoughts and words often provide the most exact and

[1] Imitation means merely using the behavior of others as a model to guide
one's own learning. To learn by imitation consists in observing and then
learning by trial and error to reproduce the expressions observed.

[2] On this point review the discussions of emotional reactions on pages
155-158.

rapid expression with the least expenditure of energy should not be overlooked. As children mature they must learn to curtail physical reactions as well as to refine and perfect them. In learning to read silently, too much expression by body or face and articulation will obstruct the acquisition of fluency and fullness of comprehension; in learning to read orally, neglect of the dramatic factors may result in colorless, impotent expression of thought. The dramatic method, like others, is clearly useful and probably now much neglected, but its application must be well conceived. It should include instruction in limiting as well as in enlarging and guiding overt reaction.

Methods of Self-Activity

Self-activity, in the sense of ability to educate oneself, should be an objective of all forms of education. The only problem to be raised is: How shall ability to educate oneself be developed? Our answer is that self-management in learning is achieved by the very same methods by which ability to sing or swim or read is developed. Self-activity must be made a definite objective, and the pupil, under proper guidance, must be given experience in using the means that make self-education possible.

Since, in order to develop independent ability to learn, self-activity must be exercised, it is apparent that the tendency of some teachers to direct the learning of pupils in every detail is faulty. To insure continued development of self-education, especially after completing school life, more is needed, however, than mere opportunity to exercise self-management. It is necessary also to develop those intellectual interests and appetites which make further enrichment of intellectual life a dynamic want. Extreme coercion is antagonistic to development of interest as well as independent ability. These two facts, and a mistaken conception of the principles of learning, have led several writers to declare that the best means of cultivating enthusiasm and ability in learning is to throw the pupil on his own responsibility by giving him complete or nearly full freedom.

The fact that children's interests are more fully and surely satisfied by giving them guidance in the choice of materials in comparison with leaving them to their own immature judgments was emphasized in an earlier chapter. Their interests and competence in the choice of *methods* of educating themselves are likewise more likely to be fostered by guidance than achieved by their own unguided, trial-and-error effort. As Dewey has recently said, full freedom leaves the pupil —

at the mercy of chance suggestions, and chance suggestions are not likely to lead to anything significant or fruitful. . . . The teacher, as the member of the group having the riper and fuller experience and the greater insight into the possibilities of continuous development found in any suggested project, has not only the right but the duty to suggest lines of action. . . . The method of the teacher becomes a matter of finding the conditions which call out self-educative activity, or learning, and of coöperating with the activities of the pupils so that they will have learning as their consequence.

Self-Activity Requires Many Learning Techniques. — In treating each of the special methods in preceding pages, emphasis has been placed upon the types of techniques which pupils should so learn as to be able to utilize them in independent study of other subjects. Each method provides certain skills which are worthy of mastery. To meet every demand of life, the command of a wide variety of devices, with skill to apply them where they are most useful, is needed. Skill in learning requires a wealth of intellectual resources and versatility in their use. Confinement to any single method limits the pupil's equipment and adaptability. Independent ability is realized, however, only when it is made a special objective, when children are gradually thrown upon their own responsibility and guided in their efforts to utilize fruitful techniques. In every method, then, provision should be made for giving as full play to the pupil's self-activity as his ability and attitude will justify. Self-activity, then, is not a particular method and should not be a will-of-the-wisp. It should be a definite objective of all methods.

QUESTIONS AND EXERCISES

1. Dewey has recently stated: "The problem is to find what conditions must be fulfilled in order that study and learning will naturally and necessarily take place, what conditions must be present so that pupils will make the responses which cannot help having learning as their consequence." What *are* some of these conditions? Are they entirely matters of method, or must subject matter also be considered? What other factors must be taken into account?

2. In what respects is a project initiated by the pupil himself superior to projects set up by the teacher? What are some of the dangers of devoting a large portion of school time to projects proposed by the pupil?

3. Give some examples from your own experience in which drill or memorizing was required where other methods should have been used. In what subjects has the method of drill been most seriously abused by overuse or misuse?

4. In what subjects is the demonstration method chiefly useful? What is the primary purpose of a demonstration? Can a pupil learn to perform an act merely by seeing the act performed? If not, will a demonstration of the act be of any value at all?

5. What is the distinction between the demonstration and the experimental method? What concomitant learnings are possible in doing an experiment that are not possible in observing a demonstration? Except as the activities of *doing* the experiment are themselves useful, does the experiment have any educative values not found in the demonstration?

6. In which of the following subjects are projects least likely to prove effective — spelling, arithmetic, manual training, civics, history?

7. What features of a project are likely to make the work interesting to children? Is it always true that a project selected by a child will be more interesting in the carrying out than one proposed by a teacher? Illustrate. Are the games which children like best those which they themselves devised or those which adults have invented for them?

8. Taking the term "project" in its broader meaning, what requirements of method does it especially emphasize?

9. Is the dramatic method more appropriate to young children than to high-school students? Should the form of expression change with age? If so, in what respect or directions?

10. Which is more closely akin to the nature of the first-grade pupil: (a) the carrying out of practical projects requiring considerable bodily activity and manual manipulation, or (b) drill for the achievement of intellectual mastery or refined motor skills? Do children sometimes desire quiet work which requires little gross bodily movement?

11. What is the distinction between recommending self-activity in the sense of utilizing the pupil's knowledge, ability, and other resources to achieve new ends and self-activity in the sense of throwing the child entirely upon his own resources and interests? Can you think of any form of learning in which a competent teacher could not assist to make a child's efforts more interesting and productive?

REFERENCES

COLLINGS, E., *An Experiment with a Project Curriculum.* Macmillan.

HOSIC, J. F., and CHASE, S. E., *A Brief Guide to the Project Method.* World Book.

KILPATRICK, W. H., *Foundations of Method.* Macmillan.

McMURRY, C. A., *Teaching by Projects.* Macmillan.

MERIAM, J. L., *Child Life and the Curriculum.* World Book.

MILLER, H. L., *Directing School Study.* Scribner's.

MILLER, H. L., and HARGREAVES, R. T., *The Self-Directed School.* Scribner's.

PARKHURST, HELEN, *Education on the Dalton Plan.* Dutton.

RUGG, H. O., and SHUMAKER, A., *The Child Centered School.* World Book.

STEVENSON, J. F., *The Project Method of Teaching.* Macmillan.

"Symposium" by Kilpatrick, Bagley, Bonser, Hosic, and Hatch in *Teachers College Record,* September, 1921.

See also references for Chapters I and XI.

Chapter XIII

APPRAISING THE RESULTS OF EDUCATION

The results of education consist in changes both in the
nature of man and the world in which he lives. Although
these changes are hard to measure exactly, they are easy
to observe roughly. It is easy to see that our present
surroundings differ greatly from those of our savage
ancestors, and even easier to observe the differences between our habits, ideas, conventions, mores, and ideals
and those of our remote forebears. Education, by changing the ideas and habits of men, results in the building of
an engine, the writing of a book, the planting of an
orchard, the painting of a picture. The engine, book,
orchard, and picture become at once educative forces acting upon other men. Any change in the environment
exerts an educative influence upon all persons who directly
or indirectly come in contact with it. Changes in the environment, in large measure, reflect the educative influences of the time. Such changes are, however, closely
tied up with the ideas, beliefs, and habits of the men who
made them. They are, in large measure, the immediate
products of existing ideas and skills and their influence
upon later generations will be largely determined by the
legacy of beliefs, skills, and customs which are transmitted. Thus the transmission of ideas, beliefs, skills,
mores from generation to generation becomes of primary
importance. We must observe how or in what form such
acquisitions are passed on.

Transmission of Results of Education by Social Heredity of Ideas, Customs, etc. — Ideas, beliefs, and skills are, as we have seen, transmitted from one person to another, especially from the older to the younger members of society by teaching and learning. By these means changes of vast practical significance are brought about. The changes are significant not only because of their immediate effects upon the lives of those who receive them but also because they serve to increase the resistance to certain further changes and to decrease the resistance to others. Thus the common acceptance by adults to-day of the belief that diseases are caused not by the works of angry gods but by bacteria, deficient bodily functions, and other natural causes has not only radically changed our religious beliefs and daily habits but has paved the way for more far-reaching changes in our children. When once a belief or custom is accepted by adults, its inculcation into their children is favored instead of hindered by intellectual inertia. Children learn to speak a particular language, wear clothes, live in houses, and eat cooked foods so readily that it is difficult to realize that these activities were not instinctive, but the results of education. In so far as the ideas, beliefs, and habits thus acquired are erroneous or undesirable, progress toward better ones is hampered; but in so far as they are true and useful further progress is immensely facilitated. The acquisitions of one generation are transmitted to the next so subtly and surely that the term " social heredity " is often applied to the process.

Changes in the Bodily Organism. — Education also brings about in many ways changes in the bodily organisms of children. Ideals of physical prowess and beauty, ideas concerning diseases, foods, and habits of life influence, within limits, the growth and functions of the organism. Since education may thus directly affect many characteristics of the body, the question has been raised whether it may not also affect the germ cells, that is, those portions of our organic equipment which are immediately responsible for the creation of offspring. May not the acquired ideas, beliefs, skills, habits, and bodily modifications of parents be in some measure transmitted to the children?

Transmission by Biological Heredity. — There is no evidence that any results of education and experience will be transmitted by the germ cells. Whatever nature the parents originally had, apart from their acquired ideas, beliefs, and habits, their offspring tend also to have. The particular knowledge, interests, and skills *acquired* by parents are not passed on by biological heredity.

Improving the Human Stock by Selection. — Education, then, cannot improve the racial stock by the direct means of biological heredity, but it may do so, indirectly, by means of social inheritance. It may improve the race by teaching prospective parents to breed men, as they do plants and animals, by discovering the nature of the best stocks and by seeking to increase their fertility while decreasing the productivity of the poorest strains. To achieve this end, ideas and mores different from those now prevailing must be established since most persons still feel a superstitious dread of tampering with the question of who shall be born, though no other question so deeply affects the welfare of man.

RESULTS OF SCHOOL EDUCATION

Far too little is known of the results in knowledge, power, skill, interests, and ideals, that come from any given sort or amount of school education. What difference it makes whether one goes to school a thousand days or two thousand; whether the teachers by whom one is taught are paid one thousand dollars a year or five; or whether one studies Latin or English — to all such questions exact answers are difficult to find. In a rough way, sagacious parents, teachers, and observers of school education could estimate the gain made by a child, a class, or children at large. But such estimates would be subject to large errors partly because it would be difficult to distinguish the influence of education from the influence of selection and partly because it would be difficult to gauge the results of either with accuracy.

The Effects of Selection and of Training Are Confused. — It is not difficult to compare those who have had a given sort or amount of education with those who have not. But such comparisons do not measure the effect of the education in question alone. The other things are rarely equal. Thus, supposing it to be true that, at thirty, high-school graduates earned six thousand dollars a year, while those who stayed in high school only a year, or less, earned three thousand at the same age, the doubling of earnings cannot be credited to the education given by the last three years of high school until we are sure that the two groups were equal in native ability and social advantages. As a matter of fact, we can be sure that they are not equal. For a boy to graduate from high school means that, when he entered, he differed from his fellow-students who remained in high school only a year or less. In the case of a thousand pupils in the New York City high schools some of the differences between the pupils who graduated and those who left high school within four months after entrance were determined. These differences indicate the general nature of the selective influence of the school.

An Example of the Selective Action of Schools. — Those who remained to graduate from the New York high schools were three quarters of a year younger than those who left within four months after entering. The former reported at entrance that a high-school education was necessary for their intended life-work, two and a half times as frequently; and that they intended to complete the course, four and a half times as frequently. In the work of the first months they were esteemed by their teachers far above the other group in both ability and industry, and got, in the formal records of the school for scholarship, grades averaging eighty to the others' sixty. Only one in fifteen of them got an average grade for the first term's work below sixty, while half of those who left school did so.

We cannot measure the results of a certain form of education by comparing those who have had it with those who have not, unless the other conditions are all equal; and they almost never are. Any form of education acts by selecting certain individuals as well as by training them. Different sorts of education select different sorts of students as well as make different changes in them.

Inaccuracy of Opinions concerning Achievements. — A second cause of uncertainty in evaluating the outcomes of education is to be found in the marked unreliability of human judgments of the results of school learning. Until very recently, educational products and influences were appraised on the basis of someone's judgment. The appraisal was not a measurement but an opinion. Various studies have shown that opinions on all types of educational outcomes are very unreliable. Even in determining the most obvious achievements of pupils in their own class, expert teachers with the results of weeks of work, of special examinations, and other data before them, are strikingly inaccurate and variable.

Defects in Marks and Grades. — All of the traditional marks and grades, whether in reading, Latin, morals, or initiative, are subject to defects. Nobody could be sure what the mark or grade measured, or how closely it tallied with the reality. Marks in freshman algebra, for example, might be measures of inborn talent for mathematics, or of acquired power at mathematics, or of mathematical erudition, or of temporary memory, or of docility and fidelity in doing what the instructor ordered, or of sagacious divination of what the instructor desired! When we measure length or weight or volume, or temperature or electric potential, all competent persons measure the same thing. But when we measure achievement in first-year Latin or college algebra, even the most competent twenty teachers may measure twenty different composites.

One investigator found, for example, among instructors teaching the same subject in the same college to the same grade of students, that some gave ten times as many A's as others did, and less then one tenth as many failures. Another investigator found that identical students in the same course, taught during the first semester by one instructor and during the second by another, had three times the probability of a mark above 85 in the one case that they had in the other.

The general result was scandalous. It was found in the elementary courses at one university that A's were thirty-five times as common in Greek as in English. At another large university it was found that over a period of five years one professor had never permitted a single student out of nearly a thousand to fail, whereas another in the same college reported nearly three hundred per thousand as failures.

Moreover, even when we did know fairly well what we

were measuring, the mark or grade given by any one examiner might correspond only by a shockingly wide margin with the reality.   For example, let the ability to be measured in geometry be defined as the ability to answer a certain specified set of questions and to prove certain specified propositions.   In an investigation, it was found that a hundred experienced teachers of mathematics assigned grades ranging from 28 to over 90 to the same set of replies, on an actual examination paper.   That these variations were not mainly due to differences in standards in different schools has been shown by similar studies of teachers within the same school or college.   The variations are nearly as great.   Finally, when a teacher, after an interval, regrades a set of papers, the marks vary appreciably from those of the first scoring.

Causes of Variations in Grading. — The causes of such conspicuous variations in grading are various.   Teachers have different general standards, lenient or severe, and these may vary considerably from time to time.   Different weights are attached to the many items — penmanship, spelling, grammar, terseness, particular facts, general understanding, etc., etc. ; *i.e.*, different criteria of evaluation are employed.   Judgments of the relative difficulty of questions or problems in an examination are often faulty.   For example, among twenty sixth-grade teachers, each of whom judged the relative difficulty of 23 arithmetic problems, there was great disagreement : problem 1 was placed by some teachers in various positions from the easiest to the eighth in difficulty ; problem 12 from the fourth to the seventeenth ; and problem 23 from the first to the twenty-first position.   Familiarity with the work of pupils often leads to prejudices concerning their general abilities or their deservingness of praise or blame which color one's judgments of all particular products.

Broader Outcomes of Education Even Harder to Judge. — In gauging the more general outcomes of education, such results as reasonableness, trustworthiness, sociability, initiative, good will toward one's fellows, intellectual sagacity, culture, and the like, opinions are likely to be even more subject to individual bias, varying standards, and general unreliability. For decades, opinions have been divided as to whether teaching Latin in high school increased general mental resources, and such uncertainty will continue until better measures of the results become available. For every type of educational outcome there is a need for more reliable, more comprehensive, more meaningful, more refined evaluation.

The Need of Measurements. — If education is to become a science and a more effective art, it must develop means of determining with accuracy the degree and kind of all changes which it brings about. It is only when one can perceive the results produced by any form of education that one can tell whether that educative factor is potent or futile, and, if productive, in what direction and in what degree. Since laboratory studies have shown that an individual cannot learn a given task, such as guessing the lengths of intervals of time, unless he is provided with knowledge of the results of his efforts, we may be confident that educationists, as a group, will be unable to improve the productiveness of teaching unless they are able to appraise the results of any educational activity. We may expect, furthermore, that in education, as in other sciences and in personal endeavors, the more objective, clear-cut, and refined the measures of educational products are, the greater are the possibilities of determining and putting into effect improved educative procedures.

Objectives of the Science of Human Measurement. — Since about 1910, rapid progress has been made in the invention and development of measuring devices as a means of supplementing opinions. All of the new tests are designed to do what teachers have always been trying to do but have been able actually to accomplish only poorly or not at all; namely, to gauge the results of education in quantitative terms free from subjective bias.

The measurement movement began, naturally enough, with the construction of tests for the simpler achievements in reading, writing, spelling, and arithmetic. It extended first to knowledge and skills in other academic subjects from first-grade drawing to university professional subjects. There is scarcely a subject in the whole gamut of scholastic offerings at the present time for which some type of tests has not been devised. Achievement in the humbler arts of sewing and carpentry and in the higher types of musical, literary, and artistic tastes have both been approached by students zealous to improve the validity of measurement. At the present time efforts are being made to subject nearly every educational outcome to measurement. In all of this work there have been notable achievements and notorious blunders, justifiable and unfortunate enthusiasms. The results thus far achieved have been, on the whole, of tremendous benefit to education. Possibilities are bright for far more useful results. We shall, therefore, survey briefly the present status, the promising directions of development, and the possible ill effects of the testing movement.

CHARACTERISTICS OF EDUCATIONAL MEASURES

Two requirements must be met to appraise accurately any product of education. One must use a *standardized test* and a *measuring scale*. A *standardized test* is an examination conducted by means of rigidly prescribed rules. The materials used, the time allowed, the influential surrounding conditions prevailing, the giving of directions, the scoring of results must conform exactly to the standards established which can be reproduced at any time and place. The *measuring scale* is an arrangement of the test results or scores in such a way as to indicate a series of steps in ability ranging from zero ability (or some small degree of ability) to a maximum (or high) degree by known (preferably equal) units or steps. The scale is a fixed standard with which any individual or group of individuals may be compared.

A Sample Educational Scale. — The statistical devices by which educational achievements are scaled by units that are approximately equal are too technical for description here. We need merely to know that approximately comparable units on a scale ranging from zero or some low degree of ability upward may be secured. The results of tests with the Thorndike-McCall Reading Scale, for example, when properly scaled gave the following table.

No. of Questions Answered	Scale Score	No. of Questions Answered	Scale Score	No. of Questions Answered	Scale Score	No. of Questions Answered	Scale Score
0	23	9	33	18	43	27	63
1	25	10	34	19	45	28	67
2	26	11	35	20	47	29	71
3	26.5	12	36	21	49	30	76
4	27	13	37	22	51	31	79
5	28	14	38	23	53	32	82
6	29	15	39	24	56	33	86
7	31	16	40	25	58	34	92
8	32	17	42	26	60	35	96

Scale score 50 indicates roughly twice the ability of scale score 25; 26 is as much greater than 25 as 71 is greater than 70. All units are approximately equal.[1]

[1] Not absolutely equal, nor even so nearly equal as the inches on a footrule, but approximately equal; probably much more nearly equal than age, grade, raw score, percentile, or other units.

Note that answering one more question in addition to 6 already answered is a smaller accomplishment, as shown by the scale score, than answering one more question after completing 32; the latter in fact is twice as great an accomplishment.

Functions of the Scale. — The scale, such as the one on page 288, is a genuine measuring device. It enables the teacher, for example, to ascertain more exactly how much progress a class, or a pupil, has actually made. One pupil who, during a month, increases his achievement from scale score 33 to 37 (from 9 to 13 correct answers) has improved the same amount as another who advances from scale score 63 to 67, although the latter answers 27 questions on the first and only 28 on the last test. The merit of the scale is that it tells us with much greater accuracy what a test result *means*. Each unit of the scale score means a definite and uniform amount, just as an inch or a pound is the same wherever it is found.

Age and Grade Averages or " Norms." — It is now possible to construct age or grade norms, by averaging the scale scores obtained from large numbers of representative pupils. Below are given the Thorndike-McCall reading norms for grades in terms of scale scores.

Grade at mid-year	2	3	4	5	6	7	8	9	10	11	12
Average scale score	26	33.7	39.6	44.9	50.9	56.0	59.6	61.5	62.9	64.5	66.8
Difference between a grade and one below		7.7	5.9	5.3	6.0	5.1	3.6	1.9	1.4	1.6	2.3

The third row of figures shows that progress in achievement in this reading test from grade to grade is by no means uniform. The increase from grade 2 to 3 is very great compared to the differences between adjoining grades above grade 7, a fact that could not have been ascertained except by the use of a scale.

The table of grade scores enables a teacher, furthermore, to compare the attainments of any pupil, or a whole grade, with the achievements of other classes of the same, or higher or lower grades. The uses which may be made of such age and grade scores will be discussed after a brief survey of the kinds of educational products which may now be tested.

PRESENT STATUS OF THE TESTING MOVEMENT

Following the scheme of classifying the results of education adopted in Chapters VI and VII, we may note the following achievements.

1. Measures of Information. — Information is relatively easy to measure and as a consequence objective devices have already been prepared which enable a teacher quickly, economically, and without prejudice to determine the major attainments in nearly every elementary-school subject. For information acquired in the high school, dozens of useful instruments are available. Even in colleges and graduate schools — which are usually slow to adopt new methods — the " new " types of examination are being rapidly adopted. It is, indeed, hardly probable that any type of information at any scholastic level cannot be measured. It is equally improbable that improvements in teaching cannot be achieved by intelligent use of objective tests and scales.

2. Measures of Abilities to Think, Judge, Reason, etc. — Since thinking, judging, reasoning, and otherwise using facts depend in part upon the possession of facts, measuring information tests one of the phases of these abilities. Measuring information, however, does not fully gauge ability to think, judge, and reason. The intellectual skills represented by these terms can be, and, to a considerable extent have been, measured. Tests in reading comprehension, in solving problems in arithmetic and algebra, in using data from geography, history, civics, and other subjects, in managing mechanical contrivances, in judging facial expressions, or samples of poetry and prose are examples of useful means of measuring, at least roughly, various complex intellectual operations. By such instruments as Watson's Test of Fair-Mindedness, with which a person's reactions to religious, political, economic, social, racial, and other problems are determined, the rôle of personal bias in thinking and judging is in some measure ascertained. Measures of the more complex mental abilities, then, as well as of the mastery of facts, are demonstrably possible.

3. Measures of Motor Skills. — Tests and scales for writing and drawing were among the first to be introduced into schools. Measures of other scholastic, artistic, athletic, mechanical, and vocational abilities have since been produced. It is not apparent that, in the field of motor skills, any insurmountable difficulties block the way to accurate measurement. In one of the more difficult types, musical ability, tests of native aptitude as well as achievement have been notably successful.

4. Measures of Conduct. — Measures of conduct have come more slowly than tests of information, intellectual proficiency, and motor skill, because more time, ingenuity, and money are required both to construct such tests and to use them after they are available. The recent quickening of the interest of the school in tests of conduct has been followed by energetic and widespread activity by specialists to provide practicable instruments for measurement. During the year 1927 there appeared more than 200 publications concerned with measuring conduct in some form. Included among these contributions were reports of efforts to devise measures for such types of conduct as stealing, behavior during examinations, lying, aggressiveness, carefulness, persistence, sociability, resistance to suggestion, tendency to show anger and fear, open-mindedness in behavior, speed of making decisions, aptitude for managing details, facility in shifting from one activity to another, preferences for various types of activity, self-confidence, self-assertion, tendencies to collect and hoard, and so on. Although less advanced, the movement to measure conduct does not appear yet to have encountered insurmountable difficulties nor does it appear likely that it will do so in the future.

5. Measures of Interests, Appreciations, Attitudes, Ideals, etc. — As suggested in Chapter VII, an enormous number of acquisitions may be included under such terms as interests, feelings, emotions, appreciations, attitudes, inclinations, ideals. It is frequently asserted that such subtle reaction tendencies cannot be measured. Although it is true that measurement in this field has not advanced as far as in some others, it is quite untrue that interests, appreciations, emotional dispositions, and the like cannot be measured. The brute force of present accomplishment is sufficient evidence to the contrary. Although the methods used are still crude, time consuming, and expensive, rough quantitative appraisals of tendencies to anger and excitement; to discriminate and exercise preferences for different types of literature, poetry, music, drawings; to feel and express interests for different types of recreational and other activities; to be inclined toward honest or dishonest, kindly or cruel, social or antisocial, expansive or repressive behavior have already been achieved. In many cases the interest, attitude, or reaction tendency is gauged by direct measures of conduct. It is not now possible and perhaps may never be possible to measure all human reactions and reaction tendencies cheaply with pencil and paper tests, any more than it has been possible, in medicine, to diagnose physiological behavior cheaply and quickly by group methods. That tests have not been provided at five cents apiece for these more complex and subtle traits is no evidence that they cannot be developed. Indeed, any human characteristic that we can now perceive to exist can, by sufficiently ingenious application of techniques now available, be gauged more objectively and accurately than is possible at present.

Summary. — In summary, it may be said that, while the tests now available in inexpensive forms and usable by relatively inexperienced examiners are mainly designed to measure the narrower products of education, such as information and skills in the common subjects, technical experts are busily engaged in developing tests and measures of the other phases of educable abilities. This work, furthermore, gives every promise of being successful.

VALUES OF TESTS AND MEASUREMENTS

The measurement movement aims to decrease the element of subjective bias and to increase the objectivity, the accuracy, fullness and minuteness of appraising the products of education. By so doing it provides means of increasing the potency of education in several ways which may be briefly summarized.

1. Measurements Develop Respect for Education by Increasing Its Fairness. — The average correlation between the grades given in a subject and a student's real achievement in it is, in even the best American schools, so low that the ratings are six tenths as erroneous as they would be if they were assigned at random by a child as in a lottery. If 900 pupils pass and 100 fail by the official ratings in a subject, nearly half of those who failed really did better than some of those who passed. It is demoralizing to students to find that their official ratings depend so little on real achievement and so much on irrelevant matters, bias, and mere chance. More objective and accurate statements of achievement, by making possible a fairer comparison of a pupil's attainments with those of other pupils or with the pupil's own previous abilities, breeds respect for education and increases its effectiveness.

2. **Setting Up Standards of Achievement with Respect to Capacity.** — When tests of achievement are used in connection with measures of capacity, the treatment of each pupil may be made even more fair and fruitful. The pupil gifted with a high degree of native capacity is then expected to do more and better work than the average. He is thus protected against habits of idleness and conceit which might result were he constantly praised for merely excelling pupils of inferior endowment. Pupils of meager native talents are similarly protected against rebukes, scorn, and discouragement for inferiority in gross attainments. Each pupil's work becomes healthier and more fruitful when appraised in terms of his own capacities. Objective measurement, then, increases the effectiveness of education by setting up standards of achievement in terms of varying capacities.

3. **Adjustment to Individual Differences.** — As a result of the combined use of tests of capacity and achievement, the adaptations of education to individual differences can be more successfully achieved. The use of the Accomplishment-Quotient technique, the classification

and promotion of pupils in homogeneous groups, the provision of fair competition and attainable rewards for effort, and other practices may be more effectively put into operation.

4. Educational Diagnosis. — For the diagnosis of special difficulties in any subject such as reading or arithmetic, in social or moral adjustment, athletic or aesthetic participation, measures both of capacity and achievement are necessary. Remedial measures, to be most effective, must be accurately prescribed so as to correct the inappropriate and strengthen the desirable habits. Education and reëducation should be conducted so as to utilize the strengths and relieve the weaknesses in capacities which are revealed. With the development of standardized tests of particular abilities and aptitudes — as in reading, athletics, and music — the accuracy of diagnosis and the effectiveness of education and remedial instruction have been markedly increased.

5. Education and Vocational Guidance. — As in the field of medicine, so in education, prevention is superior to cure. Prevention of difficulties is furthered by the early discovery of strengths and weaknesses. Aptitudes and inaptitudes can be gauged only by adequate tests and measures. It is obviously unwise and wasteful to ask students to undertake to master those subjects, activities, or vocations for which they are by nature unfit. It is now possible to determine roughly, for many levels of school work and for several vocations, the degree of aptitude which a pupil possesses before the time for specialized instruction is reached. Only ingenuity and experimentation are needed to make possible more accurate guidance over a wider range of activities.

6. Improving Records and Reports. — The use of objective tests and measures makes it possible greatly to increase the significance and value of school records. When such records have a definite and common meaning for everyone, they reveal an educational history which may be full of important signs concerning future limitations and possibilities. Until we do systematically use objective measures as records, all reports and grades are indefinite and likely to mislead; all comparisons of institutions and individuals are insecure; and all predictions are hazardous.

7. Comparisons of Productiveness of Different Educative Means. — The work of comparing the merits of different institutions, different classroom methods, different organizations of materials, different time assignments, different time distributions, different incentives, etc., etc., can be unbiased, accurate, and precise, can, in a word, be scientific, only when the results produced by the different agencies can be objectively measured. It was not an accident but a necessity that the scientific work in education advanced step by step with the development of instruments of measurement. Every further improvement in testing and measurement, moreover, makes possible further advances in the science of education. By the use of measures of native equipment in conjunction with tests of acquired abilities, the influence of education can be distinguished from the influence of selection. Thus the difficulty of appraising the effectiveness of education mentioned earlier in the chapter may be overcome.

8. Determining Objectives of Education. — In many ways, precise, objective measures aid in the determination of the tangible objectives of education. In the accepted subjects, like spelling and writing, exact measurement reveals what facts or skills the pupils possess at any time, which ones need and need not be taught and what amount or level of ability the world requires. Thus tests have shown that the high degree of quality in writing formerly sought and the many words formerly taught in spelling are too rarely useful in life to justify the costs of learning them, and that many of the abilities commonly required in life need little attention in formal drills since they are learned in other activities. Again, the invention of measurements of honesty or trustworthiness has resulted in revealing in a way never before possible the degree and types of dishonest behavior that exists among school children. These objective pictures of misconduct indicate the character of educational endeavor needed to improve conduct. Similarly, tests of pupils' abilities to distinguish good from bad literature, drawings, music, moral conduct, health knowledge and habits, and personal manners have indicated definite objectives for educative endeavor. Measurement, then, has served to set up aims of education as well as to make them more definite.

DANGERS AND LIMITATIONS OF THE MEASUREMENT MOVEMENT

The fact that the measurement movement in education is sound in method, useful in practical operations, and essential to scientific progress does not guarantee it against misunderstanding or stupid and extravagant uses. Like all other creations of science such as surgery, electricity, and air navigation, educational tests have been debated, unduly praised, and unduly criticized. As with other developments, cautions against abuse and misunderstanding must be heeded. The main hazards are as follows :

1. **Use of Age and Grade Scales as Ideals.** — It should be understood that the " norms " which accompany most tests are norms in the statistical sense only ; they

are tables representing the average achievement of different grades or ages. They portray not an ideal achievement for a given age or grade, but rather a distinctly mediocre performance — the performance equaled or excelled by half of the pupils upon whose scores the average is based. Only ignorance of the simplest statistical devices could lead to a tendency to be satisfied with mediocre attainments by confusing scales of averages with ideal norms. The source of this difficulty lies in ignorance and not in tests and measurements.

2. Use of Test Materials and Methods as Models: Danger of Uniformity. — A second fear is that teachers will use the reading passages, compositions, drawings, and other materials employed in tests as models for instruction and demand that pupils imitate them in order that they may do well on later tests. This is, of course, a more severe condemnation of teachers than of tests. While many tests would, in fact, serve admirably as models for the guidance of learners, such is not their primary function. Where both functions may be served at once the use of tests becomes even more fruitful. Most tests, however, are strictly diagnostic devices and should no more be conceived as establishing models for the learner than the physician's prescription of a barium sulphate meal before an X-ray test or a day of starvation, followed by a biscuit and water which is retrieved by a stomach pump, should be mistaken for a model of an ideal regimen in hygiene. Medicine has found measurement and diagnosis, indeed, essential even when painful. Education will find them equally essential and generally less painful. In both fields standardized, rigid diagnosis can and should be used to foster, not to hamper, proper prescription for individual cases. Again, only misuse of measures results in " deadly uniformity." If teachers emphasize primarily test materials and expect their pupils merely to equal test norms, they are grossly misusing these instruments. The remedy for these practices is not to abolish tests but to educate teachers.

3. Emphasis upon the More Tangible Results of Education in Teaching. — As was stated above, the first and least expensive tests are those designed to measure the simpler facts and skills in the fundamental subjects. When tests are used primarily to measure such results and when teachers' efficiency is gauged primarily in terms of the measured improvement of her pupils in these functions, there exists a genuine danger that such facts and skills will receive undue emphasis. Without minimizing the value of these humbler products, the teacher must maintain her efforts to realize the broader aims of education. To limit her endeavors to the attainment of outcomes that may now be easily and cheaply measured would be a prodigious misfortune for her pupils. This difficulty is one which the test movement will, in time, correct by developing measures for the other abilities which comprise the broader objectives of education. The constructive policy, then, is not to abolish or curtail such measures as we have but to increase greatly our zeal in contriving tests which will measure other desired outcomes.

4. Fear of Conflict between Objective Tests and the Finer Life. — It may be said, however, that only the baser parts of education can be counted and weighed, and that the finer consequences for the spirit of man will be lost in proportion as we try to measure them — that the school will become a scholarship factory, turning out lawyers and doctors guaranteed to give satisfaction, but devoid of culture. This is a part of the general fear that science and measurement, if applied to human affairs

— the family, the state, education and religion — will deface the beauty of life, and corrode its nobility into a sordid materialism. This fear is groundless, based on a radically false psychology. Whatever exists exists in some amount. To measure it is simply to know its varying amounts. Man sees no less beauty in flowers now than before the day of quantitative botany. It does not reduce courage or endurance to measure them and trace their relations to the autonomic system, the flow of the adrenal glands, and the production of sugar in the blood. If any virtue is worth seeking, we shall seek it more eagerly the more we know and measure it. It does not dignify man to make a mystery of him. Of science and measurement in education as elsewhere, we may safely accept the direct and practical benefits with no risk to idealism.

Conclusion. — There are, then, some fanciful dangers and some real ones with which those using measurements will have to contend. If scales of average attainments are mistaken for ideals, if test materials are uncritically confused with instructional matter, if diagnostic methods are not distinguished from teaching procedures, if teachers accept no aims in education except those apparent in the commercial test catalogue, the influence of testing will be deleterious, indeed. Such misuses of measments are, however, as unnecessary as they are stupid. They should blind no one to the essential soundness of the measurement methods and the great practical value of their applications. For such abuses as exist, the best cure will come from the development of better measures for more abilities by scientists and wider and more intensive use and study of the instruments by teachers. Needless to say, tests, like teachers, must keep pace with the development of improved materials and practices which the years will surely bring. Tests, like teachers, may exercise a potent influence in improving practices and establishing new educational aims.

1. Is it true that the average adult of thirty to-day knows more than the average adult of thirty of one hundred years ago or does he merely know different things?

2. If you believe that the average man to-day knows more than the average man of a century past, to which of the following do you attribute the difference?

    a. Superior native intellectual capacities

    b. Greater effort in learning

    c. Fewer superstitions

    d. Better schools

    e. Gradual accumulation of ability through biological inheritance of the abilities acquired by each generation

    f. Greater availability of knowledge

    g. Greater amount of knowledge

    h. Harder struggle for survival

3. In what respects is the transmission of culture, conventions, etc. like, and in what respects unlike, biological heredity?

4. Aside from improving education, what other ways are there of increasing the competence and character of people in the world?

5. Give some illustrations of confusing the effects of education with the effects of selection of superior persons. How may tests of capacity be used to distinguish between the effects of native ability and education?

6. Defend or criticize this statement: "As tests of physical capacities have made possible better application of the principles of hygiene, so tests of mental capacities will make more effective the application of the principles of education."

7. Most modern education theorists, like Dewey, stress the importance of emphasizing the individuality of people both by adjusting all education to each individual's native equipment and by cultivating especially each individual's special talents. In what ways has the measurement movement made these functions possible and productive?

8. Suggest some uses that a teacher might make of the Accomplishment-Quotient technique.

9. A teacher was greatly disturbed to find that although she felt she had taught more effectively during the year than ever before, her

class barely equaled the "norms" for a series of educational tests. Is it possible that she had taught more effectively than usual? How could she have found out? Is it possible that to equal the norms would have been an extremely high attainment? Is it possible that it would have been too great an achievement?

10. Should a teacher aim at getting every one of her pupils as near the norm for her grade as possible?

11. To what extent is it true that except as reliable tests are developed we shall be unable to determine accurately whether we are over-emphasizing or underemphasizing particular information, skill, and conduct traits and unable adequately to set up any very intelligible objectives of education?

12. What are some recent innovations in educational administration and in teaching which are due primarily to the development of tests? Which, if any, of these do you believe to be unwise? Do you believe that testing, as a general method in education, is responsible for such errors or were they due to misuse of tests, or misinterpretation of test results?

13. Have tests, in general, drawn attention to or away from the nature of the child? Has this effect been wholesome or otherwise?

14. In what respects has the philosophy of education been influenced during the last twenty years by the results of tests and measurements?

REFERENCES

BROOKS, S. S., *Improving Schools by Standard Tests*. Houghton Mifflin.

LEVINE, A. J., and MARKS, L., *Testing Intelligence and Achievement*. Macmillan.

McCALL, W. A., *How to Measure in Education*. Macmillan.

MONROE, W. S., DEVOSS, J. C., and KELLY, F. J., *Educational Tests and Measures*. Houghton Mifflin.

PRESSEY, S. L and L. C., *Introduction to Use of Standard Tests*. World Book.

SEARS, J. B., *The School Survey*. Houghton Mifflin.

TRABUE, M. R., *Measuring Results in Education*. American Book.

WILSON, G. M., and HOKE, K. J., *How to Measure* (Revised Edition). Macmillan.

See also references for Chapter I.

Chapter XIV

FUNCTIONS OF THE ELEMENTARY, SECONDARY, AND HIGHER SCHOOLS

The functions of the several schools must be determined in the light of facts and principles already presented in this volume. The primary purpose of every school is to foster the general aims of education which we described in the first three chapters. In attempting to achieve these ends, the schools must be so organized as most effectively to meet the needs and utilize the powers which are paramount at each stage of growth. The schools must also be administered so as most productively to meet the wide individual differences in the rate and limits of growth in various traits. How to foster at each stage the major objectives of education, how to provide for progress in harmony with the character of growth and how to adjust education to the great variations in the rate and limits of development are the three main questions to be answered in defining the functions of the several divisions of the schools.

Before attempting to state the functions of each unit of the school system, let us review briefly some of the pertinent facts about the aims of education, and the nature of growth and of individual differences.

Review of Guiding Principles

The General Aims of Schooling. — The function of each period of education in school is to enable every pupil at each stage to achieve the most productive and satisfying participation in life at that time. The purpose of schooling as a whole for each individual is to equip him to continue, after leaving school, to participate in life most fruitfully. The most productive and satisfying participation in life requires the achievement of physical vigor, mental health and balance, and of those adjustments to the physical world, to social, civic, economic, and family situations and the acquisitions of those ethical, religious, recreational, and intellectual resources which will promote most abundantly the interests of mankind as a whole. The general aim of increasing the fullness of life for each individual by promoting the welfare of society at large requires not only adjustment to the needs of each stage in development during the whole period but specialization in school to harmonize with different careers in after-school life.

The Nature of Development. — In the preceding chapters it was shown that there are no breaks or separate stages in the anatomical, physiological, emotional, or mental development of individuals between birth and maturity. It was also stated that education must be a continuous development produced by progressive reorganization of experiences on increasingly higher and more complex levels. The range of information, the level of skill, the richness of appreciations, the strength of control, the fullness of self-activity under the best forms of education show continuous increase. Since development, both as it depends on innate growth and personal experience, is continuous, the school system should similarly be one series of intimately connected links without a break.

The Transition from School to Life. — While the need for continuity among the several divisions of the school is commonly recognized, the equally valid and important requirement for a smooth and natural, rather than an abrupt and artificial, issue from the school into the life of society is less frequently mentioned. Too truly does " graduation " from school or college represent " commencement " of a new or even of " real " life. Since the " real world " is not so surely dedicated to protecting and guiding the youth to further the interests of society at large in a manner consistent with the individual's own welfare, the effects of unpreparedness for the step from school to life are even more serious than abrupt changes within the school course. The school should, therefore, in a manner consistent with the general principles given in Chapter IX, organize its work, to mitigate, if it cannot entirely remove, this difficulty. It should, in fact, see that each individual is provided with what amounts substantially to an internship, under guidance, in the responsibilities of community life.

The Nature of Individual Differences. — It has been shown that individuals develop, by nature and by training, at very different rates and that in adult life they will live on very different levels of intellect, character, and skill. Although it appears, from certain recent studies, that the influence of the school is to make individual differences smaller instead of greater, the effect of the inner maturing of native traits is so potent that variations among pupils starting to school together become constantly greater, in many respects, as time goes on. Thus in intellectual aptitude and insight, for example, individual-growth curves diverge more and more widely like the ribs of a fan. Even before maturity is reached, it is apparent that variations in intellectual aptitude alone make wide differences in vocational preparation necessary. The school, then, must at a fairly early stage provide differential education adjusted to future vocational requirements as well as to differences in capacity to learn in the social, civic, recreational, and other phases of life. The tremendous range of individual capacities raises also the question of varying the *amount* as well as the *kind* of school training. To organize the whole school system, then, so as to promote the major aims of education in harmony with growth so markedly varied, and the requirements of adult life so highly specialized, is the perplexing problem with which we are confronted.

Early Organization of American Schools. — Unfortunately, the traditional organization of American schools into the elementary school, the secondary school, and the college was unsatisfactory in several respects. The curriculum was narrow and formal. The elementary school was designed chiefly to teach tool subjects. The traditional three R's — readin', 'ritin', and 'rithmetic — formed the basal courses. The secondary school's main function was to prepare students for college; and the college, with its highly formal linguistic and mathematical emphasis, was chiefly an academy for the ministry or scholarly pursuits. The elementary and higher schools were integrated neither with each other nor with life in general. Since the earliest institutions were established, efforts have been exerted to make the several school units better related to each other and to the needs of life at each stage of maturity. In neither aim have these efforts been entirely successful.

Present Organization of Schools. — The present system is a compromise between what nature and education demand and what tradition permits. The most recent organization of the more progressive schools includes the kindergarten of one or more years, the elementary school of six grades, the junior high school of three, the senior high school of three, the college of four, occasionally a junior college intermediate between the senior high school and the traditional college, and the university graduate school. The newer units in this series, especially the junior high school and the junior college, arose chiefly as devices for spanning the gaps between, and integrating the purposes of, the older, highly distinctive units, the elementary and high schools and the college, and of providing better adjustments to vocational needs and other individual variations. Thus it may be said that the pronounced trend in school organization is in the desirable direction of harmonizing the activities of the school with the characteristics of human nature. The movement, while in the right direction, has much distance to cover before an ideal combination of continuity and specialization is achieved.

Recognizing the facts then that school education at all levels should be guided by the same general objectives, that it should be a continuous process conforming to the requirements of each point in the curve of growth for each of many different natures, and that, to do so effectively, it must result in a transition from school to life that is smooth and natural rather than abrupt and artificial, we may proceed to discuss certain possible improvements in school organization.

The Lower Elementary School

The elementary school, as the phrase is here used, extends to the beginning of the junior high school, or grade 7. In many progressive communities it includes one or more years of kindergarten education, and if the newer nursery schools establish their value, it may extend downward nearly to the cradle.

Since children are not usually required to attend school before the age of six, the kindergarten and nursery schools are, on the whole, institutions in which school life is substituted for home training in some measure by the choice of parents. There is rapidly accumulating evidence, however, that the better types of these primary schools invest the small fraction of children's time for which they make provision more profitably than the average home does. It is probable that attendance in school before the sixth year will gradually approach universality.

Curriculum of the Kindergarten and Nursery Schools. — Studies of the capacities and interests of young children indicate the advisability of placing little emphasis before the age of six upon either the acquisition of those intellectual resources known as the formal tools — reading, spelling, arithmetic, writing, etc. — or upon abstract intellectual analysis. Instead, early education should emphasize the acquisition of the most vital adjustments of children to their material surroundings and to other people. Special emphasis is placed upon general muscular adaptations to people and things; upon sound moral, emotional, and volitional reactions in private life and in social relations; upon wholesome reactions to and appreciations of habits which foster physical health, and mental serenity and balance. Knowledge is provided and intellectual insight fostered in connection with the establishment of good habits of working and playing, eating and resting, managing simple implements and apparatus, reacting to other children and adults and to situations and things commonly encountered in the local community. By listening to good music; observing pictures and other objects; by producing simple objects of art by modeling, constructing, drawing, coloring; by singing, speaking, dramatizing, dancing, and the like, aesthetic appreciations and artistic creativeness are cultivated. By means of individual and group games, additional forms of wholesome recreational activities essential to normal growth in the early years are provided. Thus the school — by offering wider and more significant social contacts, more varied and representative features of community life, a richer store of materials and apparatus, more desirable models of speech, manners, and morals, more suitable pictures, music, and games, and better methods of guidance — affords educational opportunities which few homes can equal.

School for the youngest children, then, emphasizes direct experience with the immediate environment rather than indirect contact, through verbal descriptions or otherwise with things more distant in time, space, or significance. It emphasizes thought about concrete realities rather than about abstract characters. Yet these and other similar distinctions are matters of degree rather than kind. The kindergarten child enjoys pictures and descriptions of distant things as well as observations of immediate events. He can imagine a play world as well as see one. He can deal with abstract symbols — his oral language is distinctly abstract — as well as with concrete realities. He can perceive abstract facts — for colors, sizes, shapes, are abstract — as well as particular things. While the young child's training should emphasize immediate motor, emotional, and intellectual reactions to his tangible surroundings, guided with a minimum of coercion, inhibition, and confinement, it should be expected also to foster appreciation of the more remote, intangible, and abstract features of experience. The transition from kindergarten to first grade should be no more abrupt than the change within the kindergarten school before and after the Christmas vacation. Thus first-grade work differs from that just described only in degree.

The Elementary School

The elementary school, in the newer organization, consists of grades one to six inclusive. Children normally enter between the ages of six and six and a half years of age and are expected to remain six years. By spirit and law in America, the elementary school is designed to give a fundamental education to all children irrespective of sex, native ability, race, or social status.

Functions of the Elementary School. — The main functions of the elementary school are: (1) to provide for each child six years of experience designed to enable him to make at each step in the period adjustments to the most essential phases of life and to equip him with the various types of resources previously described in Chapter III. To adjust this general education to each child requires a considerable degree of specialization in accordance with individual differences. Consequently the elementary school has a second function, namely, (2) to determine as accurately as possible the native intellectual capacities, the physical, emotional, temperamental, recreational, aesthetic, and other aptitudes of children. Since some pupils will find it necessary or advisable to enter a vocation in the middle teens, a third function is essential in some degree, namely, (3) to explore the vocational interests and aptitudes of pupils and to provide some measure of vocational adjustment for those who will leave school at the earliest legal age. Since all of these functions are general, and have therefore been described in previous chapters, the discussion will be confined to a few comments on the phases of elementary-school work in which the need of improvement is most urgent.

The Elementary Curriculum Too Narrow and Academic. — Despite rapid progress in the right direction, the program of the average elementary school is too narrow and academic in character. Traditionally the elementary school has been primarily devoted to teaching the fundamental subjects, the three R's, and closely related disciplines. In representative schools to-day, more than half of the time is spent on reading, writing, spelling, and other language arts and arithmetic. These subjects are taught, moreover, in a too restricted and formal fashion. Artificial exercises, like drills on phonetics, multiplication tables, and formal writing movements, are used to a wasteful degree. Subjects such as arithmetic, language, and history include content that is intrinsically of little value. Nearly every subject is enlarged unwisely to satisfy the academic ideal of thoroughness. That the typical school overemphasizes instruction in these formal, academic skills as a means of fostering intellectual resources and neglects important phases of the other nine objectives set up in Chapter III is a justifiable criticism.

While this criticism is sound, care must be exercised in attempts at improvement lest the development of essential resources be neglected.

Improved Methods of Developing the Fundamental Educational Resources. — Many of the facts and skills sought in the traditional linguistic and mathematical subjects are genuinely fundamental tools essential to the economical attainment of other objectives of education. Merely to reduce emphasis upon them by wholesale curtailment, or by throwing them to the winds of incidental training would not improve the situation. Improvements should take three forms: (a) the elimination of all unessential facts and skills; (b) the improvement of methods of learning and teaching the essentials, and (c) the improvement of the values of the *content* by means of which each tool is developed. Each of these forms of improvement may be explained in a paragraph.

Determining Essentials. — What the essential facts and skills are may be determined by surveys of the uses to which they are put in out-of-school as well as in-school life of representative individuals. By such studies it has already been shown that only a fraction — according to one study less than a fifth — of the arithmetic taught a decade ago is frequently used outside of school, even by adults. Words children were taught to spell, rules of grammar they were required to memorize, the quality of writing they were forced to achieve, normal business and social intercourse rarely or never demands. Elimination of unessentials by scientific study, then, is one step in improving the curriculum.

As such studies are made, it is found, however, that there remains a substantial body of " minimum essential " skills. For accuracy, fluency, and comprehension in reading, there is now a greater demand than ever before. In view of the widespread use of written communication, ready and accurate written expression is more important now than it has previously been. At the same time, the increase of personal contacts in most phases of life emphasizes the need of effective oral expression. Radical curtailment or neglect of instruction in such intellectual tools, therefore, cannot be countenanced.

Improving Instruction. — Instruction should be improved, not neglected. The elementary school has fallen heir to faults in methods of teaching the fundamental subjects as serious as in the choices of content. Were the improved organization of material and methods of teaching which could now be put into effect actually adopted in all subjects, the saving in time and energy would be considerable.

Improving Content. — The typical elementary school of the preceding decade has permitted too marked an isolation of studies from each other and emphasized unduly the development of formal skills. Thus, in reading — the subject which received the most time — too little attention was given to the intrinsic value of the material read. In many schools little attempt was made to do more than teach the mechanics of the reading process during the period devoted to this subject. We now recognize that reading is taught better if the content is rich in value — if it has intrinsic worth in cultivating information and appreciation concerning some one or more of the phases of life which we have set up as the objectives of education. Reading can, moreover, be taught so as greatly to facilitate spelling, writing, and speech and to be facilitated by these activities. This practice of combining subjects so as always to kill several birds with one stone will make possible a considerable saving of time and marked increase in power.

By combining the three sources of improvement — the elimination of all save essential material, the improvement in methods, and the organization which gives every element in the learning situation intrinsic value — the time and energy required to establish competence in the use of the essential intellectual tools can probably be reduced appreciably. Any time and energy saved in this way can be used to enlarge experiences needed to foster the other objectives of education without neglecting the fundamental intellectual resources.

Need of Specialization in the Elementary School. — Although great improvements have been made in recent years, the elementary school has not yet made its program satisfactorily adaptable to individual variations in intellectual capacity and to differences in recreational and vocational aptitudes and prospects. To too great an extent, the intelligence and ability of the average children in a class determine the character of teaching. For the superior pupils, adequate enrichment of content and rate of pace are not arranged. For the dull, the deplorable system of failure and repetition of work, sometimes for a full year, is far too common. In the last analysis it is the school, and not the dull pupil, that has failed. The purpose of the elementary school is to give all its pupils, whatever their abilities may be, the experiences it is best for the common good that they should have. The adaptation to individual differences required to satisfy this aim is far from realized as yet.

Adjustment to Vocational Prospects. — In the elementary school some attention should also be given to vocational possibilities. Many pupils will not remain in school long after the elementary period. By the time of completing six years, or by the age of twelve or thirteen, vocational fitness, in so far as it is determined by general intellectual capacities, can be roughly gauged. Special talents for handwork, music, drawing, literary expression, public speaking, mechanical ingenuity, and other skills may also be roughly appraised. Especially for those who will turn relatively early to the work of the world, provision should be made for effecting a smooth and successful transition to the responsibilities of life in the community in which institutional guidance is no longer provided.

Need of Exploring Capacities. — To make possible adaptation to individual differences in intelligence and the cultivation of special talents of vocational and recreational value, native capacities should be systematically explored during the elementary school period. By means of available measures of general mental ability and particular talents, careful observation of performance in the many school subjects and activities and intelligible cumulative records of achievement, the elementary-school officers should arrive at as comprehensive an appraisal as possible of the talents and limitations possessed by each pupil. By the end of the sixth school year, these data can be, and should be, adequate for fairly reliable educational and vocational guidance. While refined predictions, at this early period, of future success in particular courses or vocations are not possible, the probability of satisfactory future achievement in each of five or six rough levels into which educational institutions and vocations may be grouped may be determined in the elementary school. Using the means now at our disposal it is possible to make a useful estimate concerning whether a given pupil has the intellectual capacity essential to complete successfully the work of the first-class liberal college, of the junior college, the senior high school, or only the junior high school. Classifying vocations by Taussig's method into five levels — (a) professional occupations, (b) semiprofessional occupations, (c) skilled occupations, (d) semiskilled occupations, (e) unskilled occupations — it is now possible to make a useful estimate concerning the level most suitable for each pupil's career. To provide the best possible guidance for the future which present means permit is a function of the elementary school.

Maintaining and Enlarging Contacts with Social Life.
— To fulfill the general functions of the elementary school, intimate contacts with the life of the community must be maintained. Beginning with direct experiences with relatively little emphasis upon things and events distant in time, or space, or abstract and complex in character, the school introduces the child gradually into the life of a modern community. As experience and native capacities increase, the school should attempt to extend experience and to give it broader and deeper meaning. Direct experience is progressively extended by contact with geography, history, and the other subjects which deal in an explanatory and interpretative way with the immediate and local world by placing it in the course of time and the range of space. By introducing slowly the racial inheritance of facts and materials from the arts and sciences, the meaning of the more obvious and tangible world is enriched. By proper combination of the abstract subjects and direct experience, the broader and deeper principles and their bearing on current life and its problems may be grasped. Thus gradually the pupil grows until by the end of the elementary-school period he will be equipped not only to participate in considerable measure in the life of the community by act and insight, but also to continue to utilize constructive means of continuing his usefulness and understanding.

THE SECONDARY SCHOOL

The functions of the junior and senior high schools — which together cover the average pupil's ages from twelve to eighteen — are, in general terms, identical.

They are as follows: (*a*) to continue to provide, without a sharp break, but on a higher level, experiences and instruction designed to foster the major objectives of general education; (*b*) to make this instruction adaptable to the capacities and vocational prospects of different individuals; (*c*) to explore further individual talents and vocational fitness; and (*d*) to provide vocational guidance *for all* pupils completing the elementary school. For a certain number who will complete their full-time schooling during the high school period and then take their places in society, the school must assume the following functions: (*a*) to provide, in a measure, vocational preparation; (*b*) to round out education in such a way as to smooth and make successful the transition from school to life; (*c*) to vitalize the functions of the school in such a way as to make pupils desirous of continuing to utilize educative facilities in adult life.

It is apparent that the first four functions of the secondary school are identical with those of the elementary school, whereas the last three represent new obligations concerned with introducing the pupil effectively to his particular career in the life of the community. In discussing these functions of the secondary school, some of its present deficiencies will be noted.

Causes of Deficiencies in General Education. — In the first place, it must be said that the high schools have not satisfactorily provided for all the experiences and instruction necessary to foster the major adjustments and resources which comprise a general education. For this deficiency two factors are mainly responsible. The first is the antagonistic pressure of tradition established by the early secondary schools and the second is the demand for an extraordinary degree of specialization at this level if all children are to be educated in a secondary school. A brief description of these influences will, therefore, be in order.

Unfavorable High-School Traditions. — Traditionally the secondary school has not been an institution for the education of all adolescents according to the abilities that they have, but an academy for the instruction of relatively few youths favored by high intellectual endowment and superior social and economic resources. The main purpose of the original secondary schools was to prepare a highly select group of pupils by formal methods and abstract subject matter for the work of still higher institutions.

Until recently the curriculum of the high school consisted chiefly of the linguistic and abstract subjects — English, Latin, and modern languages, algebra, geometry, physics, chemistry. All subjects, including the last three, were taught in highly linguistic, logical, and abstract form with little reference to modern life and its needs.

The Present Academic High School. — In a considerable measure, many of the secondary schools of the present day are similar to the traditional academy. The curriculum is still highly linguistic, mathematical, and abstract; the methods, formal. The subject matter, methods, and standards of attainment are so exacting that barely half of the adolescent population is sufficiently well endowed intellectually to complete the work successfully. In these schools, vocational interests, aptitudes, and preparation and the needs of the other major concerns of life at large are little heeded.

The Trade School. — A later development at the secondary level has taken the form of trade schools devoted primarily to vocational education. In these schools emphasis has veered from the linguistic and abstract subjects of the traditional type to work conspicuously practical and technical. These schools are designed primarily for youths of more limited intellectual or financial resources who wish rapid preparation for earning a living in some trade. But in the trade schools, as in those of the academic type, education has failed to foster, in the degree desirable, insight and efficiency in the conduct of the affairs of life in the large.

The Newer High Schools. — Between these extremes lie a number of more progressive institutions which are attempting to make available a broader education for a wide range of ability, to explore vocational fitness, provide guidance, and, in some measure, preparation for a particular vocation to be assumed immediately or remotely after years of higher education. Aside from the antagonistic pressure which early traditions have created, other factors make the aims of these schools difficult to realize. These difficulties are due chiefly to the demand for great specialization at this period.

Need of Adjustment to Wide Differences in General Ability. — Although differences among pupils in the present academic high schools are wide, they will be greatly increased by admitting the large number of pupils now eliminated by sheer incapacity to do the present type of complex and abstract work. Since individual variations in intelligence and other capacities become more pronounced as the age of maturity is approached, they are at the high-school level approximating a maximum. To adjust materials and methods to this wider range of capacity will require a radical departure from present methods. Indeed, it is frankly doubtful whether it can be done in such a manner as to make full-time school attendance of the less gifted pupils contribute to the welfare of society as a whole.

Need of Adjustments to Vocational Prospects. — Unless it proves socially profitable to eliminate a considerable portion of the pupils who enter the primary school from full-time participation in the work of the high school, the higher curriculum must be adapted not only to a wider variety of capacities than was necessary in the elementary school but also to more sharply defined vocational prospects. Utilizing the data accumulated in the elementary school and the results of further observations, and achievement and aptitude tests, a more exact prediction of vocational possibilities must be made in the junior high school. When all facts are taken into account, we believe it will be found that the best interests of the individual and society will be served by providing a certain number of the pupils least gifted in intelligence with the equipment needed to begin their vocational career by the completion of the junior high school period or even earlier in a few cases. Other individuals will advance their own welfare and that of society by securing but one more year, others by two, others by three additional years. Thus although the great majority of children should spend some time in the junior high school, not all of them should be expected to continue to the completion of the senior-high-school course. Each child should have as much high-school work as the common good requires.

Need of Vocational Preparation. — If this policy is sound, it becomes necessary to determine vocational fitness and to provide both guidance in a proper choice of a life work and some measure of preparation for it. The degree of preparation desirable depends so much on the provisions made by industrial concerns for technical training that it is impossible to make a general rule except that in any one community, at any one time, the schools should supply the training which cannot otherwise be secured. For those who are to enter soon upon their vocational careers, the school should bring to a culmination the broad range of education and experience essential to a fruitful participation in all other phases of life in the community, including the continuation of education in adult life.

Need of Proper Transition from School to Industrial Life. — Aside from the requirements of specialization to meet individual needs, the secondary school should make additional provision for the transition of many youths from the guidance of the school to the responsibilities of out-of-school life. As we have stated in Chapter IX, the change should be gradual and not abrupt. The youth should be prepared for all phases of community life. He must be enabled to develop a disposition to make later use of educative agencies as a means toward personal improvement and social betterment. For reasons also given in Chapter IX, we believe that education in the last years of school should be an enterprise in which the schools and industries and other agencies coöperate. Either by alternating between periods of educative activities in the school and in other institutions or by devoting part of every day or week to each, the pupil should learn to take his place, without bewilderment, in the economic world. By this coöperative enterprise, he should also be induced to take an active part in the social, civic, religious, recreational, and intellectual activities which are most appropriate to his nature and calling. The most effective means and the most appropriate institutions to utilize in continuing his education should be made manifest by instruction and made desirable by fruitful employment during the period of transition. The period of transition becomes, in effect, a period of interneship in living in society. The guidance of the school is justified for the same reasons that observation and assistance of the young physician during his interneship are deemed essential.

Summary. — The chief functions of the secondary school or of education from 12 to 18 may be summarized as follows: (*a*) The continuation on a higher and more complex level of the broad and general education begun in the elementary school. (*b*) The specialization of general education to conform to the wide range of intellectual capacity and to the vocational requirements of the students. (*c*) The appraisal of intellectual and vocational aptitudes and the provision of vocational guidance for all. For those who are to leave school early, the functions are: (*d*) The furnishing, in some measure, of vocational preparation. (*e*) The fostering of a disposition favorable to continued use of educational facilities. (*f*) The providing of a suitable transition from the protection of the school to the responsibilities of life.

INSTITUTIONS FOR HIGHER EDUCATION

The last decade has witnessed an unparalleled development of institutions for education beyond the high-school age, or, roughly, beyond the eighteenth year. The colleges have made provision for a rapidly increasing number of men and women seeking a " higher " or " liberal " education. In 1926 there were more than twice as many college students as in 1915 and more than six times as many as in 1890. During the last quarter century, other institutions such as public and private commercial and vocational schools, " finishing " schools for women, institutions for dull, delinquent, and physically handi-

capped pupils, continuation schools, university extension courses, correspondence schools, classes for adult
education, evening schools, corporation schools, summer
schools, intersession courses, and junior colleges have
been established and are recruiting students from the
college and higher age levels.

What the detailed functions of the higher schools, or
of education from 18 to 22 and later should be, we
shall not try to state. Recent attempts to provide full-
time education in the junior college, the college, professional and vocational schools for a larger proportion of
persons over 18 than ever before are clearly experimental, and the advantages achieved for the welfare
of society are uncertain. Expert opinions still differ
concerning who should be taught, what should be taught,
and how it should be taught in these full-time institutions.

For reasons presented in earlier chapters, we may
state that the institutions of higher education should
probably be frankly devoted to the education of the
most gifted young men and women who give greatest
promise of ability to serve as leaders in furthering the
interests of mankind. To fulfill this purpose, the higher
institutions must find means of restricting their efforts
to those persons of sufficient intellect and character to
profit richly by them; they should attempt to disclose
to these select students the present status and future
needs of society; they should try to discover ways of
bringing to bear upon these issues the facts and techniques now available; they should assist each student
to discover the particular type of future service to which
his native talents and acquired abilities are best adapted,
and, finally, they should endeavor to equip him with
ability and fire him with zeal to pursue this line of
service for the common good.

Because of the great variety of sciences and arts that may profitably be studied, and the great variety of careers that may profitably be prepared for by young men and women at these ages, any definite statement of what percentage of youths should attend institutions of higher learning or what courses and activities should be there pursued would be hazardous in the extreme. But few of the possible types of instruction on this level have been tried. Inasmuch as there are many considerations, as stated in Chapter IX, to be urged in favor of entering one's life work earlier while taking advantage of part-time education instead of continuing full-time schooling after eighteen further studies of results obtained from various types of part-time education (such as day, night, extension, and correspondence courses) combined with vocational enterprises in comparison with full-time school attendance will constitute one of the most significant experiments in democratic life.

QUESTIONS AND EXERCISES

1. Weigh the advantages and disadvantages of sending children from ages one to four to the nursery school. What, in general terms, are the most important educational needs during these years?

2. On what basis would you judge the effectiveness of the kindergarten? In what ways should individual differences be recognized in this school?

3. Which of the ten major needs of education listed in Chapter III are least adequately satisfied by the present elementary school? In which have the greatest advances been made since you were in the early grades?

4. In which respect has elementary education been most deficient: (a) in adjusting the work to the developmental (age) status of the pupils, or (b) in adjusting it to individual differences at each grade level?

5. In general, has the treatment of such subjects as arithmetic, geography, history, civics, etc. been on too high or on too low a level for

the intellectual insight, interests, and needs of the pupils? Is it likely that the old theory that "education is preparation for life" has had any influence on this situation?

6. If pupils were to continue to receive some education until they are twenty, would the problem of adjusting the curriculum to the needs, interests, and abilities of pupils be simplified? Illustrate.

7. What is the distinction between developing the three R's incidentally and developing them by careful management in content and activities of immediate usefulness in other subjects or situations? What procedure is recommended in the text?

8. Why has the high school failed to become a school for *all* adolescents?

9. In 1890 there were approximately 200,000 pupils in the high schools of the United States; there are now probably nearly 3,000,000. What changes in the high school, and in society, have been chiefly responsible for this growth?

10. What kind of pupils would you advise to take the following subjects in high school: practical arithmetic; French; Latin; geometry; domestic science; music; English composition?

11. What high-school subjects were most valuable to you? Why? Which were least useful? Why?

12. If the high school opens its doors to larger numbers of pupils, should the subjects usually called "extracurricular" be extended or diminished? Are these subjects likely to remain indefinitely "extracurricular" or are they likely to become as definite a part of the curriculum as any others?

13. Compare the advantages of vocational training under the direction of the high school with vocational training under the management of industrial corporations.

GENERAL REFERENCES

BONSER, F. G., *The Elementary School Curriculum*. Macmillan.

CHAPMAN, J. C., and COUNTS, G. S., *Principles of Education*. Houghton Mifflin.

CUBBERLEY, E. P., *Public Education in the United States*. Houghton Mifflin.

GRAVES, F. P., *A Student's History of Education*. Macmillan.

HILL, P., and Others, *A Conduct Curriculum for the Kindergarten and First Grade*. Scribner's.

HORN, J. L., *The American Elementary School*. Century.

KEITH, J. A. H., and BAGLEY, W. C., *The Nation and the Schools*. Macmillan.

PARKER, S. C., *A Textbook in the History of Modern Elementary Education*. Ginn.

PECHSTEIN, L. A., and JENKINS, F., *Psychology of the Kindergarten-Primary Child*. Houghton Mifflin.

REISNER, E. H., *Historical Foundations of Modern Education*. Macmillan.

SECONDARY SCHOOLS

BRIGGS, T. H., *The Junior High School*. Houghton Mifflin.

COUNTS, G. S., *The Selective Character of American Secondary Education*. University of Chicago Press.

COX, P. W. L., *Curriculum Adjustments in the Secondary School*. Lippincott.

DOUGLASS, A. A., *Secondary Education*. Houghton Mifflin.

GRIZZELL, E. D., *The Origin and Development of the High School in New England before 1865*. Macmillan.

INGLIS, A., *Principles of Secondary Education*. Houghton Mifflin.

KOOS, L. V., *The Junior High School*. Ginn.

MONROE, P. [EDITOR], *Principles of Secondary Education*. Macmillan.

PECHSTEIN, L. A., and McGREGOR, H. L., *Psychology of the Junior High School Pupil*. Houghton Mifflin.

RUSSELL, W. F., *Economy in Secondary Education*. Houghton Mifflin.

SMITH, F. W., *The High School — A Study of Origins and Tendencies*. Sturgis and Walton.

SMITH, W. A., *The Junior High School*. Macmillan.

UHL, W. L., *Secondary School Curricula*. Macmillan.

HIGHER EDUCATION

KOOS, L. V., *The Junior College Movement*. Ginn.

SNOW, L. F., *The College Curriculum of the United States*. Teachers College Bureau of Publications.

THWING, C. F., *A History of Higher Education in America*. Appleton.

SPECIAL EDUCATIONAL INSTITUTIONS AND PRACTICES

ALMACK, J. C., *Education for Citizenship*. Houghton Mifflin.

BITTNER, W. S., *The University Extension Movement*. (United States Bureau of Education, Bulletin, 1919. No. 84.)

DAVIS, C. D., *A Study of the School for Apprentices of the Lakeside Press.* Donnelley (Chicago).

DOOLEY, W. H., *Principles and Methods of Industrial Education.* Houghton Mifflin.

FEDERAL BOARD FOR VOCATIONAL EDUCATION, *Ninth Annual Report to Congress, 1925.* Government Printing Office.

FOGHT, W. H., *A Half-Time Mill School.* (United States Bureau of Education, Bulletin, 1919, No. 6.)

KITSON, H. D., *Psychology of Vocational Adjustment.* Lippincott.

MORRIS, J. V. L., *Employee Training.* McGraw-Hill.

NOFFSINGER, J. S., *Correspondence Schools, Lyceums, Chautauquas.* Macmillan.

PROCTOR, W. M., *Educational and Vocational Guidance.* Houghton Mifflin.

SNEDDEN, D., *Vocational Education.* Macmillan.

WHEELER, J. L., *The Library and the Community.* American Library Association.

INDEX